FRANK LLOYD WRIGHT

IN WORD AND FORM

■

WORLD ARTISTS SERIES

BRUCE COLE
Series Editor

Frank Lloyd Wright, 1953
Photograph by Pedro E. Guerrero

Sept. 1999

Dear Shel,

   In honor of the
new year, I present -
at last - a copy of
my little book on FLLW,
a fascinating character
who obviously deserves
fascinating enthusiasts
like you and Lana,

         Best wishes,

         David

FRANK LLOYD WRIGHT

IN WORD AND FORM

■

by David Michael Hertz

G. K. Hall & Co.
Simon & Schuster Macmillan
New York

Prentice Hall International
London   Mexico City   New Delhi   Singapore   Sydney   Toronto

G. K. Hall & Co.
Simon & Schuster Macmillan
866 Third Avenue
New York, NY 10022

Library of Congress Catalog Card Number: 94–5357

Printed in the United States of America

Printing number

1 2 3 4 5 6 7 8 9 10

Library of Congress Cataloging-in-Publication Data

Hertz, David Michael, 1954–

    Frank Lloyd Wright in word and form / by David Michael Hertz.
      p. cm.
    Includes bibliographical references and index.
    ISBN 0-8161-0536-7 (alk. paper)
    1. Wright, Frank Lloyd, 1867–1959—Criticism and interpretation.
2. Wright, Frank Lloyd, 1867–1959—Written works. 3. Organic
architecture. 4. Architecture—Aesthetics. 5. Architecture—
Philosophy. I. Title
NA737.W7H46   1995
720'.92—dc20   94-5357
                                           CIP

For Eleanora

TABLE OF CONTENTS

■

Illustrations follow page 82.

LIST OF ILLUSTRATIONS

■

To preserve a consistent chronology of Frank Lloyd Wright's architecture, I have followed William Allin Storrer's catalogue of Wright's complete works. Dates of each architectural work are for the moment in the design process when the definitive shape of the finished work emerged. The actual structures were completed afterwards. Unless otherwise specified, this practice is continued throughout the text. See William Allin Storrer, *The Frank Lloyd Wright Companion* (Chicago: University of Chicago Press, 1993).

ACKNOWLEDGMENTS

■

With great pleasure I thank Bruce Brooks Pfeiffer, director of the Frank Lloyd Wright Archives at Taliesin, and his associates for their kind assistance. In the spring of 1990, Mr. Pfeiffer suggested I write O. P. Reed. That was certainly wise advice. As a result of that advice, I can also thank O. P. Reed for his lively and invaluable correspondence about Frank Lloyd Wright. From Mr. Reed's letters, which I have received steadily for the past few years, I have learned much about the historical background of Frank Lloyd Wright and cultural life in early twentieth century America.

Among others who gave me generous portions of their time during the course of my research were Edgar Tafel and Robert Pond. Mr. Tafel has published a well-respected book on Frank Lloyd Wright himself. As a result, he is one of the best known of the former Wright apprentices. Robert Pond was a Taliesin Fellow in the early 1950s, working with Mr. Wright on a number of important projects, including the legendary Bartlesville tower. He has been working in the Architect's Office at Indiana University for twenty-six years and is currently Associate Director of Design there. His presence a secret in Bloomington, Robert Pond is less widely known than Edgar Tafel. His insights were also of great value. Kim Yang, Marilyn Nissen and Ray Fischer of Florida Southern College also will be remembered for their kind help and assistance. The same must be said for Kurt VanEss of the Steelcase Corporation in Grand Rapids, Michigan.

This is my second study on Frank Lloyd Wright, and the insights gained from many who spoke with me during my first project, *Angels of Reality,* are gratefully remembered as well. Once again, I would like to thank Oscar R. Muñoz and Margo Stipe for their help in obtaining the architectural photographs and drawings. The drawings and prose of Frank Lloyd Wright are copyright © The Frank Lloyd Wright Foundation. All rights reserved.

Finally, I would like to thank Bruce Cole, Distinguished Professor of Fine Art at Indiana University; John Stone-Mediatore; and my editors at G. K. Hall/Macmillan—Helen Ronan, Donna Sanzone, Jennifer Karmonick, Sabrina Bowers, Doug Rose—for their help and encouragement with this project.

INTRODUCTION

■

Frank Lloyd Wright was one generation away from the American frontier. Wright's father, a peripatetic minister and musician, wandered the open road of the undeveloped country in search of a livelihood. Wright, paralleling his father's meanderings, was an American nomad who roamed the vast lands of the country's mid- and southwest, marking the terrain with prairie houses and desert homes while an industrializing America, vital but crude, carelessly blotted the countryside in its energetic ignorance. Nineteenth–century Romanticism, in its American strain, retained a stronger hold on Frank Lloyd Wright than nineteenth-century Europe did on the continental modernists. His Emersonian organicism made him a twentieth century environmentalist, an anachronism in terms of Modernist ideology, but a prophet in relation to architectural concerns of the late twentieth century.

There are many books on Frank Lloyd Wright, but few that deal with the issues implied by the complex connections between Wright's ideology and artistic creations in a sophisticated and evenhanded way. The chief source for all biographies is Wright's *An Autobiography*, his own version of his controversial career. It first appeared in 1932 and subsequently underwent many revisions and republications. It is scandalous that the *Autobiography,* finally republished in 1992, had been out of print for over a decade, for it is one of the important literary autobiographies written by an American. It has had a great impact, drawing both young architects and new clients to Wright's thought. The many resurgences of interest in Wright's career have traditionally been directly affiliated with its readers. Perhaps the recent republication of the autobiography, included in the projected six volume edition of Wright's collected literary works, will attract new Wright enthusiasts once again.

What many commentators have missed—and this includes Wright himself—is the close connection between Wright's architectural works and the rich pattern of visionary metaphor that he left behind in his extensive prose works. The Wright autobiography, a neglected classic in American cultural history, is just one work among his many essays and books that merit serious rereading today.

When an important artist is relatively mute, saying little about his work, we must gauge the merit and content of his work from the traces of meaning and style in the creations themselves. Such is the case with Wolfgang Amadeus Mozart, who had little time or inclination to write about his notions of creativity and musical composition. But when an important artist has a great deal to say about his work and creative processes, we must be prepared to turn to every scrap of his writing to search for a richer understanding of intent and meaning.

As far as I know, this is the first of the many books on Wright to examine the architect's numerous writings in relation to his actual architecture and to draw clear connections between these two activities throughout Wright's long career. I show how Wright's literary and critical sensibility developed in conjunction with his architectural creations, one sometimes stimulating or anticipating the other. This gives us a fresh and relatively unknown view of Wright's development.

Let me offer a few detailed observations on how the argument of the manuscript works. I move through the main achievements of Wright's career, noting when and how important verbal formulation punctuates architectural innovation. One important example is Wright's first great period, the "Prairie house" era (1901–10). This extraordinary outburst of creativity alone would have guaranteed Wright's place in the history of world culture. But Wright's architectural forms are framed and couched in the language of aesthetic argument. In my treatment of the Prairie house period, I illustrate how the germination of Wright's ideas first occurred in prose, then evolved into architectural practice and eventually culminated in prose essays once again. After Wright's Oak Park era followed a long term of estrangement in his life and a series of catastrophes that would have ruined a weaker personality—the dissolution of the Oak Park practice, his divorce, the subsequent murder of his lover, and relentlessly horrendous publicity. None of these managed to crush Wright's creative mind as he changed, adapting from the life of the suburban bourgeois to the unsteady existence of an alienated social rebel and twentieth-century Romantic. From 1910–24, Wright's writings and buildings were conceived in closer relationships to one another as he moved back and forth from Japan to work on the Imperial Hotel and to defend in print its unorthodox nature. Another crucial instance of Wright's dual career as architect and writer is the transitional period from the late 1920s through the early 1930s. Essentially unemployed during the Great Depression, Wright rejuvenated his moribund architectural career by writing a massive series of books and articles, working out important new ideas and attracting new enthusiasts and clients through his readership. After Wright's remarkable renaissance, which was highlighted by the great successes of Fallingwater and the Johnson Wax Administration Building, he maintained a steadier balance between writing and building. Turning first to one and then to the other, he allowed words and forms to feed on one another, stimulating new spin-offs and developing older ideas, encouraging the continual processes of the creative and contemplative mind to work in a continuous flux. This steadier rhythm lasted until the architect's death in 1959.

Word and form correspond in a prism of everchanging interconnections in the mind of Frank Lloyd Wright. Wright's diverse topics in his books—utopian theories, architectural aesthetics, theories of originality and influence, and the psychological unfoldings revealed in the autobiography—show in approximately twenty books and many smaller publications a commentator whose ideas derive from and inspire his structures and designs. Often his most important critical statements either foreshadow or summarize a period of significant architectural achievement. At times, a period of critical reflection allows Wright to rest his architectural eye from the trials of practice. Often this period of rest and reflection leads to a new burst of creative activity. It is this dramatic interaction between ideas and buildings that I bring out with a greater clarity, which, I hope, will be of interest to both professional and tyro.

Simply reading *An Autobiography*, contrary to the opinions of many Wright devotees, is insufficient for understanding his thought. From a theoretical point of view, many of his other books and essays are far more important. Among them are the Hull House lecture of 1901, the introduction to the 1910 Wasmuth catalogue, the 1912 book on the Japanese print, the 1931 Princeton lectures, and the London talks of 1939. And here I am listing just some of the high points of the early theoretical writings, omitting a whole catalogue of shorter articles and addresses. Branching off from his earlier essays is a series of later publications that introduce Wright's utopian plans for an environmentally sound America. *The Disappearing City* (1932), *Architecture and Modern Life* (1937), *When Democracy Builds* (1945), *The Natural House* (1954), *The Story of the Tower* (1956), and *The Living City* (1958) are some of the important publications that mark this group of works. Distinct from these utopian writings is yet another late series of books and essays that deal with Wright's roots and influences. *Genius and the Mobocracy* (1949) and *A Testament* (1957) are the high points of these works, writings which offer great intrigue as they allow us to investigate from a psychoanalytic perspective Wright's notions of originality and influence.

A number of recent books, including those by Brendan Gill and Meryle Secrest, have based much of their commentaries on Wright's massive correspondence with architects, clients, apprentices, critics and others. Wright was an energetic correspondent, writing a voluminous amount of letters during his long life. He was an even more energetic author of critical books and essays, many of which have been neglected. Although I have consulted Wright's letters, my purpose here has been to bring out the relationship between his published criticism and architectural works as they occurred naturally and chronologically during the course of his life.

This work on Wright traces the metaphorical patterns of valuation in Wright's autobiography and key critical essays as a means of reconsidering his principal architectural works. It interprets his development through his evolution as a creative personality, underscoring the critical moments of psychological self-realization as they are described in the crucial theoretical essays and the large autobiography, moving back and forth from Wright's criticism to discussions of Wright's buildings. This book is perhaps the first among many recent studies on Wright to offer critical readings of the major books, essays and addresses in what Wright himself would have described as the organic rhythm that relates them to his architecture.

The key concepts in Wright's criticism are based on a collection of metaphorical notions which he continually develops in his prose. Often Wright explains his work in a complex set of repeated images that borrow attributes from other art forms and cultures. These are some of the key concepts in Wright's works: a Sullivanian understanding of architectural grammar; the Froebelian sense of geometric, crystalline form; the elusive concept of symphonic form in space; a correspondence between forms in nature and Wright's conception of organic architectural form; the metaphorical relation of the tree and the cantilever; Laotze's notion of empty space as the definition of form (as opposed to the ornamented wall of the West); the oriental notion of decentering; and the aesthetic of Japanese prints. Like Claude Debussy, another modern master who was caught between the nineteenth and twentieth centuries, Wright was able to re-energize late Romanticism in the West by first incorporating attributes from non-western art and then achieving a unique synthesis of his own.

Wright's preoccupation with poetic notions of form lasted throughout his brilliant, topsy-turvy, and gloriously sustained career. (He was active as an architect from the 1890s through 1959!) The text on Wright that follows is a succinct summation of the main issues in Wright studies, documenting Wright's statements about his own buildings in relation to the works themselves and analyzing the ideological commitments in his writing and his architectural creations together. The structure of the manuscript follows the dynamic structure of Wright's life and career. For the first time in a critical book on Wright that surveys the span of his entire career, readings of Wright's important works of criticism are offered in the chronological order in which they were originally written, in conjunction with the architectural work he was doing at the time.

The limited but key images reproduced here encompass a tour through Wright's oeuvre: Wright's early period of gestation under Sullivan; the prairie house era; the lean years of neglect punctuated by a few triumphs such as the Imperial Hotel; the later periods of professional triumph that began with the publication of the *Autobiography* and culminated with the highly publicized creation of the Johnson Wax Administration Building and Fallingwater; the final organicism of late works such as the David Wright residence, the Gammage Auditorium at Arizona State University, and the Beth Sholom Synagogue in Elkins Park, Pennsylvania. My first concern has been to show the interrelated development of Wright's important books and essays in relation to his architectural work. In selecting the architectural works, much of Wright's tremendous output had to be omitted in order to allow enough space to emphasize the connections between his writings and buildings.

I offer the reader a concise introduction to the study of Frank Lloyd Wright. Experienced scholars who wish to expand their knowledge of Wright's criticism should also find this study useful. The scholarly apparatus is included to aid both scholar and Wright enthusiast. The appendix is a chart that shows the chronological relationship between Wright's architecture and major literary works, while the selected bibliography attempts to include the indispensable publications that have appeared since Robert L. Sweeney's comprehensive bibliography of 1978. Anyone who reads this short study will have a clear sense of where the main issues are in the work of a man who has been touted by many historians and critics as the greatest American artist to date.

I

ORIGINS: THE WISCONSIN HILLS, CHICAGO, AND LOUIS SULLIVAN

■

William Russell Cary Wright, Frank Lloyd Wright's father, was the son of a Baptist minister from Westfield, Massachusetts.[1] William Wright was born in 1825, studied at Amherst College in the late 1830s, and worked as a music teacher in Utica, New York. In 1851, he married Permelia Holcomb. The couple moved to Hartford, Connecticut, where William studied law and joined the Bar in 1857. In 1857, the Wrights relocated to Lone Rock, Wisconsin. William Wright was at first successful in Wisconsin, but he was unable to make a substantial living there. In 1864, his wife had a miscarriage and died shortly afterward. She left him a widower with three children.

Anna Lloyd Jones, Frank Lloyd Wright's mother, was born in Wales in 1842. She moved with her immigrant family, a clan of idealistic Unitarian farmers, to Wisconsin in 1845. In 1846, the Jones family settled in Hillside, Wisconsin, near the Wisconsin River and the tiny village of Spring Green.

William Wright met Anna Lloyd Jones soon after the death of his first wife. The circumstances of their meeting are unclear and vary according to different accounts. Richard Twombly surmises that since Anna Jones was teaching school and he was county school superintendent, Wright may have met her in his professional role, perhaps while lecturing to his teachers or interviewing candidates for positions.[2] Another authority, Grant Manson, proposes that William may have impressed Anna with his musicianship while conducting vocal music at a modest recital near Spring Green.[3] More recently, Brendan Gill has advanced yet another possibility, asserting that Anna Jones was actually a boarder in the home of the first Mrs. Wright, and dead set on capturing the man of the house—who appeared to her as a relatively elegant easterner—as soon as he was available.[4] In any case, William Wright was seventeen years older than Anna, and she was certainly impressed with his musical talent and professorial manner. They married in the summer of 1866, hardly a year after the close of the Civil War.

Frank Lloyd Wright was born on June 8, 1867 in the obscure Wisconsin town of Richland Center. He was the first of three children. In that same year, Mutsuhito, victorious over the military feudalism of the Japanese *shogun*, began to systematically westernize his country. Wright would open the west to the aesthetics of the east just a few decades later.

It is commonly forgotten that Wright spent a good part of the 1870s in Rhode Island and Weymouth, Massachusetts, where his father worked as a minister. Young Wright spent some important formative years in the northeastern United States, but his father kept the family on the move, unable to throw down strong roots in any one location. The wandering existence of the Wrights is captured by the list of locales to which William Wright dragged his family on the dusty roads of nineteenth-century America: Lone Rock, Wisconsin; McGregor, Iowa; Pawtucket, Rhode Island; Weymouth, Massachusetts; and Madison, Wisconsin. William Wright was unable to establish a lasting role for himself in any of these communities.

In 1876, Frank Lloyd Wright's mother went to the Philadelphia Centennial Exhibition, where she saw examples of Japanese art and architecture and an impressive display of Friedrich Froebel's (1782–1852) building blocks for children. These are two early influences on Frank Lloyd Wright that are generally noted for their importance by Wright historians.[5] Since she had already divined that her son would be a great architect, Anna Wright decided to purchase the Froebel blocks for her child. Young Wright was able to work with the simple geometric forms of the blocks, manipulating them into various toy constructions. Froebel's system enabled the boy to touch the fundamental shapes of the blocks, first getting the feel of the forms firmly in his fingers, and then turning the shapes on different placements along varies axes, bringing out varied symmetrical arrangements. By suspending a Froebel block and twirling it, Wright would have seen different optical illusions suggesting a variety of composite forms. Throughout his life he would acknowledge their usefulness. Wright recalls the excitement that he shared with his mother over the Froebel "gifts" in *An Autobiography*:

> She had seen the "Gifts" in the Exposition Building. The strips of colored paper, glazed with "matt," remarkably soft brilliant colors. Now came the

geometric by-play of those charming checkered color combinations! The structural figures to be made with peas and small straight sticks: slender constructions, the joinings accepted by the little green-pea globes. The smooth shapely maple blocks with which to build, the sense of which never afterward leaves the fingers: *form* becoming *feeling*. The box had a mast to set up on it, on which to hang the maple cubes and spheres and triangles, revolving them to discover subordinate forms.[6]

The simple forms of geometry that Wright first encountered through Froebel's toys—circle and sphere, square and cube, triangle and tetrahedron—were to intrigue him throughout his long life. The principles of organicism, the notions of three-dimensional crystalline form, and the concept of rotational schemes for three-dimensional forms are common to Frank Lloyd Wright and Froebel, and have even been traced as far back as Froebel's teacher, Christian Samuel Weiss (1780–1856).[7] Wright's architecture thus has a direct link to educational and aesthetic theories developed during the German Romantic period.

Wright was one of the first great American artists to emerge from the frontier of the open road. He came from a family of wanderers and immigrants, and his home life was marred by significant disruptions. Unlike Henry James (1843–1916) and his brother William (1842–1910), Wright was not the scion of an established and well-settled New England aristocracy. The James family, friendly with Emerson, fantastically wealthy, and firmly connected to the most respectable elements of New England culture, was a well-established New York brood. Another contrasting example is the musician Charles Ives, one of Wright's contemporaries and perhaps the first important American composer.[8] Ives came from a far more socially prominent background, although his family subsisted on his father's modest income. The Ives's were a major Danbury family, with prestige and money. They were civic leaders with important social acquaintances, one of whom was also Ralph Waldo Emerson. And Ives married into the family of the Reverend Joseph Hopkins Twichell, a prominent Hartford minister who knew, among others, the novelists William Dean Howells and Mark Twain, as well as the poet John Greenleaf Whittier.

Young Wright, more like Whitman and Melville, came from a comparatively nondescript and unsettled background. As a boy, Wright led a peripatetic existence, moving from Wisconsin to Iowa to New England and finally back to Wisconsin. William Wright, as Twombly has said, "was good at everything except turning a profit." The father that emerges in Wright's autobiography is an impressive, but introverted, stern man, who increasingly turns away from his failures in everyday life and retreats into his private world of music and books. Wright lost contact with his father while still very young. Wright's father divorced Wright's mother Anna in 1885, winning in court but losing his family in the process. Then only eighteen year old, the son never saw the father again after the divorce was settled in

William's favor. William Wright, an American nomad until his end, wandered to—among other places—the Nebraska towns of Wahoo, Omaha, and Stromsburg; to Saint Joseph, Missouri; and Des Moines, Iowa. He finally died in Pittsburgh in June, 1904.[9]

Much of Wright's career can be seen as an attempt to recover a link to his absent father and achieve artistic distinction worthy of his approval. Wright never forgot the power and beauty of the keyboard works of Beethoven and Bach that his father used to play. William Wright, who was a musician as well as a preacher, may have been an underrated talent. He composed music and played the organ and piano. Wright has a penetrating account of his father's music-making in *An Autobiography*, which describes the stern parent playing his Bach furiously as the young Frank Lloyd Wright, tearful and exhausted, pumps the organ bellows. Wright remembers alternating moments of terror and then the exaltation that followed as he was deeply moved by the musical performance of his self-absorbed father. Wright also recounts the impassioned manner in which William Wright composed music by running back and forth from his piano to his writing desk, a pen jammed into his mouth, ink stains growing on his lips and cheeks.

Through his father's influence, the formal rigor of the European musical masters unquestionably made a lasting impression on Wright. He attempted to express a spatial approximation of a highly similar kind of integral unity in his architectural works. Wright's metaphorical approach to architecture enabled him to conceive of space and time as interchangeable concepts. On numerous occasions throughout his long career, Wright would repeat his father's pet phrase—"a symphony is an edifice in sound"—as he would describe his attempt to create a symphonic edifice in space through the motivic integration of forms in his architectural creations.[10]

Wright had to bear the strain of disrupted family life and extremely modest financial circumstances during his early years, but his maternal relatives provided a rich cultural background. Wright's mother's immigrant family, the Lloyd Joneses, is distinguished by its interest in innovative liberal education, the arts, and cultural issues. Wright's two aunts, Nell and Jane Jones, founded a liberal Unitarian school in Hillside, Wisconsin. His uncle Jenkin Lloyd Jones (1843–1918) was a charismatic and influential Unitarian minister active in the Chicago area. Jenkin Lloyd Jones joined with Jane Addams to organize the Chicago center of the Arts and Crafts movement at Hull House. Jones's friendship with Addams later led to a direct intersection with the career of Frank Lloyd Wright, who gave an important address at the Chicago settlement in 1901. Along with his uncle and Jane Addams, Wright became a charter member of the Chicago Arts and Crafts Society when it was founded in 1897.[11]

Shortly after his father left, Wright studied for three semesters at the University of Wisconsin at Madison. Although he may have received useful instruction in engineering from Allen D. Conover, he was unable to focus his energies successfully at the university. Conover, the dean of engineering, also had a lively private practice. He hired Wright to help in his private business in the afternoons for thirty dollars a month.[12] Most probably, Wright learned more during his work as an assistant in Conover's office than he did at school, for Conover, though building in a derivative Richardsonian style, was receiving some of the most important architectural commissions in Madison construction at the time.[13]

In the August 28, 1886 issue of *Unity*, a Unitarian publication, William C. Gannett refers to a "boy architect" who was instrumental in designing the interior detail during the construction of Unity Chapel, a small church in Helena Valley, Wisconsin. In the article, Gannett also notes that the church was designed by Joseph Lyman Silsbee, a Chicago architect and friend of the Lloyd Jones family. But it is especially significant that Wright was mentioned in the article, for it is the first known published reference to Frank Lloyd Wright as an architect.[14] He was nineteen years old.

Later in 1886, Wright left school to take a job with the same Joseph Lyman Silsbee who had designed the church in Helena Valley. Since Silsbee had received an important commission from Jenkin Lloyd Jones to build All Souls Church in Chicago, Silsbee was probably returning the favor by giving young Wright a chance in his office. This significant contact was of crucial importance to young Wright, who had been abruptly forced into a new role as head of his immediate family.

Silsbee's Richardsonian Shingle Style was imported from the east. It emphasized the natural texture of the rough shingle and was distinguished by the hipped roof and a more horizontal scheme than the comparatively cluttered and vertical Queen Ann style, its immediate predecessor. Silsbee served as a conduit, a vessel through which the force of Richardsonian architecture flowed into Frank Lloyd Wright. Later, when Wright worked with Sullivan, he once again would reconsider the achievement of Richardsonian architecture, especially in the context of finding applications for Richardsonian Romanesque and Gothic styles in the developing concept of the tall building.

It is quite possible that Wright had already familiarized himself with Silsbee's manner while helping Silsbee during construction of the chapel near the Jones homestead in rural Wisconsin. In any case, Wright benefitted greatly from his first extensive exposure to architectural practice in Silsbee's Chicago offices. Here Wright received instruction in draftsmanship from Silsbee, who was a master at the art, and he struck up an important friendship with Cecil Corwin, a young architect in the office. Wright's design for the Unitarian Chapel at Sioux City, published in 1887, reflects the fledgling's growing mastery of the Shingle Style. Wright's aunts, Nell and Jane Jones, commissioned him to actually build another of his designs. This was to be only the first of the schools Wright constructed for them at Hillside, Wisconsin. The finished school, now demolished, demonstrated Wright's command of the Shingle Style, but showed little of the rebellious originality that the young architect was to display within a few years.

After Silsbee refused Wright a small raise, Wright left for a short period of time to join the architectural firm of Beers, Clay and Dutton.[15] Quickly Wright began to suspect that his new employers, who were short of talented draftsmen, needed him more than he needed them. Feeling unable to progress and learn at his new job, Wright quickly returned to Silsbee. He received his raise.

It is around this time that Wright moved with his mother to Oak Park, Illinois, a growing upper-middle class Chicago suburb about thirteen miles west of Lake Michigan.[16] According to Grant Manson, the Reverend Augusta Chapin, a Unitarian minister, invited the Wrights to stay as guests in her home on Forest Avenue. Wright began to travel to work among the increasing ranks of Oak Park commuters.[17]

By the mid 1880s, Louis Sullivan and Dankmar Adler had risen to prominence as the most innovative architects of their day. They were hard at work on the Chicago auditorium, then one of the most massive and ambitious architectural projects ever undertaken in the United States. President Grover Cleveland was on hand to lay the cornerstone in 1887.

Sullivan had originally met Adler through John Edelmann, Chicago architect and member of the Cliff Dwellers Club, an Emersonian men's club on Michigan Avenue. Adler, a more settled man, was over a decade older than Sullivan, and he already had set up a respected architectural practice in the Chicago area. Adler had acquired sophisticated engineering skills during the Civil War by designing bridges for the Union Army. Later, he used much of the same engineering techniques when planning some of the first tall buildings in America.[18]

Louis Sullivan, retracing the steps of Henry H. Richardson, had studied in Paris at the Ecole des Beaux-arts. Sullivan admired the Italian Renaissance masters and the operas of Wagner. His greatest talents were in the areas of design and ornamentation, for he was able to rival the exquisite detail of European craftsmanship in huge new American buildings. His major works, such as the massive Wainwright Building in St. Louis (1890–91) or the Guaranty Building in Buffalo (1894–96), remind one of giant Renaissance palazzos, greatly enlarged. His large buildings are usually in three parts: base, shaft and cornice. The base holds the large halls of the typical Sullivan building. It is usually punctuated by a large arch with rich ornamentation celebrating the significance of the entrance.

Sullivan's elaborate ornamentation generally connects the shaft, with remarkably detailed spandrels, and the cornice, which often dramatically finishes off the building in carefully crafted patterns in terra-cotta. The lyricism of his ornamentation belies the mass of his huge structures, drawing connections between the European predecessors that had been conceived on a smaller scale. Works such as the Bayard building, Sullivan's only structure in New York City, are remarkable for the evocation of movement and dynamism in the static form of the tall, symmetrical building. With its intricate and flowing ornamentation, the Bayard building is all movement, continually transforming in the shifting transitions between daylight and city light.

Although Sullivan is generally considered as father of the American skyscraper, William Le Baron Jenney is really the architect who first used the steel frame in a tall building in the mid 1880s. Le Baron Jenney, like Adler, was a brilliantly gifted engineer, and Jenney also gained important engineering experience in the Union Army during the Civil War. Jenney served in the Army Corp of Engineers and on the staff of General U. S. Grant, rising to the rank of major by the end of the war. Both Jenney and Adler were well prepared to apply their practical experience to new building technology in late nineteenth-century Chicago. Jenney, a mentor of Chicago architects, also helped train Louis Sullivan, William Holabird, Martin Roche, and Daniel Burnham. Nonetheless, Wright credits Sullivan, Adler's eccentric partner, with conceiving the first skyscraper with a formal design that properly reflects its size and mass, for Jenney, like Adler, was less an original visual artist and aesthetician than he was a technician.[19]

Daniel Burnham and John Wellborn Root are two other important architects who wrestled through the evolution of the steel frame around the time that Wright came to Chicago. Burnham, the powerful champion of Beaux-Arts neoclassicism in the Chicago area, is responsible for much of the city's present lakeside landscaping. John Wellborn Root was another bright young architect who also happened to be the brother-in-law of Harriet Monroe, a critic and editor who would rise to great importance in American cultural history. Together the two men formed the influential architectural firm of Burnham and Root.

The importance of the steel frame is easily noted by comparing two Burnham and Root structures, the Monadnock building and the Reliance building. The Monadnock building (1885–92), with its thick weight-bearing walls, lacking the strength and economy of the steel frame, seems almost oppressively massive when viewed in relation to the steel-framed Reliance building (1890–95).[20]

Sullivan and Adler needed talented draftsmen to help them with the complex ornamentation for the Auditorium Building. Frank Lloyd Wright was in the right place at the right time. Wright had little formal schooling, attending the University of Wisconsin for only a brief stint of undergraduate education. His chief professional training came from his close relationship with Louis Sullivan, an apprenticeship which was to last seven years. Since Sullivan's prominence in architectural history is indisputable, Wright was fortunate. At an impressionable age, Wright was directly exposed to one of the most important precursors and innovators of early Modernism.

In 1887, Wright started with the firm of Adler and Sullivan at $25 a week, hired as an apprentice with the understanding that he would help with drawings for the new auditorium.[21] Wright and Sullivan became very close, far beyond a mere relationship of employment. A protegé of great talent, Wright served in the capacity of what he always described as "the pencil-in-hand" for the master architect. While he was drawing for Sullivan, the two of them took time to discuss books and ideas that pertained to the worlds of arts and letters, as well as to architectural practice. Whitman, Wagner, Herbert Spencer, Rousseau, Victor Hugo, and others were topics of their conversations. Sullivan's mercurial temperament resembles Wright's in some ways. But his High Romanticism and penchant for flowery ornamentation mark him as a distinctly different artistic personality.

In June 1889, Frank Lloyd Wright, then twenty-two years old, married Catherine Tobin, a young lady from Kenwood, a fashionable neighborhood in south Chicago. They moved to Oak Park shortly after the wedding. Wright's extended contract with Adler and Sullivan enabled him to finance a new house in this growing suburb.

While working for Sullivan, Wright began to experiment in his own home, which he built on the corner of Chicago Avenue and Forest Street. He started in the Shingle Style that he had mastered during his apprenticeship with Silsbee.[22] Soon, however, he left it behind for a unique architectural adventure that took place within the changing interior of his own home. Although the eclecticism of his taste at the time is reflected in the varied stylistic choices made in the frequent remodelling of his home, Wright's strong personality quickly began to dominate the emerging nature of the home, which was continuously altered to fit the needs of his growing family.[23]

In 1889, prominent Chicagoans decided to hold a world's fair in the developing city.[24] The fair was in large part an American response to the 1889 *Exposition Universelle* in Paris; it marked the emerging importance of Chicago as a major American city and center of international commerce. The fair, which came to be known as the World's Columbian Exposition, was organized at around the same time as the founding of the University of Chicago, the Newberry Library, and the Chicago Symphony. It was located on Chicago's south side, incorporating the still-present Midway Plaisance, which today cuts across the University of Chicago campus, and large lakefront areas to the north and south (now part of both Jackson

Park and Grant Park). Planning and building the fair was a vast enterprise that spanned almost five years. It opened on May 1, 1893.

The clashing architectural ideologies represented at the fair were to have a germinative influence on young Wright. Most of the major conflicts and stimuli that sparked his creative life were present on its grounds. They were particularly manifested in the Japanese Pavilion, Sullivan's Transportation Building, the urban planning of Daniel Burnham and John Wellborn Root, and the landscape architecture of Frederick Law Olmsted. Many scholars have noted that Wright's prairie houses display important stylistic affinities with the Japanese Pavilion exhibited at the fair. This structure, known as the Ho-o-den, was based on a monastery from the ancient Fujiwara period which may have been built around A.D. 1053.[25] Wright also saw reproductions of Mayan, Aztec, and other native American architecture elsewhere on the fairgrounds. These indigenous architectural styles would later receive a modern reworking in Wright's use of concrete textile blocks.

Other non-European architectural styles may also have made an important impression on young Wright. Among them were the Ceylonese Building, with an octagonal room and a sloping roof, and the Turkish pavilion, with overhanging eaves, broad horizontal lines, and abstract ornamentation.[26] The emerging technology of the approaching twentieth century, demonstrated in the engineering and building materials of the fair (including new uses of steel, concrete, and electricity) was to have a lasting impact on Wright as well.

Burnham and Root's neoclassical plan for the fair left a permanent stamp on the city of Chicago. Burnham's Chicago Plan of 1907–09, which has given today's city much of its present lakeside shape and interlocking system of inland waterways, is based on ideas and experience garnered in the planning for the 1893 fair. The fair was an ideal preparation for the more extensive Chicago Plan, for it was truly massive in size and scope, essentially a medium-sized city in itself. The site spanned 633 acres and visitors would have had to walk approximately 150 miles to see all of the exhibits.[27]

Most of the huge fairgrounds did not feature the exotic architectural alternatives that attracted the eye of the young Wright. The heart of the Columbian Exhibition was "the White City," a complex of buildings with classical façades, colonnades, and an allegorical statuary graced by a large lagoon. The White City was the utopian vision of how an ideal city should look in a Eurocentric America. Cleverly, the architects of the White City recycled images from classical Greece and Rome, Renaissance Italy and— most obviously—Beaux-Arts Paris.

The plaster structures of the fair were designed for temporary use only. But the White City was to have a lasting impact on the American cultural consciousness. The academic classicism of the layout for the fair made it clear that the revolutionary developments of Chicago architecture had little status in the eyes of some of its outstanding proponents and practitioners. It marked a shift in taste, a turning away from the Gothic rewritings in the buildings of Richardson and Sullivan, and it was, for many, a kowtowing to the Eurocentric styles of eastern architects. Even the iconoclastic young Wright experimented with academic neoclassicism as a result of the fair. Its impact on architectural criticism lasted until the mid 1920s.[28] And it set a bad example for Europeans who were looking for legitimate signs of originality in the midwest and elsewhere in America. Later Wright learned how little sophisticated Europeans cared for the derivative Beaux-Arts architects of America. But it was the easterners who dominated at Chicago in 1893, eclipsing the great talents of the Chicago school for years to come.

Wright worked closely with Louis Sullivan on the preparations for the Transportation Building, and probably helped with the drawings for the intricate ornamentation and Richardsonian receding arches of the "Golden Doorway" (fig. 1). Sullivan's exotic design stood out as a single, rebellious statement of originality. Perhaps impressed because his work was so radically different from their many American imitators, the French gave Sullivan a citation for his ornamentation.[29] The striking orientalism of Sullivan's highly ornamented arches over the entrance to his pavilion is a remarkable contrast to the pseudo-Grecian designs for the fair at large. Most architectural historians, including Manson, laud Sullivan for his design, but point out his relatively insignificant role at the fair. Sullivan, relegated to an obscure site on the subsidiary lagoon, away from the highly visible "Court of Honor" overlooking Lake Michigan, did not command the planning of the fair in any significant way.

Sullivan's building was an impressive 960 by 256 feet and contained many samples of the trains from America's powerful nineteenth century railroads. According to Wright apprentice Edgar Tafel, some of the first automobiles were displayed there as well, thus making an intriguing connection between the future of architecture and the future of transportation in industrialized America. It is certainly appropriate that the prophet of modern architecture in urban America would house the mechanical transportation that would characterize the twentieth century. Nevertheless, the fair contributed significantly to the rise of derivative European styles in American architecture instead of an opportunity for a proud assertion of the Chicago School's prominence and originality. The firm of Adler and Sullivan dissolved shortly after the fair ended. After his gifted partner Root died at a tragically young age, Burnham increasingly became a proponent of the Beaux-Arts style in America. With Sullivan's decline, the neoclassicists dominated Chicago architecture.

II

EARLY
TRIUMPH IN
OAK PARK

■

Style is important. A style is not. There is all the difference when we work with style and not for a style.

Frank Lloyd Wright, *The Natural House*

In 1893, Wright left Sullivan's atelier in disgrace, fired for his moonlighting. Although he was bound by a five year contract with the firm of Adler and Sullivan, Wright had been building homes for his own private clients, without telling the head architects at the office. Working secretly from 1890–93, Wright may have designed as many as ten houses, which he always referred to as his "bootlegged" projects.[1] Sullivan, knowing about the burden of Wright's growing family, had been kind enough to allow Wright advance pay on his contract. He became furious when he found out about his apprentice's activities.[2] However, the split was inevitable, for Wright had become a fully finished architect and was ready to go it alone. Grant Manson speculates that Wright launched his own practice around May 1893, about the time he won a competition for a boathouse design in Madison, Wisconsin.[3]

The traits of Wright's teachers and precursors are all clearly evident in the early designs done in secret in the Chicago area. In the Thomas H. Gale and R. P. Parker homes in Oak Park, Wright worked his way through the Queen Ann style. However, in these homes, as well as in the W. S. MacHarg house (1891), Wright discarded the shingles of Silsbee for clapboard siding, displaying an ability to take some initiative of his own.[4] Both the Warren McArthur (1892) and the George Blossom (1892) homes still stand today in Kenwood near the University of Chicago. While the

McArthur home is done in a kind of Silbeesque derivation of the Richardsonian Suburban manner, the Blossom house is in a more abstract colonial style, again featuring Wright's new preference for the smoother effect of clapboard siding.[5] It is Wright's one experiment with Jeffersonian academicism (fig. 2).

In summation, these homes, while promising and original in many of their details, are all Sullivanesque or Richardsonian or Silsbeesque. Wright was searching for his own voice as he worked through the styles of others. The more he worked on his own, away from Sullivan, the greater the temptation he must have felt to experiment with other styles distinct from what he had done with Sullivan, and to synthesize his own ideas.[6]

Two projects stand out amongst Wright's efforts during his years with Sullivan, one done with his approval, the other done in secret. The James Charnley house (1891), technically an Adler and Sullivan project, shows the hand of Sullivan's gifted apprentice clearly for the first time. The sheer pragmatism of the symmetrical design for Charnley prefigures many of Wright's later notions, and the grouping of symmetrical windows around the prominent front entrance clearly anticipates Wright's own design for the William H. Winslow house in River Forest, completed just a short time later. Most historians agree that the Allison Harlan house (1892) in Kenwood is Wright's most significant "bootlegged" project. Here the wide eaves of a hip roof protrude beyond the boxlike form of the house, sheltering a balcony directly underneath. The elegant French ornamentation on the balcony and windows, unusual for Wright, displays a lightness and sweep not typical of Sullivan. In the interior, the impressive two-story stairwell already shows Wright's fascination for open space and clean rectangular forms.[7]

After leaving Sullivan's firm, Frank Lloyd Wright swiftly built an architectural practice that resembled the system of apprenticeship and patronage established centuries before by European Renaissance masters.[8] He soon gathered an entourage of apprentices, craftsmen and artisans who could help him execute his projects, and he maintained this custom for the remainder of his career. Among the talented people who gathered around him were William Drummond, Albert McArthur, Walter Griffin, Marian Mahony, George Wills, Andrew Willatzen, and Frank Byrne.[9] His base of operations was his home and studio at Oak Park, where he built many of his prairie houses. From Oak Park, Wright quickly spread his name throughout the country, designing new buildings for a number of midwestern states, and landing a commission as far away as Buffalo, New York—the important Larkin Administration Building—in 1904.

Almost immediately after he left Sullivan and Adler, Wright designed an innovative home in River Forest, Illinois for William Winslow, with whom he had worked previously in Sullivan's practice. The front exterior of the home demonstrates a fascination with pure geometric design and a clarity of line that is markedly distinct from the Sullivanian manner. The only echo of Sullivan, who Wright will later acknowledge as his "Lieber Meister" (Dear Master), is a single ornamental band tracing the balanced tripartite arrangement of the two windows punctuated by the front door (fig. 3). The rear of the home is a busy conglomeration of irregular angles that result from a pragmatic concern with the functions of the family that dwells within the home.[10] Here Wright allows the activities of the Winslow family to determine the shape of the home, experimenting with a free, asymmetrical form that is both pragmatic and pleasurable. For the first time in Wright's work, inner space begins to control the appearance of outer form.

In 1896–97, Wright collaborated on *The House Beautiful* with his client William Winslow and William C. Gannett, who had first mentioned Wright as a "boy architect" in 1896. The book is a significant early document of Wright's attentiveness to natural forms. The elaborate page decorations in black and red show Wright's complete mastery of Sullivanian ornament and offer some early indications of his own unique sense of geometric precision. But most important are Wright's remarkable photographs, which highlight the intricate symmetrical patterns in plant shapes. They precede the actual book in a thin, fourteen page booklet sewn to the front page. Later Wright would create metaphorical analogies for many of these shapes in his designs.

At the same time, Wright's burgeoning creativity overflowed from book illustration to the design, engineering and construction of an impressive tower that rose out of the Wisconsin hillside. The "Romeo and Juliet" Windmill Tower of 1896 is an important foreshadowing of Wright's mastery of geometric forms. Built on the grounds of what would later become the Taliesin North estate in Spring Green, Wisconsin, the tower still stands today. The structure is an interlocking union of a pure lozenge and a complete hexagon, with the diamond piercing the hexagon at one end and jutting outward to form what Wright described as a "storm prow" at the other.[11] In turn, the hexagon locks the diamond in a firm embrace. This interpenetration of simple geometric forms will appear in Wright's work throughout his life, especially in his later work.[12]

When the firm of Adler and Sullivan dissolved in 1895, Frank Lloyd Wright was already undertaking Japanese-style alterations in his own home at Oak Park, and adding his new studio, offices and waiting room. The new facility, adjacent to the home facing Forest Street, opened with a separate entrance onto Chicago Avenue. This effectively partitioned the streamlined forms of Wright's professional headquarters from the earlier Shingle Style design of the residential wing. Wright was now beginning to apply ideas advanced by Horatio Greenough and Ralph Waldo Emerson decades before in their calls for a native American architecture. And he was about to find a way of realizing Emersonian organicism in his own concept of "organic architecture," and beginning to formulate his notions of the prairie house style.

Wright's developing anticlassicism and dominating individualism is evident in his relationship with Richard Bock. Wright commissioned Bock, who had collaborated with Wright on earlier projects, to help him work out the exterior of the Oak Park studio. In his colorful memoirs Bock makes a clear distinction between the work he did for Wright on the Isidore Heller house (1896) in Hyde Park and the strange new style Wright wanted for his studio in Oak Park. Whereas Wright was content with an extremely Sullivanesque frieze for the Heller house, Wright now wanted sculptures of large storks with scrolls of architectural plans on each pillar framing the entrance to his studio. For the terminal of a projecting pier, Wright thought up the idea of a hulking, Rodinesque statue of a man, known as "The Boulder," who appears to be supporting the weight of the roof. Bock's hilarious account of his work on the statue gives us a sense of Wright's personality:

> The modeling of the figure presented an amusing incident. Nothing could go on unless Frank had his finger in the pie, so what had been laboriously completed with the model wrenching every bone and muscle in his body, Wright would come along and want to change. This made me very impatient, so I finally locked all the doors to my studio and thus prevented him from coming in. Pacing up and down in the hall outside, he threatened to break in, but I paid no attention and completed the figure as I had originally designed it, and he was perfectly pleased.[13]

The Oak Park home and studio proved to be Wright's architectural laboratory, in which, room by room, he could experiment with different styles and possibilities. While the neoclassical mail-order frieze winding around the foyer entrance to the home is one of Wright's last flings with academicism, the intricate inglenook displays Wright's growing fascination with the hearth as a focal point in domestic design. The four large Sullivan pieces, plaster moldings removed from the site of the Auditorium construction and placed in the corners of the living room ceiling, must be viewed along with Wright's growing sense of space, evident in the couches set into the window bays. In the remodelled dining room of 1895, the complex Sullivanesque pattern for the lighting fixtures is strangely at odds with the Japanism of the subtle, *tatami*-sized wood panels that frame the room.

The new dining room of 1895 and the studio and offices that Wright soon built immediately adjacent to his home reflect his growing interest in pure geometric shapes. As Henry-Russell Hitchcock and others have proposed, the taut, refined formalism Wright displayed in his designs for the dining room and studio may be a direct result of his early knowledge of Froebelian concepts.[14] But the dining room surely reflects Wright's increasing awareness of Japanese aesthetics. The large studio, an interlocking pattern of square and octagonal forms, is carefully proportioned in relation to a smaller library, which is based on a network of rotating octagons. Here the revolutionary Wright truly emerges.

In the studio, the great breakthroughs to come are most clearly evident in the use of simple geometric forms such as the octagon to relieve the monotony of the box and facilitate human movement. Unlike the more static octagons of Jefferson, Wright's forms create a sense of process, as though architecture could express the continuous flux of human movement. The rotating angles of the varied octagons in his library, hidden in the recesses of his studio, brings the eye upward toward the band of windows that refresh the interior space. The variations of the form help create a sense of ample room and variety in an otherwise cramped area. Wright does not reinforce the notion of a single shape from a single fixed point of view, but chooses to vary his octagonal forms, rotating them at different angles radiating from the center of the small room. Free movement and rotation in space are implied by Wright's shifting forms. In the larger workroom of the studio chambers, a low ceiling leads into a magnificently vaulted central area, opening up as if Wright had constructed a cathedral to celebrate the work of his architectural practice. The design for the added studio wing indicates Wright's growing understanding that architectural forms conduct the process of natural human movement and that forms generate profound psychological repercussions in the human mind. It is a clear indication of future work and displays architectural concerns that will intrigue Wright for his entire life.

The steadily growing evidence of Wright's powerful originality becomes increasingly clear in his work of the late 1890s, which led steadily toward the final evolution of the prairie house. The Chauncey Williams house (1895) in River Forest, Illinois still resembles the Richardsonian Shingle Style of Silsbee in terms of its steeply pitched roof, but the Roman brick work and long horizontal lines at window level display young Wright's developing originality. Because of the uninhibited exposure of natural materials and the experimentation with clear geometric forms, a number of commentators have also noted the Williams house as an early example of Wright's Japanism.[15]

The Heller house (1896) in Hyde Park and the Rollin Furbeck home (1897) in Oak Park have a romantic ornamental and sculptural exterior that is reminiscent of Sullivan. In spite of their rather heaped, pyramidal form, they also both have startlingly flattened hip roofs and subtly projecting eaves that seal off the top of the homes, drawing the eye along the lines of inhabited space.

Manson calls the Joseph Husser house of 1899 "the last stop before the Prairie House."[16] The now demolished Husser house was a complex, exuberant form, made out of a busy series of interacting rectangles, hexagons and octagons. It featured a significant amount of Sullivanian ornament. However, the two extending octagons, protruding from the main trunk of the structure, both with views of Lake Michigan, paralleled Wright's development of octagonal patterns in his own study and library just a few years earlier. Also, Wright decided to eliminate the sunken basement, which he always detested. Now he raised the basement to the ground level for the first time, foreshadowing innovations in the forthcoming prairie style. Hitchcock identifies Wright's growing admiration for Japanese aesthetics in the flattened hollyhock patterns around the hearth.[17] Wright's abstractions of natural forms, inspired by his identification with the Japanese aesthetic sensibility, marks his increasingly confident assertion of a style distinct from Sullivan's.

Born without money or prestige, Wright had to use his wiles, especially when young and unknown, to gain access to the world of the wealthy. It is much more important for an architect to gain connections to the financially well-established than it is for a poet or novelist, or even a composer or dramatist. The cost of building with the aesthetic dimension as a primary concern is astronomically higher than the financial resources necessary for composing or writing. We have only to think of the price of steel, wood, glass, and cement as compared to the cost of paper to understand the distinction.

His marriage to Catherine helped young Wright meet many established families in the Oak Park area, and a number of them soon became important clients for his architectural projects. His married life and architectural practice developed harmoniously and rapidly in Oak Park. Also important is Wright's early practice of presenting his novel ideas about architecture in the form of written lectures. In this way, he was able to frame his revolutionary inclinations in explanatory prose, thereby winning over new audiences and clients. At least four of these lectures are extant: "The Architect and the Machine" (1894), "Architect, Architecture, and the Client" (1896), "A Philosophy of Fine Art" (1900), and "Concerning Landscape Architecture" (1900).[18]

1901 was a crucial year of architectural triumph and theoretical realization for Wright. The steady emergence of his style that had begun with the Winslow house of 1893 came to a clear culmination. In 1901, while Frank Lloyd Wright was building the revolutionary Ward Willits house, Freud had just published the *Interpretation of Dreams*, Picasso was painting promising but rather conservative post-impressionist paintings in Paris, and Albert Einstein was beginning to work out his theories of relativity. All of these figures would transform the shape of modern life, but Wright's innovative sense of time and space would have no less of an impact on the culture of twentieth century, for his lifework, which would have its most concentrated impact on the domestic sense of modern life, brought a new concept of fluid human movement and aesthetic beauty into the home.

Three obvious successes in domestic architecture mark Wright's emergence in 1901. The Frank Thomas House in Oak Park, which, according to Wright, "opens like a flower" from its central core or stem around the hearth, is the first pure prairie house (fig. 4). The Davenport House in River Forest is a tiny masterpiece of detailed craftsmanship. The Willits residence, a bold experiment in Wright's personal sense of cubist form unfolding in a cruciform pattern, demonstrates the organizing power of abstract geometric structure in architectural space. Photographs of the original Willits house interior show how meticulously Wright integrated geometric, cubist patterns bathed within the subtle glow of indirect lighting. The Sullivanian ornamentation for the lighting fixture above the Willits' dining room table, which Wright designed, is really inconsistent with the overall effect of the *tatami*-sized geometric forms of the room. The clean lines of the grille pattern for the dining room lighting fixture is consistent with the cubist concept of form evident in the exterior and throughout the house. Thus, it is a more consistently organic structure that marks Wright's growing sense of control over form and material.

Some of Wright's most important early commissions came from his two aunts, Jane and Nell Lloyd Jones, who were liberal educators running a private school in Spring Green, Wisconsin. Wright built a conventional structure for them in 1887. This was the first Hillside Home School. By the turn of the century the Lloyd Jones sisters needed more room.

In 1901, Wright built a second Hillside Home School for his aunts in Spring Green. This school, which still stands today, is remarkable for the way it incorporates the shape, color and texture of indigenous materials into its sandstone ashlar masonry, hipped roofs, and spread-out design. The random masonry of the lightly colored stone gives the building a rugged, understated elegance. With its long horizontal lines, hugging the land of the hilly countryside, the school is a precursor of the later Taliesin, especially with respect to the way in which Wright incorporates the asymmetrical slope of the hill into the asymmetrical shape of the school. Site and structure are sublimely combined.[19] With this impressive structure, Wright for the first time demonstrates the possibilities of the prairie house design for large public buildings.[20]

In these first works of the mature Wright, the pulse of clearly segmented structure makes a new kind of abstract rhythmic ornamentation unique in architectural history. Detail and large form are clearly related in a carefully balanced scheme, very similar to the motivic phrase and movement of the classical symphony. Here Wright combines his love for the purity of form, which he first encountered in Froebel, with the geometric precision of the Japanese print and his passion for the clarity of musical classicism. He makes an architecture of clear sections and segments, separating large spaces from smaller ones, but leading from one to the other. Ornament is one with function, working together to guide the human being through the continuous flow of space. As Wright clearly admits in his own essays, three non-architectural sources—musical classicism, Japanese aesthetics, and Froebelian geometries—are successfully merged and blended in his unique architectural sensibility.

The year of furious architectural activity also culminated in an important literary expression of Wright's ideas about buildings and aesthetics. Architectural practice and theory were united in a dramatic fusion at Hull House in Chicago on March 6, 1901, when Wright read what is now an historic address, "The Art and Craft of the Machine."

He spoke to the Chicago Arts and Crafts Society, which had begun to flourish under the guidance of Jane Addams. Addams, a close friend of Wright's uncle Jenkin Lloyd Jones, was the daughter of a small town Illinois businessman who had succeeded as a miller and banker, and then risen in politics to serve as a state senator. He had also been a friend and supporter of Abraham Lincoln, who in turn became one of Jane Addams's idols. She was a member of the first graduating class from Rockford College in 1882. A pioneer feminist, Addams had organized a variety of humanistic activities in the social settlement she founded at Hull House in the 1890s.[21] By the end of the decade, the Arts and Crafts Society began to announce a series of lectures in the monthly bulletins of Hull House, attracting a variety of artists, craftsmen, and enlightened manufacturers to its meetings.

Wright's address to the society amounted to a critical manifesto with the equivalent impact of the riotous debut performance of Igor Stravinsky's *Sacre du printemps*, which was to take place in Paris over a decade later. Just as the Stravinsky debut in 1913 marked the coming of age of modern music, the Hull House lecture of 1901 announced the arrival of twentieth-century architecture. Speaking before an audience of young architects at Princeton years later, Wright himself looked back at the Hull House lecture with a better understanding of the importance of the event as the first major literary statement of his ideas. Referring to himself in the third person, Wright describes the lecture as a declaration of aesthetic war: "Should its clumsy earnestness bore you—remember that the young man who wrote, should, in that earlier day, as now, have confined himself to a hod of mortar and some bricks. But passionately he was trying to write—making ready to do battle for the life of the thing he loved. And I would remind you, too, that in consequence he has been engaged in eventually mortal combat ever since."[22]

Crystallizing with a new clarity and power ideas emerging in his earlier speeches, Wright begins "The Art and Craft of the Machine" by marking off what he sees as the great challenge of the artist in the modern age—the artist must move with the flow of history and learn to use technology for aesthetic purposes. The "Machine" is Wright's symbol for that technology. To use the machine well is to become a successful modern artist:

In the years which have been devoted in my own life to working out in stubborn materials a feeling for the beautiful, in the vortex of distorted complex conditions, a hope has grown stronger with the experience of each year, amounting now to a gradually deepening conviction that in the Machine lies the only future of art and craft—as I believe, a glorious future; that the Machine is, in fact, the metamorphosis of ancient art and craft; that we are at last face to face with the machine—the modern Sphinx—whose riddle the artist must solve if he would that art live.[23]

Noting that two of his great precursors, William Morris, whom he calls "the great socialist," and John Ruskin, whom he describes as "the great moralist," were hostile to the role of the machine in the making of art, Wright brings out the fallacies he perceives in late nineteenth–century aesthetics. Although he is aligned with Morris and Ruskin in their call for a return to nature and natural materials, Wright argues that they are out of touch with modern culture.

For Wright, the energy of culture is never still. To explain this, Wright introduces a metaphor from Victor Hugo's *Notre Dame de Paris* that he will repeat all his life: "the book will kill the edifice."[24] The phrase comes from Hugo's extended lamentation on the gradual defacing of the cathedral of *Notre Dame* that had already gone on for centuries by the time he wrote his novel. Wright expands upon Hugo's description of how Gutenberg's printing press devalued the importance of architecture in modern society. Wright makes architecture represent "traditional-art" and the printing press represent "the machine." He ends up with the analogy that traditional art stands in opposition to the machine just as Hugo's old notion of architecture is in contradistinction to the printing press. Then Wright decides that the old relationships of meaning must now be readjusted and reversed. It is time, he argues, for the artist to make peace with the machine and work with it rather than against it. Wright claims that it is time to make the machine artistic.

One must follow Wright's sweeping perceptions of technology and culture in order to understand this, however. In Wright's view, human thought and energy move from one art form to another, just as they move from one century to another:

Architecture is dethroned.
Gutenberg's letters of lead are about to supersede Orpheus' letters of stone.
    The book is about to kill the edifice.
    The invention of printing was the greatest event in history.
    It was the first great machine, after the great city.
    It is human thought stripping off one form and donning another.
    Printed, thought is more imperishable than ever—it is volatile, indestructible.[25]

Technological products of culture, both cathedral and printing press are mechanistic extensions of the human mind and demonstrations of human ingenuity. Frequently in Wright's criticism, we can find various forms of *art envy*, which may be more crucial in understanding him than traditional notions of Freudian oedipal jealousy.[26] Here Wright is jealous of the book (elsewhere it is the woodblock Japanese print or the German classical symphony), because in earlier epochs, such as the Medieval period, the architect had more power and prestige than the writer. During the Renaissance, this privileged position had been lost to the writer. With the invention of the printing press, the architect became less important. Wright views the printing press, in a sense, as the first important creation of modern technology. It is a view that Wright will advance on numerous occasions throughout his long career. Using technology, Wright wants to reclaim for the modern architect once again some of the initial power of architecture that had fallen into the hands of the writer.

Wright sees that modern engineering and technology have already changed the nature of architecture forever. The modern architect must not use technology to falsely attempt to emulate the past. Instead, he must move with it. Observing the development of the modern skyscraper, Wright points out in a perceptive metaphor that "the tall modern office building is the machine pure and simple."[27] Once, again, the direction of Wright's argument is clear: turn an evil into a good, turn a negative into a positive, turn the killer of architecture into the force for making new architecture. In short, use the machine artistically.

Wright proclaims that artists must readjust and adapt to the present moment: "Echoes are by nature decadent."[28] There is no turning back. Hostility to modernism and new technologies will do more ill than good:

> artists who feel toward Modernity and the Machine now as William Morris and Ruskin were justified in feeling then had best distinctly wait and work sociologically. . . In the field of art activity they will do distinct harm. Already they have wrought much miserable mischief.[29]

The crucial metaphorical union will be to find new ways to join the aesthetic temperament typified by the sensitivity of Ruskin and Morris with the technological capability of the modern manufacturer and engineer. Wright advises applying Morris's notion of simplicity to the Art of the Machine. Machinery used badly can make lies. Machine "wood-carving" is an example of this, but clean, strong forms are now possible because of the machine. Wright singles out the Japanese as rare examples of tasteful designers. All people but the Japanese have mistreated wood, he argues. The machine can be used well to rectify that sin. The unnatural manipulation of occidental wood-carvers has hidden the true beauty of wood. Proper use of the machine can reveal the aesthetic properties of wood as a material:

The machine, by its wonderful cutting, shaping, smoothing, and repetitive capacity, has made it possible to so use it without waste that the poor as well as the rich may enjoy to-day beautiful surface treatments of clean, strong forms that the branch veneers of Sheraton and Chippendale only hinted at, with dire extravagance, and which the middle ages utterly ignored.[30]

The artist must ride the wave of history and participate in its inevitable flux. Modern technology will make the artist today a less monolithic figure: "the artist is the leader of an orchestra, where he once was a star performer."[31] In other words, the architect must work with the manufacturers, who are so essential to the structure of modern life. The machine, as a creation of man, must be seen as an organic entity, a product of nature: "for this thing we call Art is it not as prophetic as a primrose or an oak?"[32] The machine must be used with sensitivity, well-guided by an expert artistic sensibility, so that it, too, can create things which have an organic connection to nature.

Wright closes his essay with a frightening, prophetic depiction of the modern city as a monster already befouled and poisoned by pollution and smoke. The metaphor, a tangle of mixed images, is also a mixture of important Wrightean impulses. First, the city is the ultimate modern machine, a mechanism of great complexity. But it is also alive, an organic entity, bursting with energy, pulsating with mechanical metaphors for veins and arteries. Both alive and mechanistic, the city, however, already has taken on the size and distorted appearance of a grotesque monster:

Be gently lifted at nightfall to the top of a great down-town office building, and you may see how in the image of material man, at once his glory and menace, is this thing we call a city. There beneath, grown up in a night, is the monster leviathan, stretching acre upon acre into the far distance. High overhead hangs the stagnant pall of its fetid breath, reddened with the light from its myriad eyes endlessly everywhere blinking. Ten thousand acres of cellular tissue, layer upon layer, the city's flesh, outspread enmeshed by intricate network of veins and arteries, radiating into the gloom, and there with muffled, persistent roar, pulses and circulates as the blood in your veins, the ceaseless beat of the activity to whose necessities it all conforms.[33]

The technology of the machine has, in effect, given the city a Frankensteinian aspect. Since human carelessness has allowed the city to become sick, the modern architect must use his aesthetic sensibility to make it healthy. This already anticipates many criticisms of modern life that Wright will develop in later essays, especially when he begins to describe Usonia and Broadacre City, his symbolic conceptions of a modern architectural utopia.

At first, the Hull House lecture did not at all seem to be a success. Instead, it was a contentious affair. By Wright's own account, the architect stacked the hall with his own army of claques: "sheet metal workers," "terra cotta manufacturers," "tile and marble workers," "iron workers," and "wood workers." These were the artisans, Wright felt, who were the real creators of the great architectural renaissance in Chicago at that time.[34] In spite of his supporters, the architect recalls that he was either shouted down or ignored by the many disciples of Ruskin and Morris, who rejected his notion of the artistic possibilities of the machine. Wright withdrew from the Society after the lecture, but he had ushered in a new era of modern culture with this significant address.

Following the Hull House lecture, Wright's architectural activity gathered into a tremendous intensity that changed the history of modern architecture. The crucial sequence of buildings designed from 1902–5 documents his quick rise to prominence. Among the best of the buildings are the houses for Arthur Heurtley (1902), William E. Martin (1902–3), and Edwin Cheney (1903), all in Oak Park. These homes are distinguished by the bold modernity of their facades, their economy of form, and the high degree of privacy they offer their inhabitants.

Wright is particularly successful in integrating form and function in the Heurtley house (fig. 5). In this jewel of the early Oak Park period, the subtle interplay of exterior brick and mortar creates a hypnotic horizontal flow. The long, low lines of the roof emphasize the sight lines created by the rich coloring and even spacing of the exterior pattern. The entrance is Wright's trope on the early American arch. Its elegant voussoir is a sophisticated modernist reworking of more rugged Richardsonian predecessors and it lures the dweller into the home as if it were offering the peace and security of a fortified cave.[35] The entrance voussoir is echoed in the impressive voussoir over the fireplace in the upper floor. One of Wright's boldest strokes here is that he chose to locate the main activity of family life on the second story. Here one finds the living room, dining room, kitchen, and a large veranda perched a story above street level and sheltered under the broad roofs of the prairie house. Triangular bays on the upper floor protrude out of the solid rectangle of the main trunk of the structure, breaking up the rigor of the shape with unexpected excitement. This, too, is elegantly echoed in the small porch leading to the entrance of the home.

The homes for Heurtley, Cheney, and Martin were on the comfortable but reasoned scale of the suburban upper middle class. Heiress Susan Lawrence Dana offered Wright a chance to expand his virtuosic command of architectural form and interior design with a luxurious commission in 1902. Compared to the early Oak Park houses, the Dana House in Springfield, Illinois is a much larger structure, an oriental pleasure palace based on the sumac and butterfly motifs. The home is an elaborate complex for a wealthy patron of the arts who did much entertaining. It surrounds an earlier Italianate house, absorbing it into its new structure and entirely new aesthetics. The whole is distinguished by its extraordinary detailing, replete with stylized furniture and customized butterfly lamp-shades (fig. 6).

Wright developed techniques during his Oak Park period that he car-ried with him and expanded upon in later periods. The Larkin Company Administration Building (1903) is an important application of Wright's philosophies to commercial architecture. The Darwin D. Martin residence (1904) in Buffalo shows the implications of the prairie house in a large-scale structure and prepares Wright for the ambitious villa he would build for Avery Coonley in 1907. Unity Temple (1904, 1905–8) in Oak Park is the first large building in the United States in poured concrete. The Elizabeth Gale house of 1904 is remarkable for the way in which it applies the can-tilevered slab used at Unity Temple to domestic architecture. The Gale house's steel frame enables Wright to experiment with overlapping planes of space as free entities. Later, he will turn these planes to create a sense of intense torsion, rotating them to fit into the land at Fallingwater and elsewhere at less famous sites. The Heurtley and Gale homes, while rigor-ously rectilinear, also have features that recur later in the more rotational plans for the Morris Art Gallery and Fallingwater.

Wright's growing passion for Japanese culture, already evident in the lecture at Hull House, certainly led to his visit to Japan in 1905. Profits from this early work, especially payment for the design and execution of the home of heiress Susan Lawrence Dana, helped fund Wright's trip. In February 1905, Wright, accompanied by his wife and former clients Mr. and Mrs. Ward Willits, set sail from Vancouver on the *Empress of China*, a Canadian Pacific ocean liner.[36] Wright made it back to Oak Park by mid-May, after amassing an impressive collection of Japanese prints during his three months in Japan. The trip resulted in his subsequent exhibition of 213 Hiroshige prints at the Art Institute of Chicago in the following year. In 1908, Wright exhibited his growing collection of Japanese prints along with Clarence Buckingham in a second show at the institute. Steadily over the next two decades, Wright became one of the major collectors of Japanese prints in the United States, purchasing the work of Buncho, Eisho, Haronobu, Hiroshige, Hokkei, Hokusai, Kiyomitsu, Masanobu, Shunzan, Toyonobu, Utamaro and others.[37] His interests also ranged beyond the print to rare textiles and art objects.[38]

The W. A. Glasner house of 1905 is distinguished by its asymmetrical angling into a small hill over a ravine. The Thomas Hardy residence (also 1905) in Racine, Wisconsin, is similar in its meticulously irregular position-ing, as it is dramatically situated on a bank that rises above Lake Michigan. Both homes are precursors for Wright's later design at Taliesin in Spring Green, Wisconsin. A number of commentators have noted the distin-guished architectural drawing for the Hardy house, especially because of the manner in which Wright's daring illustration resembles a dynamically asymmetrical Japanese print.[39] Here the asymmetrical pattern of the drawing shows the natural relationship of home to site. The home is placed diagonally in the upper reaches of the watercolor and ink drawing, and the dramatic sweep to the lake is captured in the large empty spaces in the center of the illustration with Wright's individualistic version of Japanese *noton* technique.[40]

Wright significantly refined his understanding of his metaphorical forms for the midwestern prairie in 1906. In that one year, he designed the Robie house, the Pettit Mortuary Chapel in Belvidere, Illinois, and the River Forest Tennis Club. 1907 brought the F. F. Tomek house and the Avery Coonley mansion in Riverside, Illinois. These are all ship-like in structural design, floating on the land in long horizontals. The metaphor is based in fact too. The Robie house actually uses a new kind of steel beam developed by American shipbuilders.[41] The removal of the damp basement, which Wright hated, caused his forms to sail above the land, raising them quite literally out of the ground and floating them above the prairie of lakeside Chicago. Although Wright develops a new sense of streamlined forms, now almost displaying a new kind of machismo in their clean economy of line, the earlier elements of Japanese aesthetics (overhanging eaves especially), Froebelian form, and a musical progression of interrelated motives are all displayed in these buildings as well.

The contrast between the tiny garage (1907) and main structure of the Blossom house (1892) in New Hyde Park, Illinois shows the emergence of the mature prairie style out of the language of traditional architecture. It is the garage that has the long horizontals and overhanging eaves that will become the trademark of Wright's first great period.

In 1908, Wright designed a house for his secretary, Isabel Roberts. It compares favorably to the rather stiff version of the prairie house that Wright disciple William Drummond built for himself in the lot adjacent to it in 1910. The Wright house is filled with unusual angles and unpredictable interactions between his formal planes, allowing for the subtle integration of a large porch, living room, dining room, work area, and bedrooms on three split levels. The dining room is more elongated and rectangular then the rather square porch. They balance against each other on either side of a two-story living room, but Wright is careful to distinguish the forms and to allow for utility to determine their basic nature and the points of entry leading into them. The balance of the home is slightly off-center, with the entrance located between living room and dining room. However, the doors opening onto the porch also invite the human form to move through the living room, across the hearth, and out into the open air of the porch. Today a tree is incorporated into the design, growing through the porch area. The Drummond house, while admirable in many respects, shows none of the masterful freedom with which his master manipulates the natural symmetry of the cruciform plan in the Roberts house to generate a unique dynamics of spacial form.

Unity Temple, Wright's first large scale project in poured concrete, was designed and executed from 1904–6. Wright claims Unity Temple as the first moment in architectural history where space dominates the shape of plastic form, instead of the other way around. In his autobiography, Wright recalls that he began conceiving of the project for the church by asking the liberal pastor there, Dr. Rodney F. Johonnot, why it was necessary to "point to heaven."[42] Wright wanted the empty shape of the central room of the church to generate the rest of the structure instead of a metaphorical attempt to build upward towards the heavens in search of divinity. Empty space would be sculpted in three dimensions and form would arise from the movement needed in that space. The sculptural ornamentation of the wall would be discarded in favor of the orchestrated movement of human beings. All that was needed was a "flat slab" of concrete to cover the roof. The whole would be akin to the geometrical shape of the ideal cube.

Movement was planned from the first. The noisy Lake Street side of the lot was not given an entrance. To minimize intrusive sound, the congregation enters from a side street and then moves to the left to go into the chapel or to the right into a secular meeting room. When entering the great space of the chapel, one must move around the pulpit into a "depressed foyer or cloister corridor." Egress, however, was arranged in a manner that allowed the congregation to continually face the minister at the pulpit while heading for a set of swinging doors which could be opened after services. Thus, Wright's cube form generates a continuous process of human movement through the building. "The sacrosanct space for worship" is more important here than "sculptured building material." Ornamentation, while intricate, is subdued and discretely placed, putting much emphasis on natural materials and natural lighting. Above all, the straight lines and white spaces of the ornamentation reflect the large movements of the congregation and the meditative quality of their activities within the Temple (fig. 7).

To point out the subdued white walls, straight lines, and right angles of Unity Temple is not to argue that ornamentation is absent from the structure. Wright never intended to strip away decorative pattern as if it were a kind of pervasion of aesthetic truth in the manner of the far more severe stylistics of a contemporary like the Viennese Adolph Loos (1870–1933). Instead, plant motifs abound in the Temple, anticipating the hollyhock motifs and floral patterns of later buildings such as the Aline Barnsdall mansion and the Arizona Biltmore hotel of the 1920s. And a "tree of life" leaded-glass pattern, used with more conspicuous elegance at the Darwin Martin house in Buffalo, is here more subtly integrated into asymmetrically placed openings in the concrete walls around the structure. In spite of the humble materials used, both interior and exterior of Unity Temple have an inviting humanistic softness that is far more like Leone Battista Alberti's understated visual aesthetics and Brunelleschi's Pazzi chapel than Wright would have cared to admit. The square shapes of the Temple anticipate the Mayan-like edifices Wright was to design in the 1920s. Clearly there is a connection between the organicism of his Oak Park years and the concrete block structures of later years.

By 1904, Wright may have read the Chinese philosopher Laotze, who had expressed, thousands of years earlier, a concept that had been evolving in Wright's architecture all along: "the reality of the building does not consist in the roof and walls but in the space within to be lived in."[43] When he left Sullivan's firm in the 1890s he had embarked on a path that would lead him to this formulation. With Unity Temple he finally fully grasped and implemented it. For this reason, Unity Temple is a crucial point in Wright's oeuvre that signifies the moment in which he is able to reverse the decorative poetics of Sullivan while forming his own fresh sense of beauty. Wright himself understood this completely and he wrote about it frequently. In A Testament, one of Wright's last books and published at the end of his life, Wright pinpoints Unity Temple as the moment in his career when he first intuitively sensed the importance of Laotze's statement.[44]

Wright, again drawing upon a non-European and non-architectural source, found in Laotze a writer who could help articulate the new concept for American architecture that he invented for himself in 1904 with the construction of the Temple. It was a concept that Wright first developed on his own. Later during his intense periods of reading and writing, he found what he would describe as "splendid confirmation" and "resemblance" in the words of Laotze, who expressed what Wright had been building all along. But Wright's ability to absorb and employ elements of oriental aesthetics should not be underestimated or ignored. One of the great strengths of Wright's creative mind was his ability to condense and displace a variety of earlier aesthetics and architectural shapes and to amalgamate them into a unique new formation.

The Larkin Administration Building in Buffalo was just such an unusual and revolutionary a design (fig. 8). It was one of the first office buildings to be planned from an environmental perspective, humanely designed to protect the workers in it from the noise and fumes of a busy rail and shipping area. It contained some of the first air-conditioning and fireproofing in any building in the United States. Here too, as in Unity Temple, the interior shape of the space to be used shapes and determines every other aspect of Wright's design. In An Autobiography, Wright refers to it is as "the first protestant in architecture" (and he repeatedly does so elsewhere), protesting, he claims, against "the tide of meaningless elaboration sweeping the United States."[45] It included a great hall, lit subtly from stories above, a rooftop recreation area and a penthouse restaurant. Greenery and flowers were incorporated into the interior design. The building, finished in the autumn of 1906, was demolished in 1950.

There was much controversy over Wright's revolutionary plans for Unity Temple and the Larkin Administration Building. Influential members of the committee for the construction of Unity Temple were doubtful opponents of Wright's plan, while the Larkin family, Wright recounts in his autobiography, was unable to really appreciate his innovative energies, and a bit unsettled by his many "experiments."

From the perspective of American domestic architecture, Wright's Oak Park years came to a climax in 1907 with the emergence of two ambitious projects. First was the great success of the Coonley mansion in Riverside, Illinois. Also in that year, Wright created designs for what surely would have been a masterpiece on Lake Michigan, the palatial home for Harold McCormick in Lake Forest. One was an architectural triumph, the other Wright's greatest disappointment to date. By default, one stands as the culminating statement on the large prairie villa that the other should have been.

Wright's layout for the Coonley estate is a superb expression of his notions of horizontality. Extending the home into the grounds, Wright designed the whole estate into a series of rectangular shapes built around one central, dominating rectangular core. At one end of the large rectangle is the home, with three wings intersecting at right angles. A sunken garden, stables, a garage, and service courts make up the other end of the rectangle. On the opposite side, the living room opens onto a rectangular reflecting pool. Wright designed the furniture and the interior decoration of the home in a manner that reflects the abstract geometrics of the squares and rectangles in the exterior tiling and etched in the plaster. All is carefully integrated form, but the lush woodwork and expressive friezes by George Niedecken furnish a sense of relaxed quality, warmth and subtle charm throughout.

The McCormick disappointment may well have led to Wright's disenchantment with his life in Oak Park. Wright's plans for the home were carefully designed for a site on the bluffs overlooking Lake Michigan, with a ravine and a brook running down to the lake (fig. 9). Dramatic settings such as this always inspired Wright's fertile imagination, though he had been forced to build many of his early prairie houses on relatively flat and uninteresting sites. Wright took great care to integrate the horizontals of the home and the supportive retaining walls below it into the natural shape of the land, much as he did for the later Doheny Ranch Resort project (also unbuilt).[46] When the influential Harold McCormick, heir to the McCormick farm equipment fortune, opted for a more traditional design by a derivative eastern architect, Wright must have felt an outsider in his own backyard, as misunderstood in 1907 as Louis Sullivan had been at the

Columbian Exposition fourteen years earlier. McCormick, yielding to his wife's prodding, chose an Italianate villa designed by the New Yorker Charles Augustus Platt for the choice site that might have been graced by the grandest of Wright's prairie houses.[47]

Clearly not everyone loved Wright's work, despite his early successes. Wright's controversial status at the time is reflected in the mixed review he received in 1907 from Harriet Monroe. An eminent literary sponsor for America's most brilliant members of the literary avant-garde, Monroe had important connections to Chicago architecture through her late brother-in-law Root. She had read her poem "Columbian Ode" at the opening of the great fair of 1893, where parts of the poem were also heard in a musical setting by George Chadwick, a prominent eastern composer.[48] Not concerned solely with poetry, Monroe wrote on architecture and the Chicago cultural scene at large. In an article entitled "In the Galleries," Monroe reviewed the exhibit of Wright's designs at the Art Institute of Chicago for *The Chicago Examiner*. She clearly realized the extent of Wright's rebellion against classicism in architecture, perceptively summarizing Wright's deliberate revolt against architectural academicism:

> Mr. Wright has cut loose from the schools and elaborated his own system of design. Like the art-nouveau enthusiasts abroad, he believes that the three Greek orders have done their utmost in the service of man until in modern hands their true meaning is distorted and lost. Therefore he thinks it is time to discard them and all their renaissance derivatives, and begin afresh from the beginning.[49]

Monroe realized that Wright's radical departure from western tradition made him "entirely dependent" on his own "creative force." She was obviously impressed by the power of that force, but she saw it as a mere "experiment" in the suburbs of Chicago. And she had her doubts. While Monroe praised his prairie homes, particularly the designs for the Metzger, Hardy and Coonley houses, she condescendingly damns his larger structures, belittling his most ambitious projects outside the realm of domestic architecture:

> What is the measure of success? His limitations are obvious enough. We pass by the more ambitious buildings—the plaster models for Unity Church at Oak Park, for the Larkin Company administration building. . . and for a huge, square nameless structure, all of which look too much like fantastic block-houses, full of corners and angles and squat, square columns, massive and weighty, without grace or ease or monumental beauty.

Monroe had missed the great trope of the Unity Temple. The movement of empty space, not sculptural forms, becomes the essence of the new style he created with its construction. Wright responded angrily to her review in a letter, calling her a provincial "type" of critic, the kind that ruins every-thing significant:

> The struggle behind vital work of any kind is naturally difficult enough but it
> is precisely the Harriet Monroe in this sense in society that makes the strug-
> gle unnecessarily grim and temporarily thankless.[50]

But he goes on to explain the fundamental concept of the "Prairie house" to her with persuasive imagery while chiding her for describing his designs as "squat":

> We happen to be living on the prairie. The prairie has a beauty of its own. A
> building on the prairie should recognize the features of its quiet level and
> accentuate them harmoniously. It should be quiet, broad, inclusive, a wel-
> come associate of trees and flowers not a nervous, fussy interloper, and
> should be "married" to the ground.[51]

Although Wright's work was controversial, his career had a distinct shape by 1908. From 1905, when his work was first featured in the *Architectural Record,* he had received increasing national coverage in the press.[52] He had already made his mark in American architecture by the time of the 1906 dedication of the Larkin building. Now the sheer momentum of the innovations he had developed in the earlier part of the decade carried him along. New and impressive prairie houses enabled him to continually refine his style and expand its possibilities.

Among the mature prairie houses he completed in the later part of the decade are the Burton Westcott home in Springfield, Ohio (1907); the Meyer May residence (1908) in Grand Rapids, Michigan; and the Ingalls house (1909) in River Forest, Illinois. The Westcott home is a large, mas-sive prairie house with a garden and extended wall. In terms of size and scope, it resembles the Darwin Martin house in Buffalo and the Coonley villa in Riverside. The tight cruciform structure of the Ingalls home was a more condensed version of the prairie house.[53] This home was Wright's last completed work in River Forest, the small community bordering on Oak Park. Just three blocks away in River Forest, Wright had begun his first great period, a period based largely in the Chicago area, with the 1893 Winslow house design. Now sixteen years later, the Ingalls house marked its end.

A portent of work to come, however, is evident in the startling home for Meyer May in suburban Grand Rapids (fig. 10). Built in the same year as the more severe house designed for Fred C. Robie, the May house is noted for its copper sheathing and Roman brick exterior. Both homes are located on the corners of growing residential blocks, but the Robie house is streamlined and masculine, floating with graceful power above the nar-row plot in Hyde Park, and the May house is set back in an imposing manner from the intersection of Logan and Madison Avenue in Grand Rapids. Robie, an industrialist who invented an experimental automobile, loved the efficiency and power of the modern machine. May, a successful haber-dasher, was a family man and bibliophile. Wright ingeniously customized his designs to reflect the personalities and needs of these two clients. Both the Robie and May homes are portraits of their patriarchal inhabitants. Like Fred Robie, the house he commissioned is modern, technologically sophisticated, and macho. Capturing the essence of Meyer May, his cus-tom-designed home is open and airy, highly ornamental and imposing, yet scaled to the small physical size of the successful businessman who com-missioned it.

For the Grand Rapids plot, Wright was clearly less interested in achiev-ing the consistent horizontality of the Robie house. Instead, the May house is his greatest rectilinear masterpiece, anticipating the Mayan nature of the concrete block buildings done in California during the 1920s. Here, long and rectangular golden-colored bricks are used instead of the mounds of ornamented concrete blocks in the later structures, but Wright used differ-ent colors of mortar to emphasize the monumental nature of the structur-al mass. Facing the front exterior, the viewer sees a solid brick wall on the southeastern facade, with no windows at all, rising over two stories above the land. To the left, thick mullions and square copper ornamentation echo the square and chevron patterns of the leaded glasswork and lighting fixtures of the interior, giving the home an imposing temple-like stature.

The interior reinforces the monumentality of the exterior, particularly because of the massive hearth, which features art glass instead of mortar to capture the reflections of light from the fire glowing within and the streaming light pouring in from the outside through the many leaded-glass windows on the opposite end of the room. Nowhere is Wright's sense of form as process as clearly evident as it is in the movement from entrance to foyer to living room. The exception, perhaps, might be the flow of space in the earlier Unity Temple, a work to which the May house is clearly related, and a work in which the flow of human movement directs the for-mulation of walls, screens, and the orchestration of light. In the May house, the procession of movement shaped by Wright's forms is startling and breathtaking. No photograph with a wide-angle lens or video camera can capture the opening of space in the living room. This magnificent room is flooded with air and light from the row of art glass windows. The natural light, in turn, is reflected in the soft golds and browns of the walls. The surprisingly deep placement of the hearth at the opposite end of the room, across from the band of windows, creates a large, compelling meet-ing area for family communion. Both a prairie house and a temple to the American family, the Meyer May house defies easy classification or peri-odization in Wright's oeuvre. It is a transitional work, incorporating important elements of work already done and other achievements to come in the years ahead.

In 1909, Kuno Francke, a prominent German professor of aesthetics visiting Harvard University, came out from Massachusetts to meet Wright at Oak Park. He had heard of Wright's unusual work at Harvard and decided to see it for himself. Wright showed him Unity Temple; the Coonley, Robie, Winslow and Cheney houses; and other designs not yet executed. Greatly impressed with what he saw, Francke urged Wright to move to Germany, arguing that the American public was not ready to understand the unique organicism of Wright's work and that the avant-garde of German architecture was already groping in Wright's direction.[54]

Probably Francke's visit contributed to Wright's growing dissatisfaction with his life. It was not long after the visit of the German professor that Wright ruined his architectural career in Oak Park. In the fall of 1909, Wright left the United States to travel to Europe with Mamah Borthwick Cheney, the wife of one of his clients. They had been having an affair in their provincial Chicago suburb for some time. The scandal was enormous and damaging. However, Wright was by then a famous man whose renown had already reached beyond the borders of the United States. And the appearance of Francke in Oak Park had signalled an important new opportunity.

Although Wright did not want to move his architectural practice to Germany, the visit of Kuno Francke had led to a literary project, a European publication of a catalogue of his works that would soon spread Wright's name amongst the continental cognoscenti.[55] The catalogue, *Ausgeführte Bauten und Entwürfe,* which Ernst Wasmuth published in Berlin in 1910, contained a collection of Wright drawings and Wright's own theoretical introduction, translated into German. Wright gave the essay a Whitmanian title—"The Sovereignty of the Individual in the Cause of Architecture." Actually, he had been developing the ideas of it for some time, and some of the materials had been published earlier in *The Architectural Record* of 1908.[56]

If Whitman could justly say that Emerson had found him simmering and then brought him to a boil, Wright's relation to Francke is no less dramatic. Wright's son Lloyd recounts the intense effort that went into the preparation for the Wasmuth catalogue, an effort that required the shipment of materials from the Oak Park studio, Lloyd's own labor, and the help of draftsman Taylor Wooley.[57] First, Wright set up a kind of mini-studio in the Villino "Fortuna" outside Florence, where he worked with Wooley. Eventually, Wright cabled funds for his son Lloyd to join him there as well. Together, the three of them used tracing paper to prepare Wright's original drawings and plans for publication in the catalogue. Although the help of a number of assistants was required, Wright's own distinctive style dominated the project. The many drawings he did for the project display the elegance, nourished by the study of the Japanese print, of his unique draftsmanship. Mamah Borthwick, by now as much a collaborator as a lover, stayed in Germany to coordinate efforts with Wasmuth while Wright was in Italy preparing the drawings with Wooley and Lloyd. Wright had to travel back and forth between the two locations over a period of several months.

The final version of the 1910 catalogue features one hundred plates reproduced from original drawings made in Oak Park. Ink in four colors— white, gold, grey, and brown—was used to trace the Oak Park drawings. Wright and his assistants then took photographs of the drawings that enabled them to reduce or enlarge the sketches as needed to fit the layout for the publication.

All of this effort developed in conjunction with "The Sovereignty of the Individual," Wright's introductory essay for the catalogue. Wright completed the essay, one of his major critical statements, in the town of Fiesole, Italy in June 1910. He was to draw upon the ideas in it for the rest of his life. The tract reflects Wright's defensiveness in the land of the European masters, but it is also a powerful retrospective of the ideas behind the first important period of his career. In the essay, Wright expands upon the notions he advanced in his response to Harriet Monroe's vigorous criticisms of his early buildings and his article in the *Architectural Record,* developing his thought into a sweeping explanation of the values that motivate his aesthetic decisions.

Wright had achieved the power of his Oak Park period without the traditional pilgrimage to the architectural masterworks of Europe. Now he was alienated from his community in Oak Park, rebelling against the traditional mores of life there with the adventurous Mamah Cheney. In the shadows of the European classicism against which he had also struggled, he articulated his stance.

"The Sovereignty of the Individual" is structured around a number of central metaphors that become essential to all of Wright's later work and criticism: the architectural work is wedded to and embedded in the surrounding land; the architectural work is an organic structure in the same sense as the tree or flower; the horizontal line is the line of domesticity.

Wright begins his essay by praising the great artistic achievements of the Italian masters, whose works he had obviously just seen with his own eyes for the first time: Giotto, Masaccio, Mantegna, Pisano, Brunelleschi, Sansovino, Bramante, Michelangelo, and Leonardo. The arts blend in the works of these masters, he claims. Some of the sculpture is "good painting" and some of the painting is "good sculpture." In the works of the Italians there is an "interfusion" of the arts which shows the underlying design of architecture, which he views as the greatest of the arts.

Noticing the humbler structures that he has just seen in Tuscany, Wright introduces the notion of the "folk-buildings" as a category within the larger realm of architecture. He compares the "folk building" to the "folk-lore" he discerns in literature and "folk music" in the larger world of music.[58] The legitimate "folk-structure" such as the Italian country house expresses a "joy-in-living", free of unnecessary "philosophical burden" or notion of "fine art" or "literature" just as the flower is not "indebted to the farmer . . . for the geometry of its petals."[59]

Then Wright introduces the notion of the similarity between the traditional art of Japan and the best of Italian culture, expanding upon a theme that he had already presented at Hull House: organic architecture is architecture naturally wedded to its environment. In both Japanese and Italian culture he finds an architecture happily blended in its surroundings.

Throughout Wright's work there is always the quest to find the ideal form under the surface of appearance. It is here that he finds his metaphorical connection in architectural form to the organic forms of nature. He detects a great facility for this neo-Platonic ability in the work of Hokusai and Korin, artists far removed from the usual plastic forms of western culture.[60] For Wright, these artists know how to find "the graphic soul of the thing" with "geometric analysis." Thus, Wright places the Japanese on a par with Velasquez, Rembrandt, and the "great Italians" while he introduces one of the most important concepts in his aesthetic stance: the notion of the geometric form underneath a thing (or within a thing) that gives it its unique style.

Wright, impressed with the original work of the Italian Renaissance, criticizes the derivative styles that have followed it. Any "folk-building," he argues, is superior to an artificially transplanted Renaissance style such as the Beaux-Arts.

> This is why folk-buildings growing in response to actual needs, fitted into environment by people who knew no better than to fit them to it with native feeling—buildings that grew as folk-lore and folk-song grew—are today for us better worth study than all the highly self-conscious academic attempts at the beautiful throughout all Europe.[61]

Even the native genius of the Italians had become staid because of too many unimaginative imitations, and the Renaissance reworkings of Gothic structures are faulted because they led to a kind of "scholastic eclecticism" that had no connections to a legitimate style or an architectural environment.

He argues that America is a special moment in the history of human culture because it is a blending of all the peoples of the world, all of whom bring all of the world's cultural traditions along with them. In America, the sterility of "scholastic eclecticism" typified by imitations of the Renaissance is particularly abhorrent. Something new is needed. Wright introduces individualism as a value that can help justify a new architecture that will suit human needs in a fresh way: "an American is in duty bound to establish new traditions in harmony with his new ideals of Freedom and Individuality."[62]

Expanding upon a theme he introduced at Hull House nine years earlier, Wright argues that technology must be used in an artistic way in the new architectural styles of the modern age. The Machine is a "great lever," and the artist must find "new forms" and "new industrial methods" that will work well together. The whole must flow together in a unified architectural "grammar" (an old metaphor from Sullivan that Wright often uses). Essentially, all great styles are "spiritual treasure houses" if they are approached organically. By this, Wright means that they must be understood in relation to the conditions of the present moment of architectural history. Thus, even styles that oppose his own, styles such as the Beaux-Arts or European classicism that he dislikes, can be good if understood in terms of universal principles that apply to contemporaneous building conditions. Industrial and aesthetic ideals must work together in the present moment for an architectural style to be legitimate.[63]

Wright criticizes Ruskin and Morris here, just as he did at Hull House before.[64] But now he is less concerned with them and more interested in presenting his notion of organic form, which has taken shape with a new force not evident in the earlier lecture. It is most obvious in his descriptions of style and the importance of natural materials. Legitimate style is made from organic consistency:

> What is Style? Every flower has it; every animal too; every individual worthy the name, has style in some degree no matter how much sandpaper (the University) may have done for him. Style is a free product: the result of the organic working in, and out of, a project entirely in character, altogether and in one state of feeling.[65]

The artist must search for a natural consistency with the architectural challenge at hand in the present moment and with the best natural materials at hand. This must be at the heart of all decisions involving issues of taste and pragmatic execution: ". . . before all should come study of *the nature of materials*, the *nature* of the tools and processes at command and the *Nature*—with capital N—of the thing they are to be called upon to do. By Nature with capital N I mean the word used in interior sense: the nature of an idea—a hand—a thought—a personality."[66] Nature here receives a religious signification (the capital "N" is appropriate for "Nature" just as "God" would merit a capital "G") that Wright will also employ steadily for the rest of his career. It is Wright's way of saying that nature is the closest thing to divinity or God that humankind can see.

Just as he demonstrates with totally realized examples in his catalogue of finished buildings, Wright now argues theoretically that artificial man-made symmetry is banished from his new style of architecture. The new architecture grows with the land: "it is . . . possible to spread the buildings which once upon a time in our climate of extremes were a compact box cut into compartments, and expand them into a more spacious expression of organic space—making a house in a garden or in the country the delightful thing in relation to either or both that fresh imagination would have it . . . "[67] Formerly, the climate caused the architect to design in boxes. Now Wright want to spread the buildings out asymmetrically into the shape of the land.

But there is also a sense of unity in his work: "all rooms are grouped together as a whole, as in the Coonley house."[68] For Wright, organic unity means relating the parts and the whole. The unified conception of aesthetic pattern integrates form and leads the eye through structure.

He introduces a key metaphor not present in the Hull House lecture: "the horizontal line is the line of domesticity."[69] While the horizontal line has now become a dominant metaphor in his poetic description of architecture, Wright does not advocate monotonous symmetry and repetition. Every shape is varied. For example Wright says that the Thomas house has a form that "[flares] outward opening flower-like to the sky" or that "grammar may be deduced from some plant form . . . as certain properties in line and form of the sumach were used in the Lawrence house at Springfield."[70] Once again, "grammar" is the term for the architectural consistency of each design.

Wright closes his "Sovereignty of the Individual" with a description of the three basic kinds of buildings that characterize the first great period of his career. First, Wright lists the homes that have a new relationship with the horizontals of the land and sky: "low-pitched hip roofs heaped together in pyramidal fashion or presenting quiet unbroken sky lines." The Hillside Home School and the Winslow, Thomas, Willits, Heurtley, and Westcott houses are buildings notable for their quiet, unbroken hipped roof lines, clearly illustrating this class of forms. Other examples are the Winslow stable, the Rhodes houses at South Bend, Indiana, or the Pettit Memorial Chapel in Belvidere, Illinois. Another branch of Wright's family of forms is made up of those structures characterized by understated lines that slope along the shape of the land: "the low roofs with simple pediments countering on long ridges." The Warren Hickox house in Kankakee, the Hardy house in Racine, the Dana house in Springfield, and the Davenport house in River Forest are examples of these. Finally come those works that Wright understands as "Protestant" in their protest against the distortion of architecture into a sculptural form of expression. These buildings are more economical than their comparable precursors in architectural history and they point out a new way to understand the importance of space in architecture. In the catalogue, they are "those structures economically topped with a simple flat projecting roof slab."[71] The Larkin building, Unity Temple, the design for the Lexington Terrace complex and the Gale house are examples of these.[72]

In one sense, Wright was in trouble, now anathema to the purveyors of Oak Park decorum. But his Wasmuth essay is the work of a powerful mind and his European trip was more than a furtive elopement with his new mistress. The trip abroad led directly to Wright's most important publication to date, a publication that marked a crucial point in his artistic development. Wright had formulated his new notion of architecture and had built that new architecture in Chicago and the surrounding midwest. Now he summed up the theoretical implications of his creations in a bold and convincing manner.

III

THE MIDDLE YEARS: TALIESIN, JAPAN, AND MUCH MISCHIEF

■

Afterhe left Oak Park, Wright's career quickly declined and did not rebound in the United States significantly for the next twenty years. Upon returning from his European adventure with Mamah Cheney, Wright had to face the entanglements of his marriage, the disruption of his professional life at his studio, and the voyeurism of the newspapers. During his absence, a great fuss had been made over his shocking elopement. A prurient press vilified him. His notoriety at the time is indicated by the fact that he and Mamah Cheney had even been featured as the subjects of a wrathful sermon, delivered to a packed church audience by Reverend Frederick E. Hopkins, a prominent Chicago minister.[1]

Due to Catherine Wright's eloquent defense of her husband in the press, the papers had come to refer to Wright's European voyage as a "spiritual hegira." Catherine, who remained ready to forgive him, asked Wright to consider the possibility of attempting a reconciliation. But Wright's hegira had not caused him to see things her way. He was willing to move back to Oak Park, but he wanted to remain Mamah Cheney's "protector." This was unacceptable to Catherine.[2] After realizing that they could not settle their differences, Wright moved out of Oak Park, returning to the family homestead of the Lloyd Joneses in Spring Green, Wisconsin.[3] There he designed a new home hidden in the hilly countryside.

Originally Wright may have intended the site for a new home for his aging mother. Whatever the original intention, it was only a pretext by the time he approached the wealthy Larkin family in the early spring of 1911. Desperately in need of funds for the project, he asked the Larkins for help just as a Renaissance artist would have sought out support from a princely patron.[4] What Wright really needed now was a refuge for Mamah and himself, away from the scorn of reproachful society. He called the new home Taliesin and built it into the folds of a Wisconsin hill in 1911.

Taliesin, which means "shining brow" in Welsh, has a complex iconology.[5] It signifies the poet-hero of Welsh mythology, who was an artist tainted by the experience of earthly sin, but gifted with the insight of divine knowledge. Most significant for Wright, Taliesin gains his poetic inspiration directly from nature. In the myth, Taliesin, the poet-hero, undergoes a series of metamorphoses until he is reborn in the womb of a witch and cast into the sea. Eventually, Taliesin is washed ashore and rescued by a prince. While liberating the child from the leather sack in which he has been imprisoned, the prince notes the beauty of the shining brow of the youth and accordingly gives Taliesin his name.

Wright obviously identified with Taliesin.[6] Playing upon the meaning of his hero's name, Wright built his new home into the brow of the hill on the Lloyd Jones property. He focused the axis of the structure just below the hillcrest, forming elongated horizontal wings in a graceful L-shape that followed along the lines of the sloping land (fig. 11). Wright gave his site a mythological symbolism as he named it, and he also borrowed the prestige of the fallen poet hero for himself, for he needed to claim new artistic and social self-justification in his own fallen status.

In certain respects, the new home recalls the fortified country palace of a Japanese warlord, replete with its commanding position and layers of stone wall hiding and protecting its inhabitants. Taliesin is remote, feudal, hidden in the countryside.

But Taliesin also marks a change in architectural history, offering a new conception of architecture integrated with its site. It is made of the natural wood and limestone of the Wisconsin hills, incorporating indigenous materials into a structure that merges and emerges from the land. The horizontal planes of the prairie house are now broken up in space to create terraced surfaces that function as man-made expressions of the hillside, flowing freely between interior and exterior. At Taliesin, the site shapes the man-made structure and the sight-lines built into the architecture in turn frame the natural setting. The architectural work joins in a unique embrace of its natural surroundings, forming a remarkably complex and dynamic interrelationship.[7]

Wright was continuously exposed to damaging public scrutiny in the press during this period. From this point on, Wright consistently took on the role of the defiant artist challenging the narrow middle class mores of

America. His controversial love life instigated the evolution of this persona, but this evolution was bound to take place anyway, for a variety of artistic reasons that had little to do with Wright's peccadillos. Wright now began to continually engage the press as mediator between his rebellious positions and the conservative views of the public. At first, Wright's private scandals forced him to do this, but later he learned to use the media to rehabilitate and redefine his professional reputation.

Oak Park, the initial setting of Wright's controversial affair with the upper-middle class matron, Mamah Cheney, was, by and large, a highly provincial suburb in the middle west in the early twentieth century. The new home in Wisconsin represented a retreat from the scandal and notoriety in Chicago. After great punishment from the press, Wright became for a time a misanthrope and recluse. He left the company of the conservative middle class that had supported his early rise to take on the identity of a modern "Taliesin," an artist in defiance of the narrow dictates of society.

Mamah Cheney joined him in his efforts to find a sense of self-validation and dignity, both in a public and private sense, as they struggled to define their new lives together. Wright felt compelled to invite journalists to his new home at Taliesin to hear him read a long statement on his ideology of marriage and freedom: "The solution of this case will be individual, and worked out by honest living, not by patching broken conventions, nursing wounded sensibilities, or hiding behind expediencies . . . A written contract does not make a marriage nor keep it holy . . . We depend too much on outward forms and are careless of the spirit beneath them. Integrity of life means unity of thought and feeling and actions, and therefore a struggle to square one's life with one's self."[8] While Mamah Cheney sat nearby, resplendent in an oriental gown, Wright read his statement standing by his hearth in a long crimson robe. The unorthodox dress of the couple also indicates their determination to flout Western conventions of the day.[9]

Turning to literature, poetry and intellectual writings, the two of them sought out a vocabulary to define their notions of love and marriage in their readings. Wright, always a moralist at heart, needed to find a way to justify why the conventions of ordinary marriage were too limited for him.

Catherine Tobin Wright was a traditionally upper-middle class suburban wife who had helped her husband find his way to bourgeois respectability in Oak Park. Mamah Cheney offered Wright more intellectual challenges than did Catherine. Intrigued by Goethe and Nietzsche, interested in feminist thought, she became extremely active as a translator during her years with Wright.

Fascinated with the works of Ellen Key (1849-1926), a Swedish feminist and sexologist, Mamah Cheney translated and published four of Key's books, all of them appearing in print from 1911-12: *The Morality of*

Women and Other Essays, Love and Ethics, The Torpedo Under the Ark: "Ibsen and Women," and *The Woman Movement.* Wright, moreover, even helped her with her efforts and he is listed as a co-translator of *Love and Ethics. The Woman Movement,* published by G.P. Putnam's Sons, featured an introduction by Havelock Ellis. Since both of them were beginning new lives together, Mamah Cheney gave the book an epigraph from Goethe that held great significance for them: "There is no past that we need long to return to, there is only the eternally new which is formed out of enlarged elements of the past; and our genuine longing must always be productive, for a new and better creation."[10]

Twombly brings out how strangely determined Wright was to cut himself off from his success at this time. Not only did Wright deny himself access to clients in the Chicago area, he also made it difficult for *them* to have easy access to him. Essentially, he hid in the Wisconsin hills. Most important, Wright never resided in an American city again. For the remainder of his life, his American residences were in rural Wisconsin and Arizona. He gradually became determined to attain increasing control of his personal environment. This was best accomplished with a sufficient number of secluded acres in the countryside.

Donald Leslie Johnson, in a more recent study, now finds that Wright was remarkably uninterested in important clients after his return from Europe.[11] Two of these prestigious clients were Henry Ford and one of Ford's major executives, Childe Harold Wills. Perhaps because he was still miffed by his bitter experience with industrialist Harold McCormick, Wright ignored Ford's commission to build a villa on the Rouge River in Michigan. He turned over the Wills project to Herman von Holst, who took over as head of his practice, and Marion Mahony, a talented assistant in the Oak Park studio.[12] Ford commissioned Wright before the architect left for Europe with Mamah (in 1909). After he returned, Wright seems to have made no attempt to renew contact with these clients.

However, Wright did take the trouble to complete a number of minor projects in Oak Park and Chicago. Foremost among these are the Harry S. Adams house (1913) on Oak Park's Augusta Avenue, one of Wright's last prairie homes in the locus of his first great creative period, and the more revolutionary Coonley Playhouse (1912) in nearby Riverside, Illinois. The exuberant leaded glass windows of the playhouse contain both abstract and representational elements. The balloons, flags, confetti, musical notes and other patterns prefigure the abstractions of the later Mondrian and the symbolic expressivity of Stuart Davis. In the interior, the long lines of the simple brick and wood playhouse, with clean, humble wood furniture designed for the function of the building, formed an environment of understated elegance appropriate for the Coonley children. Here Wright expands upon his experience in building the barrel-vaulted playroom for his own children in his Oak Park home, developing the pragmatic innovations for Unity Temple to formulate a new relationship between geometric pattern and architectural space.[13]

As Wright's alienation with the American midwest deepened, his Japanism became more intense as well. In 1912, he published *The Japanese Print*, a short but poetic work that sheds new light on the importance of Japanese art in the formation of his aesthetic position. Here Wright argues that the formalized conventions of the print are equal to the structural perfection of European art music. Both form an aesthetic expression of "sublimated mathematics" that gives pleasure to the knowing eye or ear.

Wright's sense of geometry leads him to compare the precision of the natural forms in the flower to the craft of the print. His predilection for natural materials is supported by his admiration for the pure colors of the print, which he finds refreshingly free from the illusory effects of elaborate *chiaroscuro* techniques common to the West:

> The use of color [in the print], always in the flat—that is without chiaroscuro—plays a wonderful but natural part in the production of this art and is responsible largely for its charm. It is a means grasped and understood as perfectly as the rhythm of form and line, and it is made in its way as significant. It affords a means of emphasizing and differentiating the forms themselves, at the same time that it is itself an element of the pattern.[14]

Although he admires the manner in which the Japanese mind eliminates unimportant detail to show the abstract form underneath objects, Wright clearly does not see geometric precision in form in a purely abstract sense. In *The Japanese Print*, he states clearly for the first time that forms signify meaning ("human ideas, modes, sentiments"). Forms that characterize various moments in Wright's career are described in this brief, important text in terms of specific significations. Forms convey a kind of psychic "spell-power," a mystical primal meaning which is continually latent in any "grammar" of forms: the square evokes "integrity," the triangle suggests "structural unity," the circle means "infinity," "aspiration" is best implied by the spire, and the spiral signifies "organic progress."[15]

It is especially intriguing to note that Wright had decided on the spiral as a meaningful shape as early as 1912. Many years later he would employ it as the central motif for the Guggenheim Museum in order to bring out the organic interrelationship of a series of paintings. However, all of these shapes seemed to have great immanent meaning for Wright. He continued to develop them in various configurations until his death in 1959.

Defining a concept first appearing in his 1900 "Philosophy of Art" lecture, Wright introduces a strikingly contemporary notion of "conventionalizing." Wright's conception of conventionalization enables him to bring together what he admires in art and nature.[16] Representation is not fixed and absolute. Instead, it is a matter of cultural interpretation and choice, and essentially specific to the subjective point of view of an artist working legitimately within a milieu.[17] In nature, Wright observes that the acorn and the oak, the fretted cone and the pine are interrelated structurally. The reduced forms of the tiny seed carry the codes for large structure into the giant tree. The two forms, small and large, are related aesthetically, thematically, and naturally. Fine art—prints, music, architecture and other refined cultural expression—must do this too: "Real civilization means for us a right conventionalizing of our original state of nature. Just such conventionalizing as the true artist imposes on natural forms . . . ." Wright views art as a body of cultural prophecy for a civilization. It therefore must be created within the context of a culture and speak to it on its own enigmatic terms:

> Art is not alone the expression, but in turn must be the great conservator and transmitter of the finer sensibilities of a people. More still: it is to show those who may understand just where and how we shall bring coercion to bear upon the material of human conduct. So the indigenous art of a people is their only prophecy and their true artists their school of anointed prophets and kings. It is so now more than ever before because we are further removed from nature as an original source of inspiration. Our own art is the only light by which this conventionalizing process we call "civilization" may eventually make its institutions harmonious with the fairest conditions of our individual and social life.[18]

"Conventionalizing" is an act of interpretation and abstraction, a spiritual act that the artist carries out for the sake of a people. The Egyptian lotus and the Greek acanthus were conventionalized in ancient stone blocks in this way, moving from the observation of nature into the shaping of available building materials. The Japanese print conventionalizes larger aspects of nature in this manner as well. Organic architecture, too, conventionalizes and reduces natural forms in order to master them within a human architectural language. The reduction to simpler forms in turn enables the articulation of vast structures, just as the acorn and cone generate the oak and pine.[19]

Wright's significant literary statements opened and closed the Oak Park era. Now Wright's criticism begins to blend with his emerging architectural expression as the two aspects of his thought move together in a closer, almost simultaneous rhythm. After he resettled in Spring Green with Mamah Cheney, Wright began work on the Midway Gardens (1911-14), an outdoor entertainment complex in Chicago. Midway Gardens is a large-scale experiment in interrelated geometric "grammar" that tested the commentary advanced in *The Japanese Print*. It also is the most oriental of Wright's works up to that point.

The complex, now destroyed, was a combination of American cafe, German beer garden, Japanese sculpture garden, and tea house. Although numerous experiments in abstract art were already under way in Europe, Wright's achievement was a complete integration of abstract architectural form and the plastic arts. As he explains in his autobiography, Wright intended to "weave a masonry-fabric" that would inform every aspect of the work, with painting and sculpture as further expressions of the geometric forms in the basic architectural motifs.[20] The Midway Gardens featured numerous sculptures by Alfonso Ianelli, a stage, and facilities for both indoor and outdoor dining. Ianelli felt an affinity for Wright's experimentation with geometric forms and created sculptures based on anthropomorphic forms and a totem pole motif to merge with Wright's development of geometric shapes.[21]

In an unpublished fragment that Ianelli sent to Wright's son John, the sculptor corroborates Wright's claims. Ianelli argues that he and Wright were independently experimenting with concepts of geometric form and space that were also intriguing the cubists in Europe, who were undertaking similar explorations around the same time.[22] The Midway Gardens embodied the early Modernism of the 1910s and the merriment of the 1920s, but the project was forty years ahead of its time and too sophisticated for a relatively young American city like Chicago. The ensuing depression and prohibition era were important causes of its demise as an enterprise.[23]

Although Wright was still active, his career had not rebounded to the level of the Oak Park period. Over the years, he had grown isolated from the mainstream of cultural life in Chicago. After all he had achieved, Wright found it especially disappointing to be misunderstood by his contemporaries near his base of operations. Still under fire at the time for his personal affairs, he sensed a foreboding of coming troubles.

After a stormy beginning, Wright was now reconciled with Harriet Monroe, the late John Root's sister-in-law. Wright was in touch with her in April 1914. Since Wright was a clever pragmatist when it came to finding a way to keep his career alive, he probably hoped to enlist the support of a prominent sponsor of the literary avant-garde. In one of the April letters, Wright boldly asks her to a write an essay explaining his work. But the other April letter to Monroe captures Wright's growing sense of anxiety. In the letter, Wright identifies with John Root, whom he praises:

> I want to thank you for the wise kindliness of your notice of my share in the Architectural Club exhibit. I am sure it was truly helpful as I seem to be-set on all sides with prejudice and sometimes evil-intent.
>
> I hope the "new movement" when it becomes such *actually* as well as in *sentiment* will have your sympathetic support. It should have it because were John Root living in the flesh he would be with it heart and soul—as his work is with us now. He was a genuine artistic influence and a power on the side of an indigenous architecture and is so still. His buildings stand today among the later spiritless attributes of the modern renaissance as oases in a

desert. Any history of the development of American Architecture will have to give a warm living place to the genius of John Root.

I believe thus stripped of all this factional professional enmity—the qualities in any artist's endeavor stand truly revealed in course of time—a belief in the immortality of the soul assures me of this. It is too soon to expect justice in these matters with present day standards—but it will come.[24]

Further evidence of Wright's growing sense of isolation can be found in his second article in *The Architectural Record,* which appeared in the May 1914 issue. The article is a proclamation of Wright's decision to break with his past, a past that even includes his own work before 1910, and it asserts his dissatisfaction with the bourgeois context of "prairie school" architecture. In the article, Wright detaches himself from both his critics and his supporters. His enemies, he writes, have attacked him in bad faith, and his followers have stood with him in equally bad faith.

First he lashes out at his critics, finding them insincere and superficial in their hostility to organic architecture: "the enemies of this work . . . have not served it well. They have been either unintelligent or careless of the gist of the whole matter. In fact, its avowed enemies have generally been of the same superficial, time serving spirit as many of its present load of disciples and neophytes."[25] Alienated from the American scene, Wright proclaims that he has only been understood in Europe, where the nature of organic architecture has been apparent to the cognoscenti.

By the end of the article, even Wright's apprentices at Oak Park, who are described as capable but limited, are dismissed as too content to use his own style as a "ready made" solution to architectural problems. Real artistic style cannot be created by such imitation: "when the genius arrives nobody will take his work for mine—least of all will he mistake my work for his."[26] This last disclaimer has been taken by some as an indication of Wright's cruelty toward his disciples instead of what it really is: an insightful summation of Wright's Romantic views on creative originality. Departing from the ebullient optimism of his earlier essays, Wright here sees architecture in a fallen state, reduced from its importance as an "artistic activity," and hopelessly in the throes of materialist forces and faddists.[27]

In spite of Wright's embattled stance, his growing anxieties, his sense of the Emersonian rhythm of punishment and reward, he could never have predicted the tragedy that awaited him just one month after his *Architectural Record* article was published. While Wright was completing work on the Midway Gardens project, one of his servants, a gardener named Julian Carleton, set fire to Taliesin and brutally murdered Mamah Cheney, her two children, and four Wright employees on August 15, 1914. Wright evokes the horror of the event in a deeply moving passage of his autobiography:

At noon as we were sitting quietly eating our lunch in the newly finished bar [of the Midway Gardens], came a long distance call from Spring Green. "Taliesin destroyed by fire." But no word came of ghastly tragedy. I learned of that little by little on my way home on the train that evening. The newspaper headlines glared with it.

Thirty-six hours earlier I had left Taliesin leaving all living, friendly and happy. Now the blow had fallen like a lightning stroke. In less time than it takes to write it, a . . . servant . . . had turned madman, taken the lives of seven and set the house in flames. In thirty minutes the house and all in it had burned to the stone work or to the ground. The living half of Taliesin violently swept down and away in a madman's nightmare of flame and murder.[28]

Devastated by the loss, his home destroyed by the fire, Wright set about rebuilding Taliesin. It was to be the first of many rebuildings and renovations of his country home. But Wright was unable to restructure his private life as easily. A long period of tumult, disruption and unhappiness began with the death of Mamah Cheney.

Probably in early 1915, just a short time after the catastrophe at Taliesin—much too short for some—Frank Lloyd Wright met Miriam Noel. Noel was the daughter of a physician, forty-three years old, and a divorcée. She had three children with Thomas Noel, the son of a wealthy Tennessee family. Living on alimony, she frequented cultivated circles in Paris after her divorce. Reading about the catastrophe at Taliesin, she took the initiative of contacting Wright by letter. He then invited her to meet him in his Chicago office.[29]

Miriam Noel was attractive, wealthy, and sophisticated. Claiming that she was an artist herself, she may have seemed a perfect replacement for the liberated Mamah Cheney, who was a feminist and intellectual. In a published interview, Miriam Noel maintained that Wright and she both possessed superior, artistic sensibilities that placed them above the morals and limitations of more ordinary people.[30] Both privately to Wright and publicly in the press, she proposed a meeting of minds, a matching of artistic sensibilities in a union of Nietzschean perfection. Unfortunately, this was not to be, and their relationship proved to be contentious almost from the start.

Noel moved in with Wright at the rebuilt Taliesin in 1915, but after only nine months she packed up and left for Chicago.[31] There she set up house in Wright's pied-à-terre at 19 Cedar Street. Petty jealousy and bickering had quickly created a rift in the union of Nietzschean perfection.

Wright's gardener had turned into a killer. Now a housemaid, Nellie Breen, turned on him as well. Wright fired Breen during his initial affair with Noel. Breen, angry and out for revenge, managed to swipe a series of private love letters that Noel had sent to Wright. The Chicago newspapers, unconcerned with the sleazy manner in which Breen had obtained the letters, published them, causing Wright much negative publicity once again. Not content with embarrassing Wright by making the turmoil of his latest romantic affairs public, Breen then initiated legal action in the Federal courts, attempting to bring charges against Wright for violating the Mann Act.

The Mann Act, a turgidly written statute that is still on the books, can make a concrete illegality out of the rather ambiguous crime of moving women across state borders for "immoral" reasons. Ironically, its chief sponsor, James Robert Mann, was a conservative legislator from Oak Park who used to sit across the aisle from Wright in uncle Jenkin Lloyd Jones's All Soul's Church.[32] Indirectly, Wright's more conventional neighbors seemed to be out to punish him for his social transgressions.

Facing Breen's attack together, Wright and Miriam Noel managed to patch up their differences. Then with the help of Clarence Darrow, the renowned Chicago attorney, Wright was able to extricate himself from his legal difficulties. Wright's relationship with Miriam Noel had an ominous, damaging beginning. More trouble soon followed.

As Wright expanded his horizons away from Oak Park, he expanded his architectural vocabulary as well. But the change in Wright's style had been forming for at least four years before the tragedy at Taliesin. One last house in the Chicago area, the Emil Bach house (1915) on Sheridan Avenue, captured Wright's new architectural language. In contrast to earlier houses which open up freely to the world outside, the Bach house is built up in expanding layers of flat planes of Roman brick, recreating the fortress-like impulse of the first Taliesin in a fresh way, but this time on a flat surface rather than a hillside. Here the solid mass is gathered along the streetfront, keeping both natural light and the gaze of passersby out of the interior, but flowering openly on the upper levels, which are safely distant from the street. As the bedrooms are cantilevered slightly outward on the second story, windows and trellises appear along the planes of the upper levels, allowing for plantings and sunlight to interact with the structure. Wright's love of nature is still evident, but its penetration into the flow of human movement is much more guarded and stylized into abstraction in the Bach house.

Some interpreters have seen the great loss at Taliesin as a stimulus for Wright's new style, but actually his interest in more massive, formal arrangements had already been evident for some years, especially in Unity Temple and the homes for Mrs. Thomas Gale and Meyer May.[33] With the Bach house, Wright demonstrated that he was clearly ready to leave the older forms and materials behind and to investigate new possibilities of structure. The final stimuli effecting the change in his work were the sunlight of southern California and the Imperial Hotel commission.

After 1916 Chicago was never again a center for Wright's activities. From 1916–22, Wright travelled back and forth from Japan. Opening an office in Los Angeles helped him keep his severely reduced practice in operation in the United States. But the Los Angeles office at first served just one important client, the wealthy Aline Barnsdall, a free-spirited radical and lover of the arts. In 1917, Aline Barnsdall hired Wright to design three houses, a kindergarten, a theater, and shops on Olive Hill, an attractive, ample site situated within view of the Sierra Madre mountain range and the Pacific ocean. The theater was never built, but Wright fruitfully redeveloped and refined its concept for successful theater and auditorium designs in the 1950s. The houses, however, were actually constructed, including the massive, monumental Hollyhock House on the top of Olive Hill. Construction and development of the Barnsdall commissions was delayed by Wright's work in Japan.

Wright's connections to Japan had been growing steadily since 1905. His prominence as a collector of Japanese prints and other art objects had helped him maintain contact with Japanese artists and intellectuals and prominent American collectors like Frederick W. Gookin, who also were well-connected in Japan.[34] Gookin, an important Chicago banker and collector of Japanese prints, probably recommended Wright as architect for the new Imperial Hotel as early as 1911. After Wright expressed interest in the commission, Gookin wrote Aisaku Hayashi, the appointed General Manager of the hotel, in Tokyo. Hayashi, in turn, was intrigued with the notion of employing a western architect who had demonstrated a deep appreciation for Japanese culture.

In the winter of 1915–16, Hayashi, his wife, and architect Tori Yoshitake set out for America with a twofold agenda. First, they planned to tour the best hotels in the United States to hunt for ideas they might appropriate and import to Japan. Next, they intended to consult with Frank Lloyd Wright. They met with Wright at Taliesin well before the spring thaw.

The visit is documented by a remarkable photograph of Mrs. Hayashi in Wright's living room at Taliesin in which the traditional Japanese costume of Mrs. Hayashi blends harmoniously with Wright's western tropes on oriental interior design. These Wrightian innovations include a Japanese print stand and a Wright-designed table.[35] The Baron Okura, chairman of the corporation that financed the project, worked through Hayashi to hire Wright to design the Imperial Hotel in Tokyo in 1916. Wright's drawings of the projected hotel were complete by the early spring and construction began in 1917.[36] (In 1918, Wright also did a private home for Hayashi, who became the general manager of the hotel.)[37]

Wright's Imperial Hotel replaced an earlier Tokyo hotel, which had been designed in the Beaux-Arts style of the late nineteenth century.[38] The earlier building had large halls, grand staircases, and high ceilings.[39] Wright's was far closer to the culture that sponsored it and the environment in which it was constructed. The long horizontals and cantilevered slabs of the Midway Gardens, already clearly akin to Japanese-style architecture, were used to great effect in the sprawling design for the hotel. Nevertheless, Wright was also determined to bring modern Western technology to Japan, and to create his own sense of a combined tradition that would be appropriate for the international nature of the functions planned for the hotel. Accordingly, Wright avoided a clearly derivative oriental style, combining the large masses of Pre-Columbian American architecture with elegant ornamentation in his own unique style. Following his inclination to find indigenous materials whenever possible, Wright decided to combine the native oya (a kind of volcanic rock made of lava that had the approximate light weight of green oak) with the more standard materials of brick, concrete, copper, and terra-cotta.[40] The oya was mined at quarries near Nikko and shipped by barge to the building site in Tokyo.

Wright's staff was a large, unique amalgam of Europeans, Americans and Japanese. The gifted Antonin Raymond assisted Wright with drawings in a capacity roughly similar to Wright's role under Sullivan many years before. In addition, Wright brought the steady and able engineer, Paul Mueller, from America. Mueller was a German-American engineer who had collaborated harmoniously with Wright for many years in the Chicago area. The majority of the work force, however, was Japanese, and the project employed about 600 people for four years.

Like the design itself, the building process was an intriguing combination of Eastern and Western cultures. In his autobiography, Wright describes his attempts to teach Western construction techniques to the Japanese workers. At times, he was successful, as, for instance, when he convinced the Japanese to adopt the usually spurned oya as a primary building material. On the other hand, he could not get Japanese workers to use western stone-planers, stone-cutters, derricks and hoists or to lay bricks by working from the inside outward. But he marveled at the skilled craftsmanship of the Japanese and learned to alter his plans to bring out their great strengths and—as he put it—to "make the most of what I now saw was naturally theirs."[41]

Wright also freely admits to errors caused by his own ignorance of Japanese culture. One instance of this was when he mistakenly delayed progress on the hotel by ignoring traditional Japanese construction practices during the rainy seasons of Tokyo. Doing away with the customary protective shed and matting exposed the construction site to water damage, setting back the completion of the hotel by as much as seven months.

Naturally, Wright wanted absolute command of the effort and he insisted on working out every detail of the design. Raymond, who had already worked with Wright at Taliesin, was responsible for drawing presentation perspectives and intricate details of the hotel. Eventually, Raymond became bored with copying out Wright's specifications. Possibly rebelling against Wright's domineering style, he left the project on bad terms. After a year of hard work under Wright's thumb, Raymond pooh-poohed Wright's insistence on unified ornamentation as mere "mannerisms." However, Raymond, who covers his work as apprentice on the hotel in his own autobiography, also begrudgingly admires Wright's brilliance: "Wright had an infinite capacity for imaginative design, and eventually everything, including sculptures in stone and wood, fenestration, rugs, furniture, curtaining, poured out from his mind as from an unquenchable spring."[42]

Raymond also gives an insightful account of Wright's many enemies in Japan, most of whom were American and British. They ridiculed Wright's grand building, referring to it as "Tutankhamen's Tomb," and challenged the structural integrity of the design. Some of the hostility directed against Wright is recorded in "A Building That Is Wrong," a review article published by San Francisco architect Louis Christian Mullgardt in November 1922. It is one of the worst reviews of a masterpiece ever published, a review even more ridiculous than the vicious early reactions of music critics first hearing Beethoven's *Ninth Symphony* (conveniently collected for modern readers by Nicholas Slonimsky in his lexicon of musical invective).[43] A brief excerpt from Mullgardt's article, which appeared in an issue of *Architect and Engineer*, gives an idea of how displeasing the hotel could be to a conservative American architect of the era: "Viewing the exterior from any angle, one sees a fortress of buff brick and terra cotta; every facade has been laminated and lambasted with a stone of exceeding rottenness, which has been much carved with patterns of Yucatanese, Aztec and Navajo piffle."

Beethoven's *Ninth Symphony* was dismissed as horrible noise by his early reviewers. But a symphony cannot collapse on a listener's head, whereas a building can. Mullgardt's vituperative attack on the soundness of the structural design of the hotel must have seemed devastating to Wright's contemporaries and infuriating to the architect himself. Mullgardt predicted imminent disaster for Wright's greatest project in Japan: "Dame Nature allots about fifty earthquakes annually to Tokyo. Every public room [in the Imperial Hotel] has been lavishly decorated with carved Nikko stone, suspended over the heads of those underneath. The stone is soft and fragile, and literally full of pockets and perforations, suggestive of a well-known cheese. Many of the pockets are filled with loose, disintegrated granules, sufficient in quantity to fill a goblet. No one can forecast when the three factors of inadequate foundation, seismic action and suspended fragile Nikko stone, will create a tragic sensation; only extra precaution can prevent an otherwise inevitable catastrophe."[44]

With American criticism like this directed at Wright, it is certainly not surprising that a number of Wright's Japanese supporters, already worried about the steadily rising costs of the project, became concerned that the unorthodox nature of the design would make the finished hotel unprofitable and possibly even structurally unsound. Wright was forced to gather supporters as he had during his controversial work on Unity Temple. Fortunately, Baron Okura and Aisaku Hayashi remained loyal to Wright, and the Baron heroically defended Wright at a tense board meeting. Usually a reserved man, Okura erupted suddenly; hissing at his opponents and pounding the table, he offered to finance the remainder of the expenses with his own money. As a result, the building was completed more or less as the architect had originally intended, but resentment lingered amongst the financiers, and Wright had to continue work under duress.

By the early 1920s, Wright had fully renewed his contacts with his former mentor, Louis Sullivan. Sullivan's own career had rapidly deteriorated in the early part of the century. His partnership with Dankmar Adler collapsed shortly after the Columbian Exhibition, bringing to an end the era of his grand Chicago commissions. Much of his energy had then been expended designing small banks in obscure midwestern towns. Although he was ailing and destitute by 1923, Sullivan still commanded prestige. Concerned friends had arranged for him to reside near the exclusive Cliff Dwellers Club on Michigan Avenue, where he would come each day to take up his new career as memoirist and architectural critic.

Years before, Sullivan's practice had been wiped out by aesthetically conservative forces similar to the ones that were now attacking his protegé. It is touching that one of Sullivan's last acts was to write a powerful essay, "Concerning the Imperial Hotel," defending Wright's work against the influential conservative opposition of American competitors. In the essay, written in January 1923, Sullivan described Wright's method as a "reinforced-cantilever-slab-system."[45] Whereas Antonin Raymond later criticized Wright's design as self-serving and unsympathetic to Japanese culture, Sullivan understood the hotel as a harmonious blend of Japanese and American cultures that seemed to defy both conventional period terms and the modernist canon. Wright's former mentor argued that there was not a "single form distinctly Japanese" in the hotel, and yet he describes it as "an epic poem . . . addressed to the Japanese people."[46]

Sullivan was essentially reinforcing Wright's own view of the hotel, a view which Wright strongly expressed himself in no less than six articles that he wrote and published in the 1920s. Attacks on his work, particularly Mullgardt's virulent review in the *Architect and Engineer,* sparked Wright into action, causing him to write his own commentaries on the hotel in self-defense. Throughout his life, Wright was able to use his anger constructively, and this was certainly the case with the controversy surrounding the hotel. He at first responded furiously to Mullgardt and others, but later displayed greater wisdom and restraint. Firing back with sallies of his own, Wright insisted that Mullgardt was a not an unbiased reviewer but a competitor who wrote stupid "business propaganda" and committed "trade assassination."[47] Finding an example of Mullgardt's own work in an issue of *The Western Architect,* Wright belittled Mullgardt's derivative architectural style mercilessly in yet another essay: "this building, this parlor for the sale of hardware . . . is but the dead past refusing to bury its dead . . . This is Mullgardt."[48]

But by cutting the revengeful passages out of the essays he eventually published, he better served the purpose of explaining the complex mixture of stylistic sources and pragmatic features in his controversial hotel. In one essay, Wright refers to his creation as a "romantic epic" in the form of a building.[49] Defending his work in "Facts Regarding the Imperial Hotel," Wright maintains that "it harks back to origins," implying that his building evokes a mystical sense of primal human impulses for shelter and comfort. His hotel, he claims, offers the deep inner experiences that only great art provides, yet it also offers a modern technological solution to the cramped quarters of the big city equal in impact to the development of the Pullman car and ocean liner. Both Japanese and western at the same time, the hotel was intended to appeal to the refined sensibility of the international traveler. Wright claims that his hotel possesses the mysterious Japanese concept of *shibui*, which "refers to a quality in a thing that asserts itself as beauty only when one has grown *to* it."[50] Wright argues that one can gain access to the metaphysical origins of the past only through continued contemplation and gradual familiarization.

But nature itself offered Wright the best opportunity to respond to his critics. Due to Wright's ingenious use of his metaphorical principles, he had been able to intuitively work out the way in which the hotel could survive an earthquake:

> To insure stability I carried the floor and roof loads as a waiter carries his tray in on his upraised arm and fingers. At the center all supports were centered under the loaded floor-slabs; balancing the load instead of gripping the load at the edges with the walls, as in the accepted manner. In any movement a load so carried would be safe. The waiter's tray balanced on his hand at the center is the cantilever in principle.[51]

Wright had noticed the seventy feet of mud at the site of the hotel and decided that the hotel could float over the mud during the tremors of an earthquake like a large battleship riding the ocean in a storm.[52] The structure, free of the rigidity of the standardized steel frame, rested on shallower supports rather than the usual deep foundation. Cantilevered from the pilings, and with loads carefully distributed along cantilevered support throughout the upper levels, the hotel rolled with the tremors of the major quake of 1923. The large pool in front of the hotel entrance, a feature that a number of worried financiers had wanted to scratch, furnished water for firefighting.

For various reasons, Wright enthusiasts often have the mistaken impression that absolutely every other building in Tokyo aside from the hotel was completely leveled in the earthquake of 1923. Actually, legend and fact diverge somewhat in the story of the hotel and the earthquake, for many of the large buildings in Tokyo were not severely damaged by the quake and also managed to sustain the shock rather well. However, it is also true that the hotel survived the catastrophe relatively unscathed, unlike a number of the more traditional neighboring buildings in the city. Some of the more drastic damage was done to buildings constructed by the very same American firms that had mocked Wright's design just a few years before. Raymond, who at the time was no friend of Wright's, had remained in Tokyo to start his own architectural practice and was there during the earthquake. In his autobiography, Raymond recounts how the newly completed Tokyo Kaikan Building broke up in front of his eyes. The Kaikan Building had been constructed with standard American techniques in a manner recommended by Wright's worst critics.[53]

Aware of his critics, and aware of what was at stake, Wright nervously awaited news about the hotel after the earthquake. When Wright received word from Baron Okura about the happy fate of his hotel, he felt absolved of all the carping and negative criticism directed at him by his enemies. He was also aware that he suddenly had a promising opportunity to promulgate his views in a wide public arena. News of the hotel's good condition came to Wright indirectly, forwarded from Taliesin to the Olive Hill site in Los Angeles, where he was working on Hollyhock House:

FOLLOWING WIRELESS RECEIVED FROM TOKIO TODAY HOTEL STANDS UNDAMAGED AS MONUMENT OF YOUR GENIUS HUNDREDS OF HOMELESS PROVIDED BY PERFECTLY MAINTAINED SERVICE CONGRATULATIONS SIGNED OKURA IMPPEHO[54]

Today the hotel recedes into myth and history, for it was destroyed by the wrecking ball of entrepreneurs in the late 1960s. We must trace our way back to its enchantment with photographs, drawings and commentaries. According to many accounts, the hotel projected a feeling of timeless contemplative fantasy, carefully incorporating the human scale into the layout of the large pond and decorative sculptures at the entrance, its grand rooms, and private chambers (fig. 12).

Over four decades after Mullgardt, Wright and Sullivan published their commentaries, the author Anaïs Nin wrote one of the most perspicacious interpretive statements of all. Nin captured the magic of the hotel, when she saw it, shortly before its destruction, in 1966.

It was dark when we landed in Tokyo. From the taxi I saw the silhouette of the Imperial Hotel built by Frank Lloyd Wright. It seemed like that of an Aztec or Mayan temple. I could see why the Japanese chose Wright to build their most palatial hotel. The sense of aristocracy, the nobility of forms, the sense of many-layered beauty in stone, tiles, wood. It was a romantic floating palace, built on piles riding in mud, which enabled it to survive the great earthquake. As I arrived, the first things I saw was the pool covered with lotus flowers. The Japanese baron who built the hotel had said there was no money for the pool. But Wright insisted it was essential to protect the buildings from the great fire that would surely follow an earthquake. And this beautiful pool did save the hotel from the earthquake-produced fire, when the city water supply failed and the hotel employees formed a bucket brigade from the pool to the buildings.

Nin noted the startling clash between Wright's hotel and the more modern and commercial building next to it, with the Wright building emphasizing the relationship between human beings and their environment, and the new hotel next to it aloof and forbidding by comparison:

Immediately adjacent was the new Imperial Hotel; in violent contrast to the garden-surrounded, romantic Wright buildings, it was a typical international high-rise, sterile, plain, monotonous. From a distance it hung like a sword of death over the last refuge of beauty in downtown Tokyo. Wright's design gave the sensation of living through many centuries; it evoked every palace or temple ever portrayed, from Egyptian to Inca. He restored to man the sense of pride and deep accumulation of experience entirely lost in modern architecture, which reduces man to an anonymous, meaningless being in an anonymous, meaningless abode, like an ant cell. Here the man who moved about in Wright's setting was a being containing memories of all the past, and strong enough to have a vision of the future, and of his metaphysical place in it. The man staying in the modern wing had no face, no identity, no existence. The restaurant was like a cafeteria. Did modern architecture know it would reduce man to a colorless, insubstantial shadow, without memory or power to evoke his own history?[55]

In a literary prose more elegant than Wright's, Nin captures the essence of Wright's vision of the hotel. Her deeply felt description is especially poignant because the hotel was closed in November 1967, shortly after she saw it. It was demolished soon after.

Wright left Japan for good in 1921, bringing to a close a long period of estrangement from the United States. Upon returning, he hoped to set up a lively practice in Los Angeles, where he had already secured the promising commission to build Hollyhock House and a series of adjoining buildings in 1917 from oil heiress Aline Barnsdall. During his long sojourn in Japan, work on the Barnsdall project had proceeded slowly and contentiously. Barnsdall attracted a number of artistic and opinionated personalities into her entourage, and some of them challenged Wright's conception for the Olive Hill site.

Notable among Wright's critics was the young director, Norman Bel Geddes, who later won renown on Broadway. Geddes found Wright unpleasantly temperamental and distinctly unconcerned about the generic demands of dramatic production. But the subtext of the Bel Geddes's version of their meeting, recorded in his memoir, reads very differently from what he might have us believe.[56] An egocentric young man himself, Bel Geddes was jealous of the way that Wright had completely captivated the wealthy Aline Barnsdall. On the one hand, Bel Geddes admits that Wright's aesthetic chatter was penetrating and compelling (even irresistible), yet he finds Wright to have been more intellectual than artistic, more didactic than imaginative. But can spellbinding talk of art really be boring and didactic? Without a doubt, the two formidable creative personalities clashed. Wright, too, was badly overextended. Distracted by the work on the Imperial Hotel, the architect often came to meetings with Bel Geddes and Barnsdall unprepared and without new plans for the theater. Defensive about this, Wright began to make grand pronouncements about the subsidiary role of theater under architecture, all of which led to an increasingly confrontational and unpleasant atmosphere for the planning of the theatrical portion of the Barnsdall commission.

As work progressed from early talks in Chicago to actual construction in Los Angeles, things began to deteriorate further. Unable to supervise the project closely, Wright's work had been entrusted to a number of intermediaries, including a troublesome contractor and the talented but then inexperienced Rudolph M. Schindler, a young Viennese architect who had traveled to the United States to become a Wright disciple. Perhaps because Wright was unable to maintain close contact with his client and perhaps because, as Norman Bel Geddes has claimed, Wright was truly unsympathetic to the demands of modern drama, Aline Barnsdall canceled her plans to build a state-of-the-art theater on the site.

Actual construction of the main house did not begin until 1920. Nevertheless, the Barnsdall mansion itself was eventually completed. Unlike anything that he had done before, it gave Wright practical experience in a new climate, enabled him to refine the use of poured concrete in domestic architecture, and helped him develop a new awareness of the ornamental possibilities of intricate pattern expressed in concrete. Abstract hollyhocks in concrete lead the eye through every detail of the large mansion, creating a unique integration of forms. They appear in frieze patterns, finial positions, or they are placed sculpturally, achieving an aesthetic unity through the use of modern technology.

With the lecture he gave at Hull House in mind, Wright now developed a new way to use the machine to create aesthetic beauty. After the fresh rectilinear formations of the Barnsdall project, it was an easy step to another concept for the modern building technology afforded by concrete: the textile block system. Working with his son Lloyd, Wright developed a plan to use concrete blocks in textile patterns to build high quality architecture at low cost. The very insignificant material value of concrete had a special appeal to Wright. By combining it with a steel skeleton especially designed to interlock each block for stability, Wright thought he could make a new form of organic architecture ideal for California.

> [The concrete block] was the cheapest (and ugliest) thing in the building world. It lived mostly in the architectural gutter as an imitation of "rock face" stone. Why not see what could be done with that gutter-rat? Steel welded to it by casting rods inside the joints of the blocks themselves and the whole brought into some broad, practical scheme of general treatment, why would it not be fit for a new phase of our modern architecture? It might be permanent, noble, beautiful. It would be cheap.[57]

Wright's California architecture led him into a new form of expression, in which he developed the concrete block as a unit of motivic architectural style. While wood, brick, and native stone had appealed to his sensibility as the most appropriate materials for building in the middle west, he found the concrete block more suited to the warm climate and brilliant sun of southern California. In the homes for Alice Millard, Samuel Freeman, Charles Ennis, and John Storer—all in the Los Angeles area and all designed in 1923—Wright built up large, square masses of concrete, integrating the structures with the striking sites chosen for each of these coastal buildings. Here Wright found new inspiration in the art of the Pre-Columbian Americas, using form and patterns that play upon the indigenous culture of the Toltecs, Incas, Mayans, and Aztecs. Large Mayan temples and ball courts are echoed in the Ennis and Barnsdall villas. Variations on subtler patterns and textures from Indian friezes are evident in the more modest structures for Millard ("La Miniatura"), Storer, and Freeman. Unlike native American architecture, Wright's own creations were all interpenetrated with air and light, and designed to allow for a natural flow of human movement.[58] Like Charles Ives rewriting Beethoven, Wright reworked his sources until he owned them and controlled them according to his powerful vision. In this way, Wright combined fresh pattern designs and low-cost building materials in defiant response to the derivative styles popular in Southern California, styles which he characteristically dismissed as "Mexico-Spanish" or "tawdry Spanish medievalism."[59]

The California homes show a sense of monumental architectural mass not evident in the earlier prairie houses, but latent in the bold designs for Unity Temple, the Larkin Building, and the Meyer May house. The expertise needed to execute the new style stems directly from Wright's work on the Imperial Hotel in Tokyo. Although Wright did not have a great immediate success with the concrete block homes, his development of their forms led to work on the Biltmore Hotel in Phoenix, Arizona as well as to late triumphs in Lakeland, Florida and Bartlesville, Oklahoma. Increasingly, Wright came to understand the concrete block as an aesthetic material that could be stretched and molded, twisted to create a torque of turning masses, or neatly fitted into attractive natural and ecologically-enlightened settings.

Developing naturally out of the earliest phases of his career, Wright's Japanism and growing interest in native American architectural forms helped him develop his own natural inclinations to work with abstract forms. Both the native and the oriental motifs that he appropriated helped him develop the aesthetic use of the machine that he had called for years before in the Hull House lecture. Now the concrete block served as an ideal unit of expression for the new aesthetics of technology. And the oriental and native American art offered an escape from what Wright viewed as the traditional western distortion of architectural expression, in which geometric structure was relegated to a lower status than the pictorial function of the wall. The Imperial Hotel, the Barnsdall house, and the ensuing concrete block houses he designed in California contained tropes on Mayan, Aztec and Japanese cultures, which he combined in his own unique manner. He was touched by Art Deco, like a number of other American artists of his period, but both the Art Deco movement and Wright's designs of this period show a similar interest in distinctly Non-European motifs that dates back to Wright's own inclinations and innovations in the 1890s.

After completing the Imperial Hotel, Wright found an attractive set of new commissions in California and was actively courting more work in Chicago. His return to the United States seemed promising at first. Nevertheless, things soon began to go wrong. As usual, there was not enough money to finance the highly innovative nature of Wright's unique designs. The California commissions, at first so promising, generated high building costs that brought Wright into financial difficulty and bad working relationships with both his clients and his son John, who was covering for him as the local architect-in-charge in Los Angeles. The concrete blocks were a cheap and promising building material, but they also created numerous construction problems and tended to allow leakage. The textile block homes, while highly innovative, did not lead to an architectural explosion in domestic design reminiscent of the earlier Oak Park period. Wright, far from the scene of the actual building, was still preoccupied with personal problems and still unable to decide on a professional direction. That the textile block homes came into existence at all is remarkable evidence of his energy and powerful imagination.

The truth of the matter was that the self-imposed exile in Japan had changed little in Wright's life. Contrary to his hopes at the time of his departure for Tokyo, he had attained no big financial success that gave him real freedom. In addition, he was still the subject of a highly judgmental public's ridicule and scorn, and his unorthodox personal life had not brought him happiness. This combination of factors was sure to breed trouble, and, indeed, the greatest crisis of his life was soon to come.

At first, a series of misfortunes and miscalculations plagued Wright after returning to the United States from his extended sojourn in Japan. Following the finalization of his divorce from Catherine in 1922, Wright began to think of returning to the base of his activities in the Chicago area, a plan that proved to be unworkable.[60] Then his mother died in 1923. The loss of this strong and supportive woman may have caused him to finally marry Miriam Noel in 1924.

Noel had been his most significant female companion since the death of Mamah Cheney in 1914. Wright's relationship with Miriam Noel was one of the great mistakes of his life. Noel accompanied Wright to Japan to live with him during his extended period of work on the Imperial Hotel. Increasingly, their relationship became stormy and unpleasant, with a series of dramatic clashes and reconciliations. Unlike the more puritanical and traditional society of midwestern America, members of the international business colonies in Japan were ready to accept Wright and his companion without much fuss. But a number of them noted the evident tension between the couple during those years, remarking, for example, on the strange manner in which Noel would stare intensely at Wright and yet frequently interrupt him when he would try to speak.[61] Antonin Raymond, whose wife Noémi was close to Miriam during their initial stay in Japan, also comments in his memoirs on the strained relations between Wright and Miriam during the Tokyo years.

Things did not improve in the United States and the wedding did little to assuage tensions between Wright and Noel. Not long after they were married, she began to frequent the offices of a Chicago psychiatrist who treated her for "advanced neurasthenia." Only five months after the wedding, Miriam asked Wright for a divorce and a financial settlement. After agreeing that details were to be worked out at a later date, Miriam Noel Wright left Taliesin for Los Angeles.[62]

One additional sad event may have instigated a turning point in Wright's career, moving him away from architectural practice and toward a new life as a writer. Louis Sullivan died in a Chicago hotel room on April 14, 1924. Fortunately, Sullivan's death came more than a decade after his happy reunion with Wright. In the years before Sullivan's death, Wright had been generous with Sullivan, occasionally offering financial assistance. Significantly, Wright was aware of Sullivan's literary efforts and had helped arrange for the publication of Sullivan's *The Autobiography of an Idea*.

Soon after Sullivan's death, Wright began work on his own autobiography. Most commentators agree that Wright had made substantial progress on the book by 1927 or 1928, and he may have begun as early as 1925 or 1926, while his life was in complete disarray.[63] Nevertheless, the autobiography required at least six years of hard work. It went to press by 1931 and finally appeared in 1932.

Further complications followed the mishaps of the early 1920s. In spite of Wright's great loss of the beloved Mamah Cheney, his unhappiness with Miriam Noel, his divorce from his first wife, and his advanced age, Wright's passionate nature led him to seek out yet more female companionship. Within six months after Miriam Noel Wright left him, he was already in the process of getting to know Olga Ivanovna (Olgivanna) Milanov Hinzenberg, a young and attractive Montenegrin woman whom he had probably met at the ballet in Chicago in late November 1924.

Wright was already fifty-seven years old and Olgivanna was twenty-six. But Wright was a charming, sensual man who spoke in a hypnotic and seductive manner. Olgivanna, though young, was not naive. She had already married Vlademar Hinzenberg, another architect active in the Chicago area. She was already a mother, having recently given birth to her baby daughter, Svetlana. By the time she met Wright at the ballet, she was separated from Hinzenberg and seeking a divorce. Certainly, she knew that she had met in Frank Lloyd Wright a notoriously famous man who had undoubtedly earned a prominent place for himself in architectural history. Wright, in turn, was smitten, finding Olgivanna beautiful and mysterious. He set about winning her affections. Within weeks, he had succeeded, and within a year, she was pregnant with his child. He moved with Olgivanna to Taliesin in February 1925, but both Hinzenberg, her enraged husband, and Miriam Noel, his jealous and unbalanced wife, were after them later that year.[64]

Miriam had herself asked for a divorce shortly after her belated wedding to Wright. Now upon learning of her replacement by a younger rival, she decided against granting Wright that divorce. Wright, however, was eager to come to an agreement with Miriam and offered her a series of reasonable settlements. Eventually, her vengeful attitude began to wear on her allies, including her attorney, Arthur D. Cloud. Cloud became exasperated with her after she rejected three different settlements he had worked out with Wright. Unhappy with her rancorous behavior and her unwillingness to settle with Wright, he resigned.

Wright's personal and financial difficulties now drove him to bankruptcy. Bank liens on Taliesin forced him out of his home, and he was eventually forced to sell his precious collection of Japanese prints in New York in 1927 at a price far below their estimated value. Wright and Olgivanna fled, first to New York, eventually into hiding on Lake Minnetonka, Minnesota, where Wright attempted to work on his autobiography. After agreeing to collaborate with Miriam Noel's lawyers, Hinzenberg managed to induce Minnesota authorities to charge Wright with violating the Mann Act and to declare Olgivanna an unfit mother. Hinzenberg also accused Wright of abducting his daughter Svetlana, and he offered a five-hundred-dollar reward for Wright's arrest.[65]

The litigious maneuvering of Noel and Hinzenberg succeeded in turning Wright and Olgivanna into fugitives from the law. Harold Jackson, Hinzenberg's attorney, accompanied by a party of police officers and reporters, found Wright and Olgivanna at a small cottage on Lake Minnetonka in October 1926. They were arrested on October twentieth and conducted to the Hennepin County Jail. The abduction charges were dismissed the next morning, but Wright still faced Federal court because of the Mann Act allegations. A tremendous public scandal ensued.

Up until this point, Miriam Noel had succeeded in extracting much public sympathy and attention in the press. But the image of the architect in the jailhouse had begun to sway many in his favor, and a number of prominent Americans, including the poet Carl Sandburg, began to press the Minnesota district attorney to drop the charges against Wright. By mid-November, Wright had managed to clear himself and leave with his new family for a rented home in La Jolla, California.

Noel's unstable nature, apparent well before the debacle in Hennepin County, became increasingly apparent to her supporters over the course of the winter. Losing ground in her legal battle against Wright, she resorted to more drastic actions. Following Wright to California, she attempted unsuccessfully to bring more charges against him, this time for abandonment. But in August, 1927 she finally agreed to divorce him.

Sadly, her health continued to deteriorate after the divorce. She pursued Wright and Olgivanna to La Jolla again in July 1928, broke into their rented house, and pointlessly destroyed several hundred dollars' worth of furniture. Noel by this time was mentally and physically unwell. She died two years later in a Milwaukee hospital, shortly after undergoing surgery to correct a stomach ailment.

The litigation and negative publicity that resulted from Wright's personal affairs made it impossible for the architect to work in the late 1920s. His architectural practice, already in a severe decline, came to a complete halt during his legal battles with Miriam Noel. A number of concerned friends began to sense that Wright's difficulties threatened to destroy him. Professor Ferdinand Schevill of the University of Chicago, Darwin D. Martin, and Mrs. Avery Coonley formed the nucleus of a group of sponsors who established a corporation designed to allow Wright to work himself out of debt.[66] Wright was able to sell his talents to this organization, which was called "Frank Lloyd Wright, Inc." This enabled him to go back to work and begin to pay his creditors.[67] The new entity issued $75,000 worth of stock against Wright's future earnings in 1927. Only gradually, with great difficulty, was Wright able to free himself of his legal and financial troubles.

Wright thrived on publicity, but he was not always able to command as much of it as he desired. He reached the bottom of his declining popularity in the late 1920s, and in 1929 he was even dropped from *Who's Who in America*.[68] But his private life had stabilized by August 1928, when he married Olgivanna in Rancho Sante Fe, California. She was to be his third and last wife.

Without question, much valuable energy had been expended on matters far removed from architecture. The period spanning from 1924-33 were extremely bad years for Wright's practice. During that period he was able to see only two commissions through construction: the Lloyd Jones house in Tulsa, and the Martin summer house on Lake Ontario. These two commissions, moreover, were inside jobs, funded, respectively, by a family member and an old patron. Wright's practice attracted little professional activity and his prodigious imagination seemed strangely dormant. Wright also conceived of a number of projects that eventually were built. But these, too, were far fewer in number than Wright's output during his peak years. Wright came up with designs for only two buildings in 1923, none in 1924, one in 1925, none in 1926, three in 1927, and none in 1928.[69] This contrasts sharply with the furious pace of Wright's creative activity before 1910. During his most fertile period in Oak Park, Wright averaged over ten building designs a year, designing eleven in 1901 and 1908, and thirteen in both 1905 and 1907. These figures, moreover, only include designs that resulted in finished buildings, and not those that remained on the drawing board.

After he left for Japan, Wright could easily have disappeared into the history books. He had already made his mark as an important innovator of the prairie house in turn-of-the-century Chicago. Indeed, many members of the architectural community were glad to write him off as a grand old man who had once done significant work, but who was no longer at the "cutting edge" of modern architecture.

If his personal problems had not forced him out of Chicago, he might have stayed put. Surely, he would have evolved new ideas there as well, but the temptation to rest on his laurels would have been greater. Instead, he first isolated himself in rural America, turning away from the city forever. Soon, he left the midwest, and, in effect, the entire country for a number of years.

At first glance, the years 1923-29 seem like years of great waste and turmoil in Wright's life. However, without them the sustained power of his architectural career would not have been possible. Isolated and defeated in some respects, Wright was actually evolving and regenerating in others. Instead of the tremendous output of the Oak Park years, he now concentrated on a smaller number of projects of great size and variety. This differs radically from the more interrelated and stylistically cohesive work of the Oak Park period. Then, he was too busy to theorize, writing significant critical statements before and after his greatest architectural efforts. Now he developed through his growing interest in architectural theorizing.

Wright's architectural rejuvenation began in the untouched desert of the American southwest. In the late 1920s, Dr. Alexander Chandler tempted Wright to design a winter desert resort in Arizona. Wright arrived on the site for the projected "San Marcos-in-the Desert" in January 1929, accompanied by his new wife and a band of apprentices. They called their campsite "Ocotillo," named after the red, flame-like triangular shape of the bloom of the ocotillo plant, and quickly set up makeshift quarters there.[70] Using inexpensive materials like plywood and canvas, Wright designed an aesthetically subtle campsite that eventually led to a new vocabulary of forms for desert architecture. Within a period of several weeks, he and his apprentices were able to build their temporary home. It gave them the opportunity to study what Wright described as the "exuberance" of desert life: the varied cacti, scorpions, rattlesnakes, and lizards (many harmless) that live in the desert environment.[71] Mountain ranges, which Wright felt were essentially formed in 30-60-90 triangular relationships, also found expression in the San Marcos design and the realized structure for the camp (fig. 13).[72]

The optimistic plans for the resort never materialized, abandoned after the onset of the Great Depression. But the stimulus of the unrealized commission effected Wright in vital ways. Far from the city, living with a group of young apprentices in the Arizona desert at Ocotillo Camp, Wright began to fashion a whole new series of nature metaphors for architecture in the late 1920s.

By 1928, he had already reformulated his idea of organic architecture in persuasive new ways. The metaphorical language in his abundant prose functioned as preparation for a rich new expression of those metaphors in architectural design. In *The Architectural Record* of 1928, Wright states that "In the logic of the plan what we call standardization is seen to be fundamental groundwork in architecture. All things in nature exhibit this tendency to crystallize; to form mathematically and then to conform, as we may easily see. There is the fluid, elastic period of becoming, as in the plan, when possibilities are infinite. New effects may then originate from the idea or principle that conceives."[73] Wright invented a new expression of open-ended, crystalline form in his Arizona desert camp. Around the time that Wright published these words, he combined the forms of rocks, butterfly wings, the sand-sails of the "desert ships," the triangular shape of the ocotillo leaf in bloom, and the triangular outlines of mountain ranges in the new forms he created for his desert camp at Ocotillo.[74]

Perhaps thinking of Thomas Jefferson's worm-walled bricks at the University of Virginia, Wright decided to fence in his camp at Ocotillo with low, angular wooden walls.[75] Box-board, battens, and canvas were used together to unite the campus in a pattern of horizontal zigzags and oblique angles.[76] The master, his wife, and his apprentices were joined in one architectural statement. Aesthetic unity and style demarcated the wilderness of the open desert. As he later wrote in 1938, the desert became a sea of sand in his poet's imagination and his series of desert tents became an assembly of ships navigating its waters; "Open in the sunlight the camp resembled a fleet of desert ships sailing down the bay."[77]

All, however, was intended to be ephemeral. Wright's real energies were not directed into the architectural practice at this time. From 1930-31, he did not construct a single building. The calamitous collapse of his practice caused Wright to find strength in new ways. With the fall of the stock market in 1929, Wright was already preparing for his next great rise.

IV

A LITERARY
EXILE

∎

A major creative artist leads at least three lives. First there are the events of private life, which may or may not be directly reflected in the artist's work. Then, there is the life of the mind lived through the created works as they take shape over the span of a career. Finally comes a life of the artist's reputation. This is the career of the reputation, the legend of the creative artist apart from the biological life or the pattern of creation of the works. Here myth, legend, criticism, public relations, and the movements of culture at large (as well as luck) will determine the fate of the artist's life.

In the 1930s, Wright's lot changed for the better. His reputation began to take on a new existence apart from his career and private life, steadily gaining a spiralling momentum that will carry him well into the next century. But this change in Wright's career only occurred after a long string of misfortunes during the 1920s that would certainly have crushed a lesser man.

By the late 1920s, Wright was bankrupt and without an architectural practice. Finis Farr, calculating Wright's annual income in relation to architectural commissions during the lean years, has estimated that Wright lived on about $2,000 a year from the completion of Hollyhock House in the early 1920s until his career revived in the mid 1930s.[1] For a great stretch of time, Wright was unable to work, unable to find peace, and plagued by an endless stream of bad publicity. When he was finally able to settle down to work once again, he was in enormous debt.

But when Wright was ready to get back to work, the rest of the country was undergoing the most massive economic setback in its history. Part of Wright's problem was the economic collapse that followed the stock market crash of 1929. Captured in the dense prose of Wright's autobiography is the catastrophic effect that the general economic disintegration of the period had on rural America: "Economic breakdown is so complete at this time that no workman's hammer is ringing in our great state of Wisconsin. Native workmen of my own countryside, laborers, carpenters and masons of Iowa County as in the next Dane County and the next Sauk County are all but starving while I watch the shingle roofs of the 1902–1903 Hillside Home School buildings falling in for lack of some such labor as theirs. All of them (yes, laborers included) are rotting away."[2] The decay of Wright's own Taliesin estate was inextricably connected to the failure of the American economy.

Architecture is a medium of expression that usually requires the support of mostly conservative patrons. Unlike a poet, who can write with paper and pencil, an architect cannot practice his art without the vital reality of a commission. Wright simply did not have any during his difficult years. Until he finally married Olgivanna in 1928, his difficult personal situation would have made it impossible for him to work if he had them. The overwhelming specter of the Great Depression, combined with the handicap of Wright's controversial reputation, shut down his architectural activity. Things did not improve rapidly after his marriage. Indentured to Frank Lloyd Wright, Inc., the artificial company set up by his worried friends, he found little in the way of architectural commissions. Taliesin remained under control of the bank, leaving Wright without a base of operations. Since bankruptcy forced him from his Taliesin estate, Wright decided once again to travel, eventually pitching a camp with his young wife and a band of apprentices in a southwestern desert near Phoenix.

By the time he reached Chandler, Arizona, however, his fortunes had already changed direction for the better. He had reached his lowest point, survived, and was actually beginning his slow and steady rise to the top of the world of architecture. Part of the change in Wright's luck had to do with a natural shift in public opinion, which had slowly moved in his favor during the bad publicity generated from his personal life. This shift was signified by Alexander Woollcott's "The Prodigal Father," an important 1930 profile of Wright in *The New Yorker*. In *The New Yorker* piece, Woollcott reassessed the work of the architect, pointing out to an educated lay audience Wright's unquestioned historical importance. He also explained why the bad publicity, which he dismissed as unfair, had made it impossible for Wright to find work. He argued that the innaccurate distortions of negative publicity had unfairly deprived Wright of clients, without which no architect can function. He also described the vicious nature of the publicity hounds and hacks hovering around Wright: "Most of . . . [Wright's] time was taken up by sleazy scandals and the ignominious procedure which our ugly divorce laws enforce, taken up by witless and vindictive indictments and all the ugly hoodlumism which the yellow newspapers can invoke when once an outstanding and inevitably spectacular man gives them half a chance. Wright gave them a chance and a half."[3]

Already an admirer of Wright's earlier work, Woollcott visited Taliesin during a lecture tour of the midwest. But he was stunned beyond his expectations by the beauty of Wright's country home. Relieved to find Wright back at work after so long a hiatus from his calling, Woollcott marveled at the newly rebuilt Taliesin and the designs for St. Mark's-in-the-Bouwerie and San Marcos-in-the-Desert. He praised Wright's architecture as a liberating force, freeing visual art from the oppressive weight of bullying precursors, allowing no single earlier style to dominate over his own self-expression. Woollcott ended his piece with a powerful statement that placed Wright back on the map of American culture: "No one in the modern world has brought to architecture so good a mind, so leaping an imagination, or so fresh a sense of beauty. Indeed, if . . . I were suffered to apply the word "genius" to only one living American, I would have to save it up for Frank Lloyd Wright."[4]

Part of the change in Wright's fortune was also caused by Wright's own energy, determination and hard work. But Wright's renaissance did not begin through his practice of architecture, the art form he had already mastered. The way back to success was found along another circuitous and difficult path. Wright had to make himself into an author who wrote about architectural theory and aesthetics. He was a gifted writer with a sensuous sense of imagery and a poetic style. Yet clarity and fluidity of expression, two qualities which he attained with great ease in his architecture, were difficult for him to achieve in his writing. Nevertheless, Wright published four important books and fourteen articles between 1928 and 1932. Many academic careers in the humanities have been built on far less.

In May of 1930, shortly after the stock market crash, Wright gave the prestigious Alfred Kahn lectures on architecture at Princeton University, thereby gaining an audience with the very Eastern architectural establishment that had increasingly overlooked him in the past decades. The Kahn lectures have great significance in relation to Wright's earlier achievements and his work to come. First, they enlarge upon key notions that had been evolving in his mind since the Hull House lecture and the Wasmuth introduction, and they bring to fruition many of the arguments developed in the *Architectural Record* articles of the 1920s. They are also an important marker in Wright's career because he expands and redirects the material of the Princeton Talks in many books and essays that he writes in the 1930s, 1940s, and 1950s. For this reason, a careful reading of the Princeton lectures is crucial in understanding the organic growth of Wright's thought.

Wright formulated six topics for his lectures: "Machinery, Materials and Men," "Style in Industry," "The Passing of the Cornice," "The Cardboard House," "The Tyranny of the Skyscraper," and "The City." The lectures flow, gradually and with some overlapping material, from Wright's introductory critique of architectural history to his explanation of specific architectural poetics, and, finally, to his imaginative depiction of utopian and dystopian visions of architecture's impact on modern life.

The first of the lectures, "Machinery, Materials and Men," incorporates paraphrases on material from the original Hull House lecture, with a brief introduction and conclusion. Wright begins with a stormy call for a free and independently-minded modern spirit:

> An Architecture for these United States will be born "Modern," as were all the Architectures of the peoples of all the world. Perhaps this is the deep-seated reason why the young man in Architecture grieves his parents, academic and familiar, by yielding to the fascination of creation, instead of persisting as the creature of ancient circumstance. This, his rational surrender to instinct, is known, I believe, as "rebellion." I am here to aid and comfort rebellion insofar as rebellion has this honorable instinct—even though purpose may not yet be clearly defined—nor any fruits, but only ists, isms or istics be in sight.[5]

And he includes a hilarious and fiery diatribe against the culturally naive American sitting in his home:

> You are sunk in "Imitation." Your much-moulded woodwork is stained "antique." Inevitably you have a white-and-gold "reception-room" with a few gilded chairs, an overwrought piano, and withal, about you a general cheap machine-made "profusion" of— copies of copies of original imitations. To you, proud proprietors—do these things thus degraded mean anything aside from vogue and price? Aside from your sense of quantitative ownership do you perceive in them some fine fitness in form, line and color to the purposes which they serve? Are the chairs to sit in, the tables to use, the couch comfortable, and are all harmoniously related to each other and to your own life? . . . If not, you are a victim of habit, a habit evidence enough of the stagnation of an outgrown Art. Here we have the curse of stupidity— a cheap substitute for ancient Art and Craft which has no vital meaning in your own life or our time. You line the box you live in as a magpie lines its nest. You need not be ashamed to confess your ignorance of the meaning of all this, because not only you, but every one else, is hopelessly ignorant concerning it.[6]

Not all of the text is vituperative, however. Wright includes a moving invocation of significant architectural achievements by diverse cultures of the human race. Wright describes architecture as a poetic calling to which all of humanity has contributed. He particularly singles out the Italians, the French artisans of the middle ages, the Mayans, the Africans, the Chinese and the Japanese. More explicitly than at Hull House or in the Wasmuth introduction, here Wright vigorously attacks weak American imitations of architecture that is unique to other times and places. He lists the "false" Pantheons, Venetian Palaces, Feudal Castles, and Queen Anne Cottages as some of the boring imitations of old styles that are ruining American architecture.

One of the problems, as Wright argued earlier, is that the power of modern technology is used to falsely imitate old masterpieces in a counterfeit way. The modern machine, instead, must be employed to bring out the natural beauty of materials. Technology is alive for Wright, and once again he turns to the image of the city as a living, breathing, pulsating organism to illustrate this point. Looking at the architecture of the ancient Greeks and Egyptians as well as the Japanese, Wright notices the intense sense of abstraction derived from ubiquitous natural forms such as the simple flower:

> But in Grecian Art two flowers did find spiritual expression—the Acanthus and the Honeysuckle. In the Art of Egypt—similarly we see the Papyrus, the Lotus. In Japan the Chrysanthemum and many other flowers. The Art of the Occident has made no such sympathetic interpretation since that time, with due credit given to the English Rose and the French Fleur-de-Lys, and as things are now the West may never make one. But to get from some native plant an expression of its native character in terms of imperishable stone to be fitted perfectly to its place in structure, and without loss of vital significance, is one great phase of great Art. It means that Greek or Egyptian found a revelation of the inmost life and character of the Lotus and Acanthus in terms of Lotus or Acanthus Life. That was what happened when the Art of these people had done with the plants they most loved. This imaginative process is known only to the creative Artist.[7]

The fascination with flower forms goes back to the earliest moments in Wright's career, especially to the important photographs of flowers published in *House Beautiful* in the late 1890s and the "Philosophy of Art" lecture of 1900. Improvising on his remarks in *The Japanese Print* (1912), the architect emphasizes here that it is necessary to apply modern technology with a sensitivity equal to the love of the flower that he finds expressed, in different ways, in earlier cultures.

"Style in Industry," Wright's second lecture, elaborates further upon some of the themes introduced in the first essay and in some of Wright's earlier publications. Now a well-formed creative artist and a master in control of his source materials, Wright gives us his clearest account of the importance of Japanese aesthetics in his own unique theoretical formulations of style and he outlines the significance of Japanese sensibility for the Western mind in general.

Rather than studying Europeans who are already copying the Japanese, Wright argues that American students should realize that the Japanese understand organic principles of pure form that are universal and available to all perceptive minds. The truths of ideal forms are therefore available for all to use, and are applicable across cultural boundaries. Wright

praises the cleverness of European artists for the way in which they have
borrowed from the Japanese. He specifically cites the Goncourt brothers,
who realized the importance of the print for themselves, and the Austrians
artists and architects, among whom he lists Joseph Maria Olbrich, Otto
Wagner, and Gustave Klimt. But he warns American artists against copying
copies, and advises against deriving notions from secondary sources.

Wright instead suggests studying the fruits of the Japanese Momoyama
period directly. He singles out the trio of Sotatzu, Korin, Kenzan and then
the more recent group of Kiyonobu, Toyonobu, Harunobu, Kiyonaga,
Utamaro, Hokusai and Hiroshige. All of these figures descend from the fertile basis of the Momoyama. However, mere imitation of the Momoyama is
not the answer, for the work of the past must be used in a new way,
according to the needs and conditions of the present moment. Wright
believes that the Japanese sensibility has a secret that will enable
Americans to use the machine sensitively. Machines can be tools to help
bring us closer to the true nature of materials if we look at how the
Japanese were able to standardize forms centuries ago with concepts such
as the *tatami* mat, which shaped formal units in 3' by 6' patterns, patterns
which for Wright echo the human form. In this lecture, the inspirational
importance of the *tatami* mat as unit finally emerges as a clear, stated part
of Frank Lloyd Wright's poetics, included in the heart of one of his most
important critical works:

> The modern process of standardizing, as we now face it on every side, steril-
> ized by it, prostrate to it, was in Japan known and practiced with artistic per-
> fection by freedom of choice many centuries ago, in this dwelling we are
> considering. The removable (for cleaning) floor mat or "tatami" of Japanese
> buildings were all of one size, 3'0" by 6'0". The shape of all the houses was
> determined by the size and shape of assembled mats. The Japanese speak of
> a nine, eleven, sixteen or thirty-four mat house.[8]

Wright intuitively understands that the *tatami*, the basic unit of the
Japanese architecture, has the function of the periodic phrase in classical
music, dividing large structure into human scale and allowing for great
flexibility and variety. Around the "tatami", "odeau" or posts of wood
come to clean terminals, joining to support the weight of ceilings and
roofs, and "shoji" paper screens are inserted and removed. The clarity of
forms is continually informed by the Shinto notion of cleanliness. To "be
clean" is to know the purity of forms and materials.

Through the machine we must return to a study in texture and pattern.
Formal pattern must be given a new prominence that recalls the importance it had before the rise of painting in the Renaissance. Architecture
had been diminished when the picture became an illusory window that
could depict a variety of imaginary worlds with the conventions of linear
perspective. That role of painting, which Wright sees as an "insubordina-

tion," had then gradually lost its importance. The role of the picture as a literal record of visual rendering had become irrelevant with the rise of the camera.

Wright uses metaphors of murder to describe how the technology of one art form eclipses the technology of another. In modern times, the camera murdered the painting as the book had once killed architecture when the printing press was invented. The machine age, in Wright's view, united literature and painting in a new art form—the cinema. The advent of camera and cinema cast painting out of its formerly dominant role: "Let us be thankful that the Machine by way of the camera today takes the pictorial upon itself as a form of literature. This gratifying feat has, already, made great progress in the cinematograph."[9] With the camera and cinema taking on new prominence, the feisty insubordination of painting had been overcome by modern technology and modern sensibility. Architecture was free to rise to prominence once again.

The third presentation at Princeton, "The Passing of the Cornice," is an important new essay that recounts Wright's growing disgust with the various neo-classicisms that had dominated turn of the century American architecture. Again, Wright describes how the writings of Hugo had a great impact on him, but this time he includes an anecdote about an accident that he witnessed during construction of the Wisconsin State Capitol building in Madison. The protruding cornice at the scene of the accident symbolized the uselessness of form without function for Wright. This is a theme that he develops throughout the talk, always returning to his view of the classical cornice as an ornament that has no meaning in modern architecture just as absurdly old-fashioned Renaissance clothing has no meaning for fashionable modern dress:

> We may well believe there is some subjective wave, that finally, perhaps blindly, gets buildings, costumes and customs all together in effect as civilization marches on. At least it would so seem as we look about us, for in the umbrageous Cornice-time immediately behind us, hats were extravagant cornices for human heads, just as the cornices were extravagant hats for buildings. And what about puffed sleeves, frizzes, furbelows, and flounces? Didn't they go remarkably well with pilasters, architraves and rusticated walls?[10]

In a passage of sweeping power, Wright imagines himself standing before the architectural sites of antiquity in Athens, raising his hand in the brilliant Mediterranean light to discover that the translucent glow allows him to view both the skeleton of his hand and the flesh around it.[11] Standing at the site, he begins to sense that Greek forms, too, were originally skeletons for an elaborately painted, highly ornamental stylistic in the plastic arts. As he views the ruins of a stone temple, Wright "gradually [sees] the whole as a great painted wooden temple."[12] Like Viollet, Wright perceives the ancient Greek cornice in stone as a metaphor for an earlier wooden temple in which the original cornice had a useful meaning—to give shelter—that had since been forgotten. The Greeks, he argues, evolved while referring back to their architectural origins, regardless of the changing materials and technology available to them. Thus, much of their own ornamental pattern had no function and was not connected to a true organic unity of purpose. This ancient foible must be avoided today, he argues, and the cornice is just one cliché among many that should be discarded in modern American architecture.

The need to eliminate box-like clichés from the vocabulary of architectural forms is covered in "The Cardboard House":

> Human houses should not be like boxes, blazing in the sun, nor should we outrage the Machine by trying to make dwelling-places too complementary to Machinery. Any building for humane purposes should be an elemental sympathetic feature of the ground, complementary to its nature-environment, belonging by kinship to the terrain.[13]

Here the ideas developed in the earlier essays emerge into the poetics of the prairie house. Looking back at the achievements of his Oak Park years, Wright explains, with more elaborate insight and detail than he offered in the Wasmuth introduction, how he developed a new sense of form for the midwestern home. Among the important insights that emerge with greater force now is an account of how Wright arrived at his decision to free the walls of a home from weight-bearing functions and to abolish the use of walls as a kind of stage for ornamental clichés. He explains that he preferred to turn the wall into a subtle screen because he wanted to express the interaction of structure and environment:

> House-walls were not to be started at the ground on a cement or stone water-table that looked like a low platform under the building, which it usually was, but the house-walls were stopped at the second story window-sill level, to let the rooms above come through in a continuous window-series, under the broad eaves of a gently sloping, overhanging roof. This made enclosing screens out of the lower walls as well as light screens out of the second story walls. Here was true *enclosure of interior space*.[14]

Wright's secret was to move the wall away from the termination of the roof and deeper into the structure. Wright rediscovers the original purpose of the cornice in the sheltering function of the roof, which now terminates in long overhanging eaves in the liberated forms of the prairie house and his subsequent designs.

He also created a revisionist conception of the original frontier fireplace. It became a tokonoma-like center of the prairie home, with a great fire glowing with refreshing intensity deep within the stonework of the home.[15] The hearth in the Wright home has great spiritual and social significance. It is a place of meditation and social gathering. Movement is planned in the empty spaces that are grouped around it, but it is always the fulcrum of human interaction in each home. Just as the tokonoma is signified with flower-arrangement, prints, and poetry in the Japanese house, Wright's hearth is made special with ornamentation and design that gives shape to the rest of each Wright home.

In "The Tyranny of the Skyscraper," Wright discusses the invention of the American skyscraper, which he pinpoints at the moment when Sullivan walked into his office with fresh sketches for the Wainwright building in St. Louis. He calls Sullivan's work a masterpiece because it was the first tall building to be conceived in one organic whole instead of a series of piled up "cornice buildings." Sullivan found a way to make a harmonious unit out of the steel frame, rounding off his huge structure with a celebration of ornament on the top. Wright finds it vastly superior to the relatively clumsy stone walls of Burnham and Root's massive Monadnock building in Chicago.

But Wright is convinced that Sullivan was followed by mediocrities who distorted the vigor of his conception. Wright expounds upon how the conceptions of tall buildings have been falsified in America through derivative emulations of Beaux-Arts mannerisms. In spite of the technological achievement embodied in the tall building, Wright finds the concentration of humanity in small areas that it creates to be a negative factor in American cities and environmentally unsound. Prophetically, Wright warns his audience about what metropolitan areas will be like in the near future: "as congestion must rapidly increase, metropolitan misery has merely begun."[16] In the last decade of the twentieth century, Wright's words seem devastatingly accurate. Wright thought the real estate entrepreneurs and builders who are developing the modern city are irresponsible profiteers, and he derided the ridiculous appearance of many of the new skyscrapers they were creating:

> So only those congestion-promoters with their space manufacturers and congestion-solvers who came first, or who will now make haste, with their extended telescopes, uplifted elephant-trunks, Bedford-stone rocks, Gothic toothpicks, modern fountain pens, and "Eversharps" shrieking verticality, sell perpendicularity to the earthworms in the village lane below, can ever be served. Nevertheless property owners lost between the luck, continue to capitalize their undeveloped ground on the same basis as the man lucky enough to have got up first into the air. So fictitious land-values are created on paper.[17]

Wright provides a gloomy view of the social and economic pressures that have shaped the American urban scene. Pressed together into constricted areas by real-estate tycoons, the sky-scrapers of the modern city have no beauty and no relation to the natural unfolding of space in human proportions.

Wright would have preferred to see the tall building spread out in the American suburbs and in the countryside, so that each form would have a sense of beauty and independence reminiscent of Sullivan's visionary Wainwright building. Instead, he claims that Americans are the "modern Romans," badly copying the clichés of other cultures in the huge conglomeration of massive buildings in their congested cities. As the Romans "pasted" Greek architecture onto their masonry arch, Americans tack on bad European clichés to their innovative combinations of steel frames, concrete, and glass. Like the Romans, American architects have innovative engineering, but derivative aesthetics.

"The City" continues the attack on urban America that Wright launches in "The Tyranny of the Skyscraper" and introduces themes that he will present with far more strident and lengthy development in his forthcoming series of writings that begin with the 1932 publication of *The Disappearing City*. In "The City," Wright turns once again to the notion of the city as a giant, monstrous organism, a concept that he develops from his Hull House lecture. Now, however, the monster is much sicker, much more diseased, and well along on the path toward its own destruction. One of the causes of the disease is the congestion caused by the massing of tall buildings in a small area. Profiteers have made the value of city real estate seem essential, when, instead, the modern machine has already rendered it unnecessary. Improved communication and transportation make it possible to spread out, but the organic use of technology has been thwarted, even perverted, by the ruse of massing tall buildings in urban areas. Eventually, the truth will become obvious to the population as the pollution and congestion become intolerable.

Wright predicts that "the city, as we know it today, is to die."[18] The city is not a proper environment for the poor, for they deserve a healthier environment that can provide them with basic human needs. The rich, too, are dehumanized by the rigid numerical grids of urban layout. Human beings must realize their innate desire to live in abundant horizontal space. Wright sees the vertical dimension of the huge building as essentially unnatural while he argues that the "horizontal line" is the proper point of reference for the healtł ˆ ıl and natural sustenance of human life. The architect argues that all congestion is bad. Not only cities, but even smaller towns are too large. The machine, the great heroic symbol of the original Hull House lecture, here takes on more significance as a liberating force that will enable human beings to leave the city, abandoning it for the open space of the countryside:

> The Machine, I believe—absurd as it may seem now, absurd even to those who are to be the first to leave—will enable all that was human in the city to go to the country and grow up with it: enable human life to be based squarely and fairly on the ground. The sense of freedom in space is an abid-

ing human desire, because the horizontal line is the line of domesticity—the Earthline of human life. The City has taken this freedom away.[19]

Intuitively sensing the rise of video, compact disc players, and stereo televisions in 1930, Wright predicts that information and culture will be spread by increasingly effective home entertainment centers. The old fashioned concert and lecture will become unnecessary. Food and supplies should be dispensed in aesthetically designed gas stations, which would also offer restaurants and meeting halls. Everything should be designed to create the greatest decentralization possible. Most importantly, each family should have at least one acre to itself.

Wright's last lecture is the most radical, advancing Wright's unique idea of democratic individualism, which at times amounts to a kind of agrarian socialism. His notions here predict many of the central tenets of his Broadacre City, a design for a new America as an architecturally conceived utopia that he will formulate shortly after the Princeton lectures. Taken together, the Kahn lectures at Princeton contain many of the best of the mature Wright's ideas, expressed in their clearest and most concise form. They sum up his earlier work and point clearly toward the next stage of his career.

Wright will continuously mine these lectures for material for the rest of his life. Within a few years after he gave the lectures, a whole new series of publications and designs emerged. Paralleling the role of the Hull House lecture of 1901, which foreshadowed the coming decade of the prairie house, the Princeton talks were a major indicator of his intellectual and theoretical maturation, a sign of vast achievements to come.

As Woollcott noted in his *New Yorker* profile, Wright's appearance at Princeton placed him in front of the eastern intelligentsia once again. Especially after they appeared in print in 1931, the Princeton lectures became a crucial factor contributing to the resurrection of his architectural reputation. Shortly after the Princeton lectures, Wright attracted a large audience when he gave two more talks at the Art Institute in Chicago on the 1st and 2nd of October, 1930.[20] The audience was young, fascinated, and full of architects. Although he was bringing in little income, the public sustained interest in his ideas.[21] Furthermore, successful lectures in Eugene Oregon, Seattle, and Denver gave Wright a renewed sense of self-confidence.

It was clear that Wright was not too old and irretrievably forgotten, as many of his younger rivals would have preferred. Those who wished to forget Wright are best epitomized by Philip Johnson, who purportedly asked "isn't he dead?" when asked to include Wright in the International Style exhibition of 1932.[22] In the catalogue for the exhibit, Johnson devastatingly referred to Wright as America's "greatest architect of the nineteenth century."[23] Contrary to Johnson's views, the throngs of the young and adventurous who came to hear Wright demonstrated that they were still interested in his work and ideas.

Most important from the point of view of his public relations, however, was the 1932 publication of *An Autobiography,* which Wright had been working on since he had gone into hiding with Olgivanna in 1925. *An Autobiography* proved to be a cornerstone of his rebounding new career. Repeatedly, the book served as a way of informing interested clients about his work, his life and ideas. Shortly after the book appeared, Wright began to get big commissions once again.[24]

The first edition of *An Autobiography* was made up of three books, entitled "Family-Fellowship," "Work," and "Freedom." It included powerful passages on Wright's mother and father, on the impact of the musical architecture of Bach and Beethoven, and the early years with Sullivan. Wright describes his father's organ playing of Bach in the same chapter as his mother's gift of the Froebel blocks. The importance of the Japanese print in Wright's aesthetic is covered in extensive passages, while some fresh material on Japanese aesthetics indicates the true depth of Wright's understanding of Japanese domestic architecture. For example, Wright explains the importance of the varied combinations of art, literature and interior design in the tokonoma and its importance as a focal point in the Japanese home in "Work" (Book II). He includes passages on Japanese radiant heating systems used in their "Korean rooms," which warm interiors through ducts under the floors. And he explains why he later incorporated his own radiant heating technique, also generating from the ground upward, in his buildings.

In some detail, Wright describes the evolution of the prairie house and the early triumphs of Unity Temple and the Larkin Building. In passages of highly personal and alluring prose, Wright recounts the origins of his Welsh family, their attachment to the Wisconsin land, his first trips to Europe and Japan, the tragedy and destruction of Taliesin by fire, and the ensuing exodus to Japan. Readers are able to learn much here about Wright's reactions to Japanese culture during his years in Tokyo and he offers an account of his experiences while working on the Imperial Hotel. Wright also describes his work on the Barnsdall mansion (a "musical romanza" in concrete) and the Millard house in Pasadena ("La Miniatura"). Long passages on Beethoven and Bach show how Wright conceives of the connection between ornament and structure in his work. He intends them to have the same meaning as the structural motif in the classical symphony. The only difference is that in music, a temporal art, space is evoked metaphorically. In architecture, a spatial art, temporality is evoked metaphorically.

The deserts of Arizona emerge as a setting for renewal and discovery in "Freedom," the third and last part of the first edition of the autobiography.

Wright recounts his work with Albert McArthur on the Biltmore hotel in Phoenix in the late 1920s. Originally, McArthur contacted Wright for help on implementing the concrete block technique which he had developed and applied on a smaller scale in California. Inevitably, Wright spent many months at the site. His hand is evident in the resulting hotel, which is probably the closest extant work to the demolished Imperial in Japan. But Wright gave McArthur full credit for the Biltmore, never claiming it as his own creation. We also discover how, while working on the hotel in 1927, Wright met Dr. Alexander Chandler, who captivated him with the notion of building a resort in the middle of the Arizona desert. Wright describes how he and his entourage built a camp for themselves on an isolated rocky mound rising from the desert sands. Wright's narrative in "Freedom" makes it clear how the variety and scope of the Arizona desert at the site stimulated a whole new range of architectural shapes in his fertile mind.

Sixty years old, isolated at Ocotillo camp, blissfully content under the open sky, Wright finds a cornucopia of new applications for his notions of organic structure. What Wright calls the "great nature masonry" of the desert generates new applications of geometric constructions made from dotted lines (he doesn't see any straight, unbroken ones in Arizona) and flat planes. And in the Saguaro cactus, Wright sees an analogy between its "interior vertical rods" and "reinforced building construction."[25] Cholla, staghorn and bignana hold similar lessons for the architect.

Wright's plans for the San Marcos resort were dashed with the economic collapse of 1929. Within a short time, the Navajo Indians claimed the remnants of the abandoned Ocotillo camp for themselves and carried off its materials into the desert, but Wright was happy that he learned about the desert from first-hand experience. When he drove to New York to consult with Reverend William Norman Guthrie about a tall building for St. Mark's Church on the corner of 10th Street and 2nd Avenue, his desert experience contrasted favorably with the tremendous urban congestion he witnessed. He became more convinced than ever of the poisonous nature of city life. The tower project, like the Arizona speculation, was another casualty of the Depression. Both experiences, however, led to later projects in the years to come.

Although the autobiography contains a wealth of information, Wright's style is poetic and elliptical. His love of densely worded nature description, prevalent throughout the work, is evident in the opening passages:

> A light blanket of snow fresh-fallen over sloping fields, gleaming in the morning sun. Clusters of pod-topped weeds woven of bronze here and there sprinkling the spotless expanse of white. Dark sprays of slender metallic straight lines, tipped with quivering dots. Pattern to the eye of the sun, as the sun spread delicate network of more pattern in blue shadows on the white beneath.[26]

The dense prose characterizes the entire work, from this opening "Prelude" to the closing "Postlude." As Wright recounts his gradual sense of renewal and rediscovery, his attachment to the land of Spring Green resurfaces, and he combines his nature description with his notion of architectural form. The pattern of one turns into the pattern of the other:

> Tall red-top, grass on the hill beyond the garden, gleaming in the slanting rays of morning sun, the tall grass everywhere, hung with a gossamer covering of spider webs of amazing size: a sunlit brilliance. All their delicate patterns were sparkling with the clinging dewdrops, myriads that turned each separate strand of each marvelous web into a miracle of light: a kind of construction that might well inspire this age, because it is a beauty we might realize in steel and glass buildings.[27]

The great message of the autobiography is the nature of the consciousness it records in words. The meticulous color descriptions, the preoccupation with the textures of natural materials, the attentiveness to subtle lighting effects, even the pleasures of other senses such as taste and hearing—all capture permanently in language the sensuous nature of Wright's mind. Numerous passages in the autobiography make it clear that the visual world was a totality of expressiveness for Wright just as the world of sounds is for a great symphonist. All visual phenomena could be mixed and blended, or separated and savored, and then combined in infinite combinations. It is this great gift of Wright's that comes through more in his autobiography than in any other of his books.

Wright's idiosyncratic style features attractive chapter headings dividing the prose up into highly irregular sections and divisions. The best passages are the many instances of sweeping lyricism, critical insight, and valuable information. The books has its faults, too. Wright jumps backward and forward in time in a stream of consciousness known best to him and easily unravelled only by scholarly experts. At times, Wright's prose becomes turgid and opaque, and, on occasion, not completely grammatical. Because of these problems, many have found the book difficult to follow. To attain a thorough knowledge of Wright's life and career, it is necessary to read the autobiography in conjunction with a serious professional biography such as Twombly's.

In spite of its faults, however, the autobiography stands as an American classic, and one of the most important books ever written by an American artist. But Wright was far from finished with it in 1932, and his life was far from over. In fact, he was merely in the middle of his career, and the furious pace of Wright's life during the next three decades could easily have generated another volume. Writing was an open-ended process for Frank Lloyd Wright. He was a compulsive reviser and augmenter. The autobiography was republished in 1943 with significant new material. In just over ten years, the original three sections had been expanded into five:

Fig. 1. Louis Sullivan's "Golden Doorway" for the Transportation Building at the World's Columbian Exhibition (1893), Chicago, Illinois *Photograph by C. D. Arnold, courtesy of the Chicago Historical Society ICHi-02279*

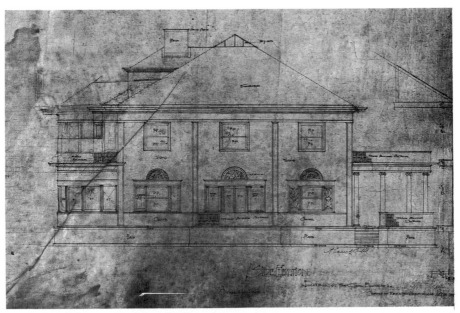

Fig. 2. George Blossom House (1892), Hyde Park, Illinois *Drawing is copyright © The Frank Lloyd Wright Foundation 1986*

FIG. 3. William H. Winslow House (1894), River Forest, Illinois *Photograph courtesy The Frank Lloyd Wright Archives*

FIG. 4. Frank Thomas House (1901), Oak Park, Illinois *Photograph courtesy The Frank Lloyd Wright Archives*

FIG. 5. Arthur Heurtley House (1902), Oak Park, Illinois *Photograph courtesy The Frank Lloyd Wright Archives*

FIG. 6. Susan Lawrence Dana House (1902), Springfield, Illinois *Photograph by David Michael Hertz*

FIG. 7. Unity Temple interior (1904), Oak Park, Illinois *Photograph copyright © 1994 by Thomas A. Heinz*

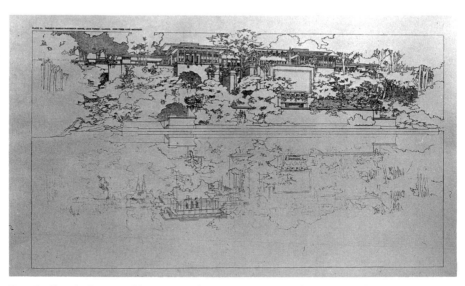

FIG. 9. Sketch for Harold McCormick House (1907), Lake Forest, Illinois *Drawing is copyright © The Frank Lloyd Wright Foundation 1963*

FIG. 8. Larkin Company Administration Building interior (1903), Buffalo, New York
Photograph courtesy The Frank Lloyd Wright Archives

Fig. 10. Meyer May House (1908), Grand Rapids, Michigan *Photograph by David Michael Hertz*

Fig. 11. Taliesin (1911, rebuilt 1914 and 1925), Spring Green, Wisconsin *Photograph courtesy The Frank Lloyd Wright Archives*

FIG. 12. Imperial Hotel exterior, with gardens (1915), Tokyo, Japan *Photograph courtesy The Frank Lloyd Wright Archives*

FIG. 13. Ocotillo Desert Camp (1928), Chandler, Arizona *Photograph courtesy The Frank Lloyd Wright Archives*

FIG. 14. Fallingwater, Edgar J. Kaufmann House (1935), Mill Run, Pennsylvania *Photograph by David Michael Hertz*

FIG. 15. Usonian House, with garden (1936), Madison, Wisconsin *Photograph courtesy The Frank Lloyd Wright Archives*

Fɪɢ. 16. S. C. Johnson & Son, Inc. Administration Building (1936), Racine, Wisconsin
Photograph courtesy The Frank Lloyd Wright Archives

Fig. 17. Pfeiffer Chapel, Florida Southern College (1938), Lakeland, Florida *Photograph by David Michael Hertz*

FIG. 18. Esplanades, Florida Southern College (1946), Lakeland, Florida *Photograph by David Michael Hertz*

FIG. 19. Taliesin West, Frank Lloyd Wright House and Studio (1937), Scottsdale, Arizona *Photograph by David Michael Hertz*

FIG. 20. Jorgine Boomer House, Phoenix, Arizona (1953) *Photograph courtesy The Frank Lloyd Wright Archives*

Fig. 21. H. C. Price Company Tower (1952), Bartlesville, Oklahoma *Photograph courtesy The Frank Lloyd Wright Archives*

Fɪɢ. 22. V. C. Morris Gift Shop (1948), San Francisco, California *Photograph by David Michael Hertz*

Fɪɢ. 24. Beth Sholom Synagogue (1954), Elkins Park, Pennsylvania *Photograph by David Michael Hertz*

FIG. 23. Solomon R. Guggenheim Museum (1956), New York, New York *Photograph by David Heald,* © *The Solomon R. Guggenheim Foundation, New York*

FIG. 25. Grady Gammage Memorial Auditorium (1959), Tempe, Arizona *Photograph by David Michael Hertz*

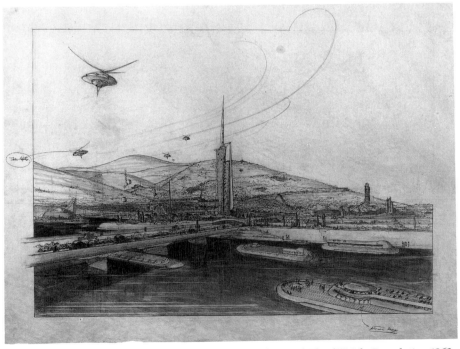

FIG. 26. The Living City (1958) *Drawing is copyright © The Frank Lloyd Wright Foundation 1962*

"Family" and "Fellowship" had grown into separate "books." "Work" and "Freedom" were retained and revised. And Wright added a new section entitled "Form," which included many of the important events in his career that took place in the 1930s as well as some new reflections on his earlier life. In 1977, the Frank Lloyd Wright Foundation released an expanded version with even more fresh material. Another edition of the autobiography, a reprint of the 1932 original was published in 1992, as part of a six-volume collection of Wright's critical and literary works.[28]

Wright had taken on the persona of the angry prophet ever since he described the modern city as a monstrous and diabolical organism in his Hull House talk of 1901. In the Great Depression of the 1930s, many raging Jeremiahs appeared, all of whom had notions about what was wrong with American society and its large cities. It is in the context of the great social unrest of the 1930s that Wright introduced his own plan for rebuilding America. Le Corbusier had responded to the destruction of Europe during World War I with his utopian plans of the 1920s. We know that Wright was perfectly aware of Le Corbusier's utopian notions because Wright published a rather envious review of the French architect's *Vers une architecture* in a 1928 issue of *World Unity* magazine. Aware of Le Corbusier's precedent, a prolific architectural theorist himself, Wright began to crystallize his utopian notions by the late 1920s. A decade after the French publication of Le Corbusier's tract, the Depression prompted Wright to conceive of an ideal society free from the economic disasters of the era.[29] Drawing upon ideas that he had developed for thirty years, he consolidated his utopian vision for the first time in a book form, *The Disappearing City*, which appeared in 1932.

In the late 1920s, Wright published nine articles for *The Architectural Record* that emphasized the microview of architectural practice by concentrating on the nature of modern materials as applied to architecture. Specific elements of modern architecture—steel, glass, and concrete, for example—received literary treatment as the basis of his architectural poetics. Following soon afterward, the Princeton lectures of 1930 were transitional works, showing the nature of Wright's building techniques and artistic style in relation to his philosophical ideas and important forces that help shape them. Subsequently taking up taking up where "The City," the last Princeton talk, had left off, Wright evolved toward a macroview of architectural theory in *The Disappearing City*.

Moving from the specific to the general in *The Disappearing City*, Wright decided to offer a new ideal for modern life, arguing in his 1932 text that a decentralized, ecologically-enlightened America is essential for realizing the ideals of individualism and democracy originally intended by the authors of the United States constitution. His assault on urban architecture became more focused and effective here than in any of his earlier writings. Asserting that the unhealthy city actually had become a pernicious element in American life, Wright described how a new integration of the population, spread out over the land, could reestablish the founding ideological commitments of the country, ideals established in the 18th century.

Wright's visionary conception of Broadacre City, first introduced in *The Disappearing City,* places him within a long, distinguished tradition of Western writers, the great utopians who decry the corruption of modern civilization, calling for either a return to or invention of an innocent, ideal vision of humankind. Unlike Plato, Campanella, Thomas More, Morelly, Fourier, H. G. Wells, and others, however, Wright is the only one of these writers who also happens to be a master architect. His double profession as architect and author makes his contribution to the utopian tradition a unique and important one.

Working out his prose in contrasting images, Wright describes an anti-utopia or "dystopia" to show the nightmarish implications of a world totally desensitized to his notions of organic architecture.[30] Dystopia, the nightmare of modern life, is the natural outgrowth of the Romantic reaction to the excesses of industrialization. John Stuart Mill, coining the phrase in 1868, contrasted the utopian, as "something too good to be practicable," with the dystopian, which he described as that which "is too bad to be practicable."[31]

Samuel Butler's *Erewhon*, which included a dystopian nightmare vision of the machine, appeared in 1872. Wright knew the book well. Butler offered Wright an important notion: a horrific description of how machines can turn against their inventors. In Butler's imaginary *Erewhon,* machines are feared because they are believed to be capable of spawning in massive numbers. Butler's Erewhonians believed that machines eventually could come to control the human beings they were meant to serve. The Erewhonians accordingly decide to banish all machines from their civilization.

Wright's dystopian descriptions link him to Butler and mid-twentieth century writers such as Aldous Huxley, George Orwell, and Eugene Zamiatin, who showed mechanization, industrialization, and technology to be dehumanizing forces that rob humanity of its dignity and identity.

The rhetoric of *The Disappearing City* is based on the opposition of Wright's notions of centralization and decentralization. In Wright's 1932 text, centralization creates a dystopian nightmare and decentralization leads to a utopian paradise. *The Disappearing City* begins with an image of modern man trapped amidst an infernal congestion of machines. He is sterilized in his urban environment: "out of machine he can create nothing but machinery."[32] He has been reduced to a robotic "puller of levers." Echoing Emerson and William Morris, Wright condemns the urban blight, which destroys the quality of life. "Perpetual to-and-fro excites and robs the urban individual of the meditation, imaginative reflection and projection once his as he lived and walked under the clean sky among the growing greenery to which he was born companion." Wide expanses of open country are needed for Wright's imaginary world to take on its intended utopian shape, a shape based on the norm of the individual walking under a clean sky among the greenery.

A key to Wright's imagery, which fluctuates between evocations of the urban nightmare and agrarian paradise, is found in the relation between human civilization and the technology it creates. In the country, the human being is master of the machine. But in the city, the human being is alienated and unsexed, reduced into a mere servant of the machine. Massed populations are better suited for autocracy and repression. A broader distribution of the population is better for democracy and freedom.

The cities of Wright's utopia are not actually cities at all. For Wright, who borrowed some of his rhetoric from Butler's *Erewhon* and Morris's *News From Nowhere,* utopia was "everywhere and nowhere," an anti-city that would replace the congestion of modern cities and spread out across the landscape as far as needed.[33] In *The Disappearing City,* Wright gives his non-city a name for the first time:

> We are concerned here in the consideration of the future city as a future for individuality in this organic sense: individuality being a fine integrity of the human race . . . We are going to call this city for the individual Broadacre City because it is based upon a minimum of an acre to a family.[34]

Broadacre City was the city that was not a city. Wright soon located it in a country that was not a country. Not wishing to refer to his imaginary country as "the United States of America," Wright decided to call his futuristic paradise "Usonia." Avoiding the real name of his country enabled Wright to conceive of breaking links with the ideological errors and cultural biases of the past. As Wright must have known, "Usonia" seems strangely familiar to Americans because it sounds like a very rapid and slurred pronunciation of the United States of America and contains the letters "u," "s," and "a." In Wright's imagination, Broadacre City became the capital of Usonia, a utopian topos that takes on increasing thematic and symbolic importance in Wright's thinking from 1932 on.

In *The Disappearing City,* Usonia is more implied than present. Wright refers to it only twice in the first edition. In writings published shortly after *The Disappearing City,* and in subsequent editions of the work, Usonia appears with far greater frequency. References to Usonia are greatly increased, for example, in *When Democracy Builds,* the revised and expanded version of *The Disappearing City* published in 1945. In this edition, Usonia is incorporated into chapter headings and featured in large sections of the narrative, growing out of ideas implicit in the argument of the 1932 text.

However, the important ideas in later versions were already present in the 1932 version, and it is important to trace their seminal appearance in Wright's thinking at that time. Already claiming to be opposed to excessive institutionalization and centralization in his 1932 text, Wright argues for a society in which each individual is free to find a sense of self through contact with the land. Wright now expands ideas nascent in "The City," his earlier Princeton lecture. Adequate space—at least an acre to a family—is essential. Whereas the "City of Yesterday" must measure space according to the unit of the square foot, the "City of Tomorrow" must measure space by the acre:

> This seems a modest minimum if we consider that if all the inhabitants of the world were to stand upright together they would scarcely occupy the island of Bermuda. And reflect that in these United States there is more than 57 acres of land, each, for every man, woman and child within its borders.[35]

Thus, the Froebelian building block of Wright's ideal society is the single family house, which is placed on the acre of land. Even factory workers will have a home on an acre plot. In Wright's scheme, domestic architecture for the individual family unit generates the structure and movement of the ideal society at large. The individual architectural unit of the family plot is a metaphorical expression of individualism. No system—communism, socialism or capitalism—can substitute for the individual:

> Therefore we should be careful how we turn upon individuality sickened by flagrant abuses in its name. But individuality is something else. Necessarily it has nothing to do with capitalism, or communism, or socialism. The 'ism' in any form has no individuality. The formula has already taken its place when the 'ist,' the 'ism' or the 'ite' may be applied. And that was why all the great religious teachers—Jesus, Abdul Bahai, and Laotze especially—wanted no institutionalizing, no officialdom, not even disciples.[36]

Wright never lost his conviction about the fundamental importance of the individual in his utopia, a conviction which first crystallized in full force in *The Disappearing City*. Even in his last years, Wright insisted that "the true center (the only centralization allowable) in Usonian democracy is the individual in his Usonian family home. In that we have the nuclear building we will learn how to build."[37]

How will the individual cultivate his or her inner resources? Wright's innovative and radical notions for hospitals, schools, and secluded "Style Centers" give us a clue. Gardens and sunlight would bring repose and normalcy in the small, decentralized hospitals scattered in the countryside of Usonia. Universities in Usonia, isolated in beautiful country retreats, would be led by an assembly of elected experts. Each expert would be chosen by his peers in each state and sent to the university campus as representative of excellence in their fields. More "father-confessors" than "professors," these individuals would lead university research in their areas of expertise. Scientists, artists, philosophers and statesmen would each elect the best of their peers to participate as "father confessors." Students would be chosen on the basis of whether they could demonstrate "inner human experience" and seriousness of purpose.[38] Innovative arts and crafts would continuously be developed in Style Centers, a combination of artist colony, research and development headquarters, and industrial planning stronghold. In the Style Center, the best and most original workmanship would be continuously developed. Style Centers would be run by innovative young architects or other "artist workers." There would be about one master for every seven students, allowing for approximately fifty students. In these centers, the most effective combinations of aesthetic sensibility, technological means, and mass production and commercial industry would be continuously developed and refined. Here Fine Art would direct the use of the machine, not the reverse—the Butlerian nightmare in which the machine controls the lives of humans. The list of products for the perfect society, developed in this hive of creativity, is enormous. A few of the items that Wright enumerates give an idea of the work that he envisions for the Style Center: "tapestries, table linen, new cotton fabrics, flowerholders, lighting devices, window-glass mosaics, necklaces, screens, fences, fireirons, all sorts of industrial art in aluminum," and much more.[39]

Religion in Usonia would be non-sectarian. The church would be universal, encompassing all earlier religions with the abstraction of musical form, "as a song without words is a song." All would be included, but the focus would be on the individual who can find spirituality without a superimposed theology. Wright would design ahistorical cathedrals to express the aspirations of human nature at its best:

Here would be a great opportunity for a pure symphony, as building. The church might, in the new city, be a church as a song without words is a song. The Broadacre church would be a rendezvous with beauty in the depths and breadths of the soul, a refuge no less individual because more profound and comprehensive for the stained and worn and skeptic. Harmony complete might in this church again descend to refresh a mortal weariness. This skeptic ego of our more sophisticated age needs spiritual recreation. No theology, now, can ever be essential. The unhistorical cathedral as a feature of the Broadacre City would be erected by and for the spirit of man to evoke again in terms of our machine-age life an organic ideal of the organic social life and new faith in the nobility and beauty of which human nature itself is capable.[40]

Wright expands these notions in later incarnations of *The Disappearing City,* and especially in the late work, *The Living City* (1958). His giant steel cathedral design of 1926, not mentioned in his discussion of religion in

The Disappearing City, offers an indication of what one of Wright's non-denominational cathedrals might have been like.

Frequently in his lectures and books, Wright organized his ideas by highlighting five or six simple concepts, then improvising on them, thereby drawing out relationships between his own work, architecture at large, and the American cultural scene. This open-ended approach allowed Wright to repeat himself in many public appearances and published writings, varying older material with new elaborations. It also enabled him to think on his feet by working over familiar material, like a good classroom teacher.

Some of the freshest material in *The Disappearing City* is presented in this way. Wright continually plays with his themes. Technology, misused, creates misery; used well, technology can also be a beneficent force for social justice. In a chapter entitled "The Nature of Modern Resources," Wright argues that five new "agencies" have made modern decentralization possible. First, electronic communication, even more powerful than the printing press, has made cramped living configurations unnecessary. He specifically mentions the coming importance of the television along with radio in this 1932 text. Agency number two is the modern transportation created by the internal combustion engine, which has made travel by automobile, ship, and airplane safe and dependable. The third agency is the use of the machine in domestic activities. Modern refrigeration, heating, and lighting make it possible for people to spread out on their own. Modern building materials are the fourth agency. Steel, concrete, and glass make architecture more flexible and inexpensive. Finally, the means of mass production are a civilizing force, making it possible to produce building materials for vast numbers of people. The combined power of these new resources is so great, according to Wright, that it can be harnessed to eliminate the unhealthy congestions of urban life.[41] Slums, traffic jams, and petty crime are just some of the negative qualities of city life that would be greatly reduced with the use of modern means to decentralize society.

The Autobiography and *The Disappearing City* had both a public and a private impact. The positive publicity generated by the appearance of these books would have been useless without the internal growth that they also prompted. Wright's words led directly to a new series of forms. In terms of Wright's artistic development, the two books proved to be the final stage of his catharsis. Wright's feverish literary activity led to a new explosion of drawings and plans, all of which stemmed from an actual scale model of his architectural utopia. After describing Broadacre City in literary form, Wright decided it was time to begin building it. He began with a scale model of a section.

According to Donald Leslie Johnson, Broadacre City was "no more than a verbalized theoretical proposition" when, in 1932, Tom Maloney and

Edgar Kaufmann, Sr. combined forces to fund building a model of it.[42] But that theoretical proposition had been maturing in Wright's mind ever since his first dissatisfaction with the modern city was voiced in 1901 at Hull House. In 1932, he had no important commissions, but was surrounded by a band of fascinated and loyal apprentices eager to work with him. Wright and his protegés set to work. Building a model for an ideal America with them proved to be a pragmatic way to develop his notions and work out his philosophical ideas with young people. The resulting model of Broadacre City was twelve extraordinarily detailed square feet of a futuristic world.[43] In the spring of 1935, Maloney and Kaufmann arranged for a traveling exhibit of the model in Madison, Wisconsin; Pittsburgh, Pennsylvania; the Corcoran Gallery in Washington D.C., and Rockefeller Center in Manhattan.[44]

Wright's greatest utopian competitor in architecture is Le Corbusier, whose *Vers une architecture* predated Wright's *Disappearing City* by exactly ten years. Like Wright, Le Corbusier also imagined the vital role an architect could play in the planning of a modern technological utopia. There are important distinctions separating the two modern masters. Le Corbusier's fantasy is static and centralized, whereas Wright's is open-ended, decentralized and metaphorical. Le Corbusier's plan for the ideal modern society radiates outward from a super-technological city at its center, "la ville radieuse," planned to localize human activity in symmetrical quadrants. Wright, responding to Le Corbusier's earlier propositions with his own plan in the early 1930s, finds the French architect's ideas reductive and dehumanizing. Man in the modern city, Wright claims, is "becoming or already become—the machine."[45] Lampooning Le Corbusier's "ville radieuse" as an example of the dystopian modern city, Wright describes the average man in it as "exhibit B . . . cog 3,000,000,128" in a sterilized urban complex. [46] Wright warns that poor and rich alike will be reduced to numbers in the grid of modern technocracy gone awry. Each will be locked into a box from which escape is impossible. Wright gives colorful examples to evoke the mechanical status of the human being in dystopia— "No. 36722, block 99, shelf 17, entrance K. . ."[47]

Except for some scattered references, Wright is curiously absent from the vast body of criticism written on utopian literature. Conversely, the many books on Frank Lloyd Wright fail to point out the utopian implications in his thought as well. It is particularly strange that even Lewis Mumford, who both knew Wright and wrote about him, failed to mention Wright in his long book on utopia which appeared in the 1920s. And yet Wright, whose frequent images of utopia and dystopia form a recurrent dialectic in his many books, may actually have been one of the most important utopian visionaries of all time. Unlike his purely literary counterparts, Wright's ideas led to actual architectural theory and many of his plans were actually implemented in fragmentary form. Even the utopian plans of other trained architects—architects such as Tony Garnier, Le Corbusier and Hugh Ferris—were far too massive and intricate to ever attempt on even an experimental basis. Wright, far more cagey and pragmatic, ironically offered more practical illumination with the figurative fragments of his poetic vision. Wright's canny metaphorical conception of a decentralized plan enabled him to build a little of it at a time while writing and talking about the rest.

Of all the great utopians, Wright is probably closest to H. G. Wells, whose *A Modern Utopia* Wright could easily have read. Both Wells and Wright share a faith in the powers of technology to generate change and improvement by continuously furnishing solutions to new problems as they appear. Both, for example, called for the use of modern manufacturing techniques to provide large-scale housing for all levels of society. Both display a willingness to discard the architectural clichés of the past for a new integration of forms based on the practical and the pleasurable. Admittedly, Wells describes an inn in Utopian Lucerne that does resemble, to an extent, an Oxford college. But he also imagines it "free from the hampering traditions of Greek temple building, and of Roman and Italian palaces; it is simple, unaffected, gracious."[48] Other features of the architecture in Wells' imaginary world have some of the well-known characteristics of Wright's work: long horizontal quadrangles; labor-saving devices of all kinds; and, especially, roof gardens, loggias and verandas to integrate indoor and outdoor life. All in Wells is imagined to improve the quality of life of the individual.[49] This, too, is a frequent point of departure in both Wright's utopian writings and realized architectural work.

Wells, who published his utopian work in 1905, just four years after Wright's lecture at Hull House, imagined a fantastic system of airplanes, trains and ships that would allow for great social mobility. Wright, too, imagined high-speed transport of all kinds, including a comprehensive system of cross-country highways. Wright's utopian drawings of the 1930s feature remarkable conjurings for domestic transport. These include futuristic aerial devices that are a cross between helicopters and flying saucers, sleek fish-like shapes for automotive vehicles, and innovative designs for overpasses on modern roadways. The fluidity of human movement was a great concern for both, but Wright was able to give us a sense of his futurism with all the grace and power of his artist's pencil.

It is of great significance that the two display a deep concern for the rights of the individual over the collective impact of their utopian visions. Both, however, prefer a kind of fluid aristocracy of merit that would allow the most capable members of society to rise to positions of responsibility. Both allow for property and ownership, entrepreneurship and the inheritance of wealth. Their conceptions run from the individual to their systems as a whole rather than the other way around. This separates them from more traditional Christian utopians, as wells as Marxist and socialist theorists. Both favor breaking apart the constraining limitation of traditional religion to create a philosophical and spiritual humanism that would encompass great masses of people from diverse backgrounds.

Both, finally, understand that utopia could no longer be placed in a specific, if fictitious, dream locale, imagined on some remote island or hidden plateau. By the twentieth century, utopia had become Planet Utopia for Wells, a dream world that encompassed an entire globe. For Wright, utopia was "everywhere and nowhere," an anti-city sprawling endlessly across the land, changing according to the varying needs of human populations. Anticipating the environmental concerns of the late twentieth century, neither Wells nor Wright see human beings as dominant over a subjugated nature. Instead, they perceive the necessity of achieving a careful balance between human civilization and the natural world.

Wright's utopian plan is grandiose and fantastic. It is therefore easy to ridicule, especially since it appears to imply an authoritarian role for the architect. This weakness seems more apparent in *Architecture and Modern Life*, a book that Wright co-authored with Baker Brownell and published in 1937. Meyer Schapiro's scathing attack in his review article, appearing in the 1938 issue of the *Partisan Review,* is one early reaction of those who dislike the implied authoritarianism of Wright's plan.[50] In Wright's ideal society, the architect, not surprisingly, would have direct effect on the shape of every area of human life, including politics, transportation, sociology, economics, education, the arts, and much more. Schapiro found this frightening, and he did not take kindly to Wright's intense hostility to the cultural dominance of large cities. Others have criticized Wright because he seems to have described what in many cases has taken place in America anyway—the repetitive spread of tedious suburban sprawl. Herbert Muschamp, in a more recent critique, has offered this point of view.[51]

There is, however, much to recommend Wright's Broadacre City plan. Not least among its positive attributes are the enlightened environmental considerations that permeate the whole concept. This seems far more attractive in the last decade of the twentieth century than it did in the years before World War II. Broadacre City gave Wright a platform from which he could articulate his stance to the public. Ironically, Wright's most famous architectural work became—for a time—a work that did not and could never exist. It was at first only a ninety page essay, then a scale model, then a more extensive literary description accompanied by some drawings. Only by the late 1930s did some fragments of it appear in scattered works of actually constructed architecture. But Broadacre City was the capital of a utopia imagined by one of the greatest visual minds of the West. On the subconscious level, the image of Broadacre City gave Wright an architectural dream vision that continually offered up new ideas that took shape on his drafting table. It provided him with a whole new vocabulary of metaphorical forms for buildings, some of which he was able to implement, others of which he could not.

Like Wells' utopia, Wright's Usonia required new ways to implement centralization and decentralization of human populations. The key concept of Wright's plan was to minimize government and bring it closer to the people. Wright shared Morris's passion for spreading out the population into a garden state. But Wright did not care to propose socialism as a panacea for the evils of the industrial cities. In all fairness to Wright—who has been unfairly branded as politically autocratic on occasion by some of his enemies—it should be emphasized that Wright argued against centralized government, finding it necessary only for fascism and autocracy. He wrote that democracy is best suited to a society of free individuals spread out over the land. Greater authoritarian control means greater numbers of people need to be lumped together. Less control and individual autonomy are linked in Wright's ideology to his favorite concepts of the horizontal line and horizontal space on the open land. Under Wright's plan, state governments would be spread out and distributed to county seats, while small towns would be gradually eliminated and reformulated into the larger units of the counties. Thus, the country and the central government would function as centers of government administration.

The basic topographical unit of the Wright plan was the acre, for Wright wanted the absolute minimum of one acre to the family. But Wright's idea was more than a matter of a spatial grid. The topographical unit implies ownership. Ownership of that acre was to allow for privacy and the cultivation of individualism. This is an important feature that distinguishes Wright from the other utopians. Everyone would be an owner in Wright's utopia, yet there would be an idealized sense of social dignity behind the overall design. Everyone would be an "organic capitalist" who would own a part of Broadacre City. Landlord and tenant relationships would be therefore abolished. Politicians would become business administrators rather than lobbyists and agents for special interest groups. Less government would be needed. The basis of government would be to provide essential services and utilities. Government services would be administered from the county. These would include postal service, gas, light, water, and gasoline (all available at the "curb" of the American roadside). No telephone poles or telegraph wires would mar the beauty of the land. The size of the county seat would be scaled to the dimensions of everyday life, allowing for interaction on a personal basis, but on a large enough scale to permit maximum efficiency.[52] A centralized government in Washington would oversee the administration of the county units, but its control over the individual would be diminished.

Wright's Usonia, and its capital, Broadacre City, could never have been realized any more than any of the European utopias. Figuratively expressed in many books and speeches, it indeed was "everywhere and

nowhere." But unlike the literary utopia of the writers and social philosophers, Wright's Usonia is a dream that is connected to many facets of his
creative life that did have actual architectural results. Wright's Usonia
began in poetic metaphor, emerged into print via the literary essay, and
developed through the science fiction sketches of Wright's fantastic pencil
and the ingenuity of his scale models. We can catch glimpses of the dream
through the many fragmentary examples that Wright was able to create
through a variety of media. The dream exists in synecdoches in the real
world: fragmented building samples, parts for a whole that can never be
seen. But Wright really did not need to build all of Broadacre City to make
his point. Lionel March aptly observed this when he wrote that "During
the last thirty years of his life Wright and his clients were building
Broadacre City whenever and wherever the opportunity arose. This is, perhaps the most audacious of Wright's attitudes towards planning. His city is
not laid out on a self-contained site . . . but it is built spot-like throughout
the existing environment, each building a center of excellence and influence."[53] Broadacre City is a complex vision that spilled into various forms
of expression: books, essays, scale models, drawings, plans and actual constructed buildings. Wright's "nowhere" became a possibility "everywhere"
because it enabled him to invent culture from the ground up—a fresh culture for modern America based on rational planning according to the
reduced scale of the individual, with technology at the service of nature
and human beings. Today we can mine his ideas for insights into how an
environmentally-minded America could look, and draw many useful
notions from them.

Wright himself did just that for the last thirty years of his life. The
Broadacre City model was followed by a growing series of Taliesin publica-
tions, which were intended to publicize and explain Wright's ideas.
Wright's texts, drawings, and illustrations (some quite detailed) are integrated in these publications. Eventually, Wright worked up his notions
into a series of books, each descending directly from the preceding one:
The Disappearing City (1932), *Architecture and Modern Life* (1937), *When
Democracy Builds* (1945), *The Natural House* (1954), *The Story of the
Tower* (1956), and *The Living City* (1958). But Usonia, which first emerged
in speculative essays, gave Wright much more than a series of books. It
provided a storehouse of literary images for architecture that would nour-
ish Wright's imagination for the rest of his life. When his vision of a magical world made perfect by architecture was complete, Frank Lloyd Wright
was ready to return to the hard challenges of building in the real world.

V

WRIGHT'S RENAISSANCE

■

Wright's new momentum as a practicing architect began with ideas. These ideas were disseminated through their publication. Eventually, the theoretical writings and lectures gave a new impetus to Wright's architectural practice. From 1923–33, Wright had been relatively inactive as an architect, but he had been rethinking his approach to architecture with numerous drawings, plans and theoretical propositions. Wright was able to redevelop his architectural vision with an utterly new dynamic intensity, and to depart from old notions and procedures to find new ones. His later career sprang organically from his earlier achievements, but he was in no way limited and boxed in by what he had accomplished earlier in his life. His earlier work did not overshadow his later achievements. Wright continued to grow and change in his creative activities.

Wright's enormous literary efforts began to produce results by the mid 1930s. The power and allure of Wright's books attracted a number of important new clients and followers. Ludd Myrl Spivey, a college president, and Edgar Kaufmann, a department store tycoon, read his autobiography, for example. Paul Hanna and Isadore J. Zimmerman, two intellectually-minded clients, and Edgar Tafel, a devoted apprentice, became fascinated with Wright while reading the published version of Wright's Princeton lectures.[1]

In the midst of the Depression, Wright first turned to publication to reach new audiences. Then he developed a second plan to spread his architectural message—the Taliesin Fellowship. The Fellowship was intended as a total environment offering complete immersion in architecture for a select group of dedicated apprentices. Wright decided to set up the Fellowship on the grounds of his estate at Spring Green, bringing his apprentices into both his professional and home life. Now respectable once again, with a supportive and charming young wife who showed a keen interest in education, Wright was in a position to present himself to young people as the grand patriarch of modern architecture that he had truly become.

The Taliesin Fellowship was designed to offer a combination of architectural training, cultural education, manual labor, and practical experience in building. Emersonian in his concern for pragmatic applications, Wright organized his fellowship program so that his apprentice architects would work with their hands. At the same time, his ancestral background as a preacher combined harmoniously with Olgivanna Wright's interest in the teachings of Georgi Ivanovich Gurdjieff, a Greek-Armenian religious leader with whom she had studied in Fontainebleau, France. Together, Wright and Olgivanna hoped to create a uniquely enriching, secular cultural environment that would convey to the young people residing with them at Taliesin the sense that architecture is a spiritual calling.

The Fellowship provided a steady income. Apprentices paid fees to work under the master of Taliesin. This was certainly reasonable since they came untrained and they needed room and board. And Wright was also generous. He is reputed to have never turned away a worthy applicant who could not come up with the tuition. Another attractive feature of the apprentice system was that it furnished a source of valuable personnel for his practice as it came back to life. Once he had trained his apprentices, he subsequently had access to dedicated and skilled help. When his apprentices showed up at building sites, his clients at times became alarmed about their inexperience. He justified using the apprentices by describing them as "honest amateurs" whose natural enthusiasm and fascination with the work at hand would more than make up for their deficiencies.

Wright, essentially a moralist at heart, was never happy in the role of pariah cast upon him by the media in the 1920s. Now he had access to the minds of young architects who chose to work under his direction in a stable environment, in the context of a harmonious home life. He attracted a wealth of new talent to Wisconsin, among them the gifted trio of Edgar Tafel, Wesley Peters, and Edgar Kaufmann Jr.

One of the most important commissions of Wright's career developed through Kaufmann Jr., the son of a Pittsburgh department store magnate. Edgar Kaufmann Sr., delighted with his son's passion for Wright's method, became a major patron. Kaufmann Sr. helped Wright build and present the Broadacre City model and hired Wright to design Fallingwater, a country house in Mill Run, Pennsylvania. This country house was to become one of the most famous buildings of the twentieth century.

The founding of the Taliesin Fellowship seemed to be the last ingredient needed to set Wright to work once again. While captivating the public imagination with his utopian visions, Wright became increasingly revitalized with a number of crucial commissions that gave him renewed visibility. By 1936, the dynamic Wright had designed a home for Malcolm Willey in Minneapolis, completed drawings for the Hanna "Honeycomb" house in Stanford, and shown his model for Broadacre City to Edgar Kaufmann, Sr. Reversing the nonproductive trend of the previous years, he completed four important new designs for buildings in 1936 that were eventually constructed.

Two of these designs were for important domestic structures that soon came to underscore Wright's new prominence. 1936 saw both the triumph of Fallingwater, an ideal vacation home for which great wealth was put at the service of artistic vision, and the first Usonian House, a modest home for the ordinary American based on Wright's organic principles.

In some respects, Fallingwater is a rotational version of the concrete slabs used at the Elizabeth Gale house and other prairie homes during Wright's great period in Oak Park. To build Fallingwater, Wright turned the geometric forms of his Froebelian-inspired planes to fit the unusual site. Unlike the houses built on the flat terrain of Oak Park, this home is anchored on a rock above a waterfall. It spills down the rocky hillside as if it had grown out of a thousand year process of erosion and natural transformation, incorporating the stream, rocks, and trees into every aspect of its plan (fig. 14). Reinforced concrete is used to create what Wright described as "a cantilever system of this extension of the cliff beside a mountain stream."[2]

The Usonian House for journalist Herbert Jacobs, on the other hand, is based on Wright's deep knowledge of the possibilities of the horizontal line and the flat plane. Based on a simple L shape, it was designed to make the refinement of Wright's architectural principals affordable for the ordinary American citizen. Developed in the late 1930s, perfected in the same decade in which Aaron Copland composed his *Fanfare for the Common Man* (1942), the Usonian House was an attempt to show the relevance of architecture to the life of the ordinary American in the era of the Great Depression. The Usonian House was more than this, however. It was also the home for the average Usonian family in Wright's architectural paradise. It was a part of Wright's imaginary world of perfection, brought into reality through the opportunity afforded by the Jacobs family. Accordingly, it provided Wright with a great opportunity to publicize his utopian notions, armed with a specific example of what he had in mind.

Once the theoretical Usonian unit had been created, the principles could be applied elsewhere, enabling Wright to elaborate on his utopian vision in actual practice. The Jacobs house is the first of a number of Wright projects in low-cost housing for the middle class. Many more examples followed in the 1940s and 1950s. Usonia remains a dream partly recorded in the architect's writings, speeches, and his many drawings and plans. But Wright's utopia also saw partial realization in a long, sustained series of completed structures. In the second edition of his autobiography, published in 1943, Wright claimed that he had already completed twenty-seven Usonian Houses in seventeen states.[3] As John Sergeant so convincingly argues, the Usonian house continued to appear in a variety of configurations, scattered throughout the American countryside.[4] Each was a fragment of Wright's utopia, which could appear whenever and wherever circumstances would allow Wright to bring it into existence. Larger fragments of Wright's utopia were the few communities of homes—communities such as the development in Pleasantville, New York—for which he managed to find the funding to build. Sizable non-residential fragments were the civic center in Marin County, California, and a college campus at Lakeland, Florida.

For the first Usonian House, Wright developed new ways to use wood, brick, cement, paper, and glass that enabled him to lower costs considerably. Long, horizontal wood boards and small, raised windows shelter the inhabitants from noise and other intrusions on the street side of the house. Large windows and glass doors open onto the garden in the backyard, affording a private zone for interaction with nature (fig. 15). Profiting from lessons he learned from the Japanese, he employed a remarkable heating system that warmed the house through the floor. In his autobiography, he listed specific ways to cut cost while still maintaining the aesthetic quality of the Usonian house. Masterful architectural planning from the outset could allow for extensive elimination of insignificant items that contributed little to the formal unity of the house. Wright did away with visible roofs, garage, basement, interior trim, radiators, light fixtures, expensive furniture, paint, plaster, gutters and downspouts.[5]

The most important trope in Wright's poetic conception of the Usonian house was to realize that the modest home must aspire to be what it was and not pretend to be the house of a rich man, thereby falsely emulating materials and structures that are inappropriate to its nature. He compared the Usonian house to a country girl who is content to wear clothes that fit her status and her labor. The opposite extreme is a modest home that pretends to be something that it cannot be, employing inexpensive materials and means to emulate more expensive and pretentious ones. This is the metaphorical equivalent of the country girl who would rather wear clothes in imitation of her "city sisters" who in turn "imitate Hollywood stars with the lipstick, rouge, high heels, silk-stockings, bell-skirt, and cock-eyed hat."[6]

Wright's love of Romantic nature metaphor found new expression in the Paul Hanna house. Here the geometric forms of the honeycomb are combined with the requirements of the human dwelling. Moving away from the rectangles of the Usonian and prairie houses, Wright decided that the hexagon was more comfortable for human movement than the simpler forms that dominate these earlier structures. Right angles, he declares, were less fit for the "to and fro" pattern of human movement than the obtuse angle.[7] The interlocking grid of hexagons in the Hanna home create the honeycomb effect for which it is named. The hexagon of this house is part of the increasing rotational sensibility in Wright's works, which leads to the curvilinear wave, circle, and spiral effects that he will create in his later years.

An early indication of Wright's evolution from the rectilinear to circular forms is one of his greatest masterpieces, the Johnson Wax Administration Building (1936) in Racine, Wisconsin. Wright described the building as "architectural interpretation of modern business at its best, as inspiring a place to work in as any cathedral ever was in which to worship."[8] Miles of long glass tubing create a crystalline effect, bending elegantly around the curves of the design. Wright described the crystal metaphor he wanted in his autobiography: "Glass was not used as bricks in this structure. Bricks were bricks. The building itself became—by way of long glass tubing—crystal where crystal either transparent or translucent was felt to be most appropriate."[9]

The glass tubing is installed in two horizontal bands wrapped around the curvaceous lines of the structure. For optimum effect, one band is placed at the six foot level, just above eye-level, according to Wright's idio-syncratic sense of scale (based on his own modest height of 5'8"). The other is higher, twenty feet above the floor at the juncture of roof and wall. Here the translucent crystal effect created by the glass takes the place of the old cornice (which Wright despised), creating a modern streamlined fluidity that is graceful and attractive.[10]

Together with skylights over the great work space and an array of care-fully placed artificial light sources, the glass tubes create soft, natural indi-rect lighting. Shadows and unpleasant extremes in winter or summer are avoided.[11] Wright had meticulously orchestrated the possibilities of indi-rect lighting in his buildings since the very first years of the twentieth cen-tury. Here, he may have created his greatest lighting composition, for he succeeded in bringing natural light into the building while blocking out the boring, undistinguished surroundings of the industrial site. Like the Larkin Building of 1903, the focal point of visual interest is created in the interior. And the work environment is created to be as pleasant and humane as possible.

Stems with circular tops, described by the architect as "dendriform columns" or "monolithic dendriform shafts," grace the entire structure, with sixty of them creating an abstract forest effect in the great work hall. Wright saw them as the essential and dominant feature of the architectural work. The Larkin Building, Wright's earlier interpretation of modern American "business at its best," is angular and rectilinear. At Johnson Wax, in contrast, soft curves of circles, ovals and ellipses dominate the structure (fig. 16). The desks and chairs Wright designed for Johnson Wax express the circles and ellipses of the hall and the dendriform columns, just as the desks and chairs created for the Larkin Building express that building's grammar.

All of Wright's large projects provoked controversy during the course of their design and construction. In the case of the Johnson Wax Administration Building, Wright's unusual dendriform columns generated suspicion. Officials of the Wisconsin Industrial Commission were worried that the columns would not stand up to the stress of the buildings. The Commission's calculations were based on columns planted at right angles to the stresses of the weight they were intended to support. Modelled metaphorically on the interior fibers of the staghorn cactus, Wright's columns were spread out at the top and supported by a mesh of steel. Weight from the broad surface of the circular top to the narrower stem was borne on a more even distribution.[12]

Wright, defiant as ever, seized upon the inevitable confrontation with these authorities to stage an enormous public relations success. First he negotiated with the Commission to permit the construction and testing of a sample column in order to illustrate the validity of his engineering principles. They agreed that if his column would meet their requirements, he would be allowed to proceed with the construction of the building. Then calling the press to the building site in Racine on June 4, 1937, Wright stood under his dendriform column, alternately kicking it and whacking it with his cane. In the meanwhile, ton after ton of sandbags and pig iron were loaded onto the large circular top of the column. The architect remained underneath, confident in the strength of the cantilevered principle underlying the shape. Only after sixty tons of excess weight were piled on the column—far more than the twelve tons needed to satisfy the state inspectors—did it finally crack and collapse. By this time, Wright had deftly stepped out of the way to view the event from a distance with his binoculars. Photographers and journalists, congregated in great numbers at the site, saw plenty of evidence of the safety of Wright's dendriform columns. After long years of suffering the abuses of the American press, Wright had finally learned to make it work to his advantage.[13]

The signal that Wright had risen to the top of his profession in America once again, perhaps even higher than he ever had during his golden years in Oak Park, came in 1938 when the *Architectural Forum* devoted its entire January issue to his work.[14] The editors of the prestigious magazine allowed Wright to design and write the entire issue, which covered the Taliesin estate at Spring Green, Kaufmann's striking country house over the waterfall, the St. Mark's Tower design, the "Wingspread" mansion for Herbert Johnson, the Hanna "Honeycomb" house, drawings for the abandoned San Marcos-in-the-Desert, the Johnson Wax Administration Building, and the Broadacre City model, as well as other drawings and buildings. The concept of the Taliesin Fellowship frames the entire presentation of Wright's works in the issue. Close to 130 illustrations of Wright's works, either in the form of photographs or drawings are provided. The issue is rich in quotations from Walt Whitman, which are interspersed under or above the numerous illustrations. An important epigraph from Thoreau's *Walden* sets the tone:

> True—there are architects—so called—in this country and I have heard of one, at least, possessed with the idea of making architectural ornaments have a core of truth, a necessity, and hence a beauty, as if it were a revelation to him. A sentimental reformer in architecture he began at the cornice, not at the foundation. What reasonable man ever supposed that ornament was something outward and in the skin merely—that the tortoise got its spotted shell, or the shell-fish its mother-of-pearl tints by such a contrast as the inhabitants of Broadway got their Trinity Church . . . the man seemed to me to lean over the cornice and whisper his half-truths to the rude occupants who really knew it better than he. What architectural beauty I see I know has grown from within outward—out of the necessities and character of the indweller and whatever additional beauty of this kind is destined to be produced will be preceded by a like unconscious beauty of life.[15]

Canonizing his work in his own issue of the *Architectural Forum,* Wright places himself amongst the great literary Americans. He was convinced that he was the architect really named by Thoreau in the preceding century. He may have been justified in that conviction.

Also featured in the issue is a review of Wright's *Architecture and Modern Life,* which Wright had recently co-authored with sociology professor Baker Brownell and published in 1937. The magazine is a magnificent example of how Wright manipulated the varied web of media that can be used to express and present an aesthetic point of view in modern culture. Elegant magazine design, poetry, literature, ideology, aesthetics, photographs and architectural illustrations are mixed together in a heady multi-disciplinary presentation of Wright's work and architectural theories.

By the late 1930s, Wright had recreated himself as the grand old man of twentieth-century architecture, not merely—as Philip Johnson had written so mercilessly—"America's greatest nineteenth century architect."[16] With his attractive young wife and his impressive new accomplishments, he was clearly a vigorous old man, happier in his senior years than he had been in middle age. Not surprisingly, around this time he quipped that he would rather die than live through his youth once again.[17] Trips to Rio de Janeiro, London, and Moscow enabled Wright to speak to architects abroad and disseminate his views. He ostensibly traveled to Rio to judge a competition, but before long he had established contacts with the press and arranged for publication of his ideas in local newspapers. In Russia, Wright met with a great number of genuine admirers and young architects who were attempting to create a new architecture under Stalin. Perhaps the most important of these trips, however, was the visit to England, for this excursion caused Wright to author still another important book—the published version of the lectures he gave there.

Wright's reputation had always remained higher in Europe than it had in the United States, and he had continuously attracted a steady stream of disciples from abroad who came to learn his ways. Unhappily, the Europeans never did offer Wright an architectural commission, in spite of his great reputation there.[18] Nevertheless, an invitation to speak to the Royal Institute of British Architects (R.I.B.A.) provided the best opportunity to send his message to European architects since his 1910 Wasmuth catalogue and the seven-issue series of the *Wendingen* magazine, devoted to his work, and printed in Holland in the 1920s.

The invitation to speak to the R.I.B.A. culminated in the London lectures of May 1939. These talks served as Wright's summation of the great projects and achievements of the 1930s, just as the "Sovereignty of the Individual," the essay introducing the Wasmuth catalogue, had captured the artistic power of the Oak Park period many years before. Wright gave his lectures over a period of four evenings at the R.I.B.A. The official title of the talks, the Sir George Watson Lectures for 1939, was "Four Evenings on an Organic Architecture, the Architecture of Democracy."[19] During the four evenings, various installments of James Thompson's color film of Wright's life at Taliesin and his major architectural projects were shown to the English audience as well.

From the outset of the lectures, not everyone was charmed with Wright's controversial opinions. By Wright's own account, as added to the 1943 edition of his autobiography, one duchess leaned over to ask "who is this charlatan from Texas who comes way over here to talk us down?"[20] Although it is hard to believe that an English duchess could have phrased such a sentence, the gist of her indignant remark becomes plausible when one discovers that Wright began the first talk by proclaiming the date of his lecture, May 2, 1939, as an architectural declaration of independence in the spirit of July 4, 1776.

To give a sense of the forces behind his own development, he described how Richardson, Sullivan, the Chicago World's Fair, and the reactionary conservatism of the American architectural establishment had impacted on his work. In order to bring out the essence of his architectural declaration of independence, Wright paraphrased Laotze on space, who, he said, "saw that the reality of a building consisted not in the four walls and the roof but inhered in the space within, the space to be lived in."[21]

In the London talks, Wright makes it clear how reading Laotze made him realize what he had understood throughout his career: since the movement of the human form in space is the dominant point of departure for organic architecture, empty space must determine the forms that are constructed around it. Humbled at first by Laotze's words, Wright realized that he had actually realized in architecture what the ancient Chinese philosopher had merely expressed in words centuries before:

I did not know of Laotze when I began to build with it in my mind; I discovered him much later. I came across Laotze quite by accident. One day I came in from the garden where I had been working and picked up a little book the Japanese Ambassador to America had sent me and in it I came upon the concept of building I have just mentioned to you. It expressed precisely what had been in my mind and what I had myself been trying to do with a building: "The reality of the building does not consist of walls and roof but in the space within to be lived in." There it was! At first I was inclined to dissemble a little; I had thought myself somewhat a prophet and felt I was charged with a great message which humanity needed, only to find after all, that I was an "Also Ran." The message had been given to the world thousands of years ago . . . So what? I could not hide the book nor could I conceal the fact. But then I began to see that, after all, I had not derived that idea from Laotze; it was a deeper, profound something that survived in the world, something probably eternal therefore universal, something that persisted and will persist for ever. Then I began to feel that I ought to be proud to have perceived it as Laotze had perceived it and to have tried to *build* it.[22]

Wright's insight into the relation between empty space and architectural form led him to reject the older, Sullivanian "form follows function" for his own "form and function are one." This was the fundamental concept behind his rebellion against "Italo-French-English" architecture, which he dismisses as a polyglot eclecticism that continually concentrated on the pictorial aspects of the architectural masses rather than their cultural function. The natural flow of human movement was of no great importance for this kind of architecture, and it was, consequently, inferior. Classicism, commercialism, academicism—these are the counter-revolutionary forces for the organic architect. A declaration of independence from these repressive influences enables the architect to see that the interpretation of life is his true calling, a calling that places him at the center of human culture.

As an example of the inorganic heritage that he had rejected in protest, Wright singled out the faulty engineering in Michelangelo's concept of the dome. Wright cleverly explained how the dome and the arch are interrelated: one, the dome, a three-dimensional expression made by rotating the other, the arch. Wright described his attempt to get away from this interdependent relationship that dominated architecture. For him, the arch was essentially a two-dimensional concept unrelated to specific three-dimensional spaces. In order for the arch to withstand the natural pressure that pushed it outward, it needs extraneous reinforcement, including chains and other devices to hold it in, just as an uncomfortably tight corset pushes an overly abundant figure into an unnatural shape.

On the second evening of the Watson lectures, Wright praised Egyptian, Gothic, and Japanese architecture while continuing his attack on classical models. He specifically extended his criticism to the ancient Greeks, claiming they knew nothing of organic architecture. He criticized modernism too, claiming it had formed a radical "left wing" to counter the reactionary "right wing" of classicism. But he found this left wing of modernism "two-dimensional," "hard," and "unsympathetic in aspect."[23] Guilty of the false sterility of the International Style, its most extreme practitioners are culprits that Wright implicates but does not name. "True architecture," he declared, "is poetry," because, like poetry, architecture is interpretation, the interpretation of human life in all its facets.[24] The architect's materials are just as sensitive as the poet's, who interprets human experience with his gift of language. To what does the great architect give meaning with his structural interpretations? Wright's answer was succinct: "Every great architect is—necessarily—a great poet. He must be a great original interpreter of his Time, his Day, his Age."[25]

The third evening was Wright's utopian lecture. In it, he laid out the elements of his particular dream vision of a perfect society. He moved from the Herbert Jacobs house, the humblest residential unit of his utopian plan, to Broadacre City as a whole, and finally to his explanation of Usonia as a new term for the ideal United States of America (he disliked the imperialism of "America" as a term for North America) that he would build. He expounded upon the implications of the Usonian house, proclaiming that he had already built twenty-seven of them. Once more, he declared that every human being deserves ample space in Usonia. If each person should have an acre, a family of seven should have seven acres.

As examples of how he had broken away from the picturesque walls of European architecture, Wright mentioned that he had already employed in his buildings the stones used by native American Indians, even stones that feature their writing on them. He borrowed creatively from the Japanese *shoji* screen in his Arizona architecture, where canvas was stretched over the stones to allow for the natural illumination of the desert sun. The light streamed through the rugged fabric of the canvas, which could serve as both roof and wall. The use of the canvas varied according to the climate of the American desert. Like the *shoji* screen, canvas could be pulled back to allow for viewing the night sky, and to cool off the dwelling in the evening.

In the question and answer period following the third talk, Wright described Chicago as "the only city in America to discover its own waterfront." He praised Daniel Burnham for bequeathing this distinction to Chicago, for he was aware that Burnham's Chicago Plan had determined the basic shape of all subsequent waterfront development in the city. Burnham, who had at one point represented the Beaux-Arts opposition that Wright despised and feared, emerged here as a very different figure. This reflects Wright's deep ambivalence about Burnham, who once tempted him with a scholarship to study European architecture in Paris. Wright admired Burnham as an urban planner, but disliked him as an arbiter of taste in building design.

Wright spoke approvingly of Burnham in the context of Chicago's waterfront planning. Appreciative of the sense of open space and dramatic positioning of the great buildings alongside Lake Michigan, Wright observed that "you may drive nearly the whole day long without going away from the boulevard and park system of Chicago."

The fourth London talk was a summarization of Wright's great renaissance of the 1930s and a social critique of the corruption that has led to the social catastrophes of fascism and depression. These same forces, he felt, also led to the strangulation of organic architecture on a massive scale. During his presentations, Wright used installments of James Thompson's film about Taliesin and the activities there. He did so to set the tone for his fourth lecture and then move quickly to specific examples of his work. He discussed a number of his major achievements of the 1930s in quick succession, while succinctly summarizing their importance and uniqueness. These works included the Hanna house, the Johnson Wax Administration Building, Fallingwater, and the Herbert Johnson mansion (known as Wingspread). He described the Hanna house as "built with thin but solid walls of laminated wood" and based entirely on a hexagonal unit system. This hexagonal system allows a greater flexibility of human movement than the rectangles of the usual boxlike architectural clichés. Fallingwater, jutting from its anchored base on a bank of rocks, "[carries] the living space out over the waterfall."[26] He explained that simpler Usonian Houses were built with wood and brick, eliminating the need for plastering. Wingspread, the great country villa in Racine, Wisconsin, is disarmingly described as the latest "prairie house." But Wright made the grand scheme of the home clear, as he illustrated how its four wings literally spread out from a huge fireplace at the heart of a great living room in the shape of a giant wigwam. Like the Robie house thirty years earlier, Wingspread was intended to have the clean sense of the powerful utility of a steamship or airplane.

The Johnson Wax Administration Building was the pièce de résistance. Wright told the audience that the dendriform columns making up the metaphorical forest of the great hall are "six times stronger than needed." With its veins of glass tubing, its forest of dendriform columns, and its great interior of open space, Wright felt that Johnson Wax was his most purely realized work of organic architecture to date.

In the London lectures, Wright made it clear, once again, that he clearly understood the implications of his achievement. Wright effectively encapsulated his remarkable architectural renaissance of the thirties. However, his confidence in his own work did not hide his sense of its insignificance in relation to the catastrophes of the 1930s and the ominousness of the approaching 1940s. Wright also saw that the terrors of modern civilization included the misuse of its technologies, the travails of economic depression and the rise of fascism.

While some of his political judgements on the Soviet Union and the fascists were obviously misinformed, Wright had an uncanny and fatefully prophetic understanding of the growing specters of modern mass murder. Aware of the dangers of the machine when misapplied, Wright concluded the lecture by addressing the abuses of capitalism and the rise of fascist militarism. He cited the use of modern technology to commit atrocities unknown before, such as the carpet bombing of entire civilian populations.

Use of technology for mass militarization or mechanized warfare against a civilian populace is antithetical to the humane use of the machine for aesthetic purposes that Wright had called for consistently since 1901. Aware of the dystopian nightmares implicit in the misuse of the machine, he saw the failure of political and industrial leaders to protect civilian populations from this danger as part of the same failure to enable modern architecture to realize organic structure on a massive scale. Wright had criticized the corrupt application of technology to poison and suffocate human beings in modern cities in the Hull House talk of 1901. Now he noted how the same grotesque misapplication of the machine leads to mass killings, amounting to an even worse perversion of human ingenuity. For Wright, architecture was the supreme expression of culture. The failure to implement architecture in a humane way for the greatest number of human beings implied the failure of culture. Wright viewed the political disasters of the thirties as one more sign of that failure.

The British *Architect's Journal* of May 1939 gives us a literary sketch of Wright at the London lectures and the atmosphere of excitement and interest he elicited from the audience: "At the end of the evening meeting last Friday the audience overflowed into the aisles. The white-haired prophet was in form, disciples and disbelievers spellbound by his natural dignity, his obvious sincerity, his easy manner—or rather, his lack of anything so superficial as a manner. He has an irresistibly persuasive voice, mellow, smooth-flowing."[27] By 1939, Wright was a seasoned lecturer, a canny showman who had learned how to bewitch his audience with his Emersonian reflections on the nature of his work and lengthy improvisations on his architectural theories.

Wright's Broadacre City model, his literary speculations on Usonia culminating in *The Living City,* and his visionary drawings lead directly into many realized projects. Some of them are smaller and isolated, like the Usonian house for Herbert Jacobs. Others are larger and offer a more sustained view of Wright's grander vision, and involve a complex of realized structures. Wright's drawings and essays are directly connected to his finished designs. The drawings and essays, too, give us glimpses of his utopia, perhaps freeing his imagination to explore the possibilities of architectural form without the immediate pressure of actual construction. But when Wright received an opportunity to really build part of his Usonian plan, he was happy to adjust his plan to fit the opportunity. He was not an impossibly rigid idealist, as he has been popularly portrayed. The gross distortion of Wright's character, the hero-architect of Ayn Rand's novel *Fountainhead*, was insanely self-absorbed, ready to detonate architectural blasphemies created in his name with the zeal of a late-twentieth-century terrorist. Unlike Roark, Rand's inflexible fictional architect, Wright was flexible and shrewd, a practical survivor when necessary. Charm and pragmatic cunning were as valuable to him as rigid idealism.

With this in mind, we can see that the closest that Wright came to attempting Broadacre City was the complex of buildings he designed for Florida Southern College in the late 1930s. The Florida Southern campus is a sizable fragment of his dream vision of Usonia. Wright wanted to decentralize the cities, which he had steadily viewed as plagued by poisonous congestion ever since the Hull House lecture of 1901.[28] Wright called for the use of the most advanced technology possible to reorganize activities that had been restricted to urban centers in carefully designed rural settings. The modern American college campus proved to be the best place to try out these ideas on a small scale.

Were he as rich as Rockefeller or Ford or Du Pont, Wright frequently claimed, he would buy up the universities in order to close them down.[29] While his fury was chiefly directed at art institutes and schools of architecture, Wright thought that institutions of higher learning created inertia and sterilization amongst the young. For this reason, he was always reluctant to call his Taliesin Fellowship program a school. His young followers were never described as students. Instead, they were "apprentices," learning from the master as they practiced their trade. Thus it is both fortunate and ironic that Wright's consistent criticism of higher education in America did not prevent the college campus—which has steadily brought urban culture to the American countryside—from providing Wright with a natural format to test out his notions of decentralization and cultural development in a rural milieu.

Wright may have met his match in Ludd Myrl Spivey, the college president who hired Wright to design the Florida Southern campus at Lakeland. Like Wright, Spivey was a smooth salesman and a charming talker, a magnetic personality who managed to persuade others to follow him in his visionary notions.[30] Spivey, like many others, was inspired by Wright's *Autobiography*. After he read it, he became fascinated with Wright's work and flew out to Spring Green. Without much prompting, Wright designed a complex of eighteen buildings for him. Spivey did not have the financial backing possible at a well-endowed eastern institution. But he had imagination, charm and cunning. Spivey used student labor to help with construction, providing work-study arrangements for his pupils. It was a practice familiar to Wright, who often used his apprentices fruitfully for a variety of construction projects at Taliesin.

Although Wright was not especially fond of universities, he was always pragmatic and he quickly realized that Dr. Spivey was offering him a chance to plan a large group of integrated buildings in a handsome setting. Wright may also have been attracted to the small size of Florida Southern College. The modest enrollment—only about 800 students—was an ideal number for a county seat in Wright's Broadacre City plan. The architect saw it as the maximum number in his plan for urban decentralization that would allow sufficient land, air and light for each person.[31] The campus had 87 acres, allowing for 87 acres per 800–1000 people.

Thomas Jefferson's plan for the University of Virginia can be contrasted fruitfully with Wright's plan at Lakeland. Jefferson's campus, begun in 1818 and almost finished by the time of his death in 1826, is the creation of an eighteenth century neoclassicist, while Florida Southern College is the product of a twentieth century Emersonian environmentalist. It is not surprising that Jefferson's plan is symmetrical and abstract in a manner markedly different from Wright's. Jefferson's university crowns the land, Wright's campus grows out of it.

But there is a remarkable similarity in the common ability to find masterful unification of a complex series of architectural works within the context of an untouched natural setting.[32] It may be a coincidence that both men were approximately the same age when they turned to the challenge of designing an academic campus. Wright was sixty-seven years old at the time of his first visit to the building site in Lakeland, Florida. Jefferson was in his early seventies when he designed the University of Virginia. But it is certainly not coincidental that both the eighteenth-century statesman-architect and the twentieth-century architect-writer were attracted to the organizational power of simple geometric forms such as the circle or octagon. Both found notions of purity and integrity in such forms. Both chose to combine an integrated patterns of walkways and buildings in an intricate and unified plan.

Wright frequently mentions Jefferson in his essays, attempting to absorb the symbol of Jeffersonian democracy for his own style of organic architecture. But Jefferson, a capable architect himself, was a classicist and Francophile, two qualities that Wright usually claimed to abhor in architectural aesthetics. Jefferson drew continuous inspiration from Andrea Palladio (1508–80), designing a miniature academic utopia for the University of Virginia, which he described as an "academical village."[33] The Jefferson design has great originality, but it is a reflection of least four earlier cultures. Its originality is in its measured re-application—tempered through the cultivated eye of the contemporary European Latrobe—of

Palladio's Renaissance Italian principles applied to Roman classicism, which was in itself already a reworking of Greek architecture.[34]

The center of the Jefferson campus is a library designed as an eighteenth century reinterpretation of the pantheon. Colonnades connect the pantheon-library to a variety of lesser structures, separate pavilions each housing both classrooms and lodgings for individual professors. The integration of scholarly and residential life was intended to be extensive. Each pavilion was modelled on a distinct Roman or Palladian precursor. Columns, cornices, and modillions were intended to serve as instructional models, pointing to the great architecture of the classical past as it universally applies to the present and future. Nothing could be farther from the taste and inclination of the rebellious Frank Lloyd Wright, who thrived on finding site-specific forms to express the human presence in relation to each natural setting, and who was known to describe imitating Greek architecture as "voluntarily going to prison."[35]

The pantheon-as-library is the nucleus of the Jefferson campus. Wright created a more complex fulcrum that generates the shapes of his campus—a combination of chapel and library connected by cantilevered balustrades. As is customary in Wright's work, the asymmetrical shapes of his Florida campus are a direct response to the environment in which he places his buildings.

Wright was captivated by the tropical abundance of the Lakeland setting. The lush vegetation, brilliant sunlight, and sloping land recur in various metaphorical configurations, as Wright allowed his imagination to soar in an improvisatory response to the possibilities of his building site. A college brochure advertising the Lakeland campus refers to the palms, bougainvillea, hibiscus, cherry laurel, crotons, oleander, and "countless fragrant flowers" in the area. The original site was a dense orange grove, affording the lakeside setting with natural shade from the Florida sun. The stately symmetry of the University of Virginia is far less indebted to the shapes and qualities of its setting.

Wright's first structure at Florida Southern was the Annie Pfeiffer Chapel of 1938; the last completed Wright design was the Polk Science building of 1959. Nils Schweizer, a Wright disciple, also built more recent structures on the campus, including a new library and a concert hall. Florida Southern is the largest collection of Wright buildings at a single site.[36] Although Wright designed eighteen buildings, only seven of them were actually realized (but the college says there are actually twelve separate structures, strictly speaking).

Groundbreaking ceremonies for Pfeiffer Chapel were in May 1938. The second World War interfered with construction, but the building was completed in 1941. The chapel's prominence on the hillside of the campus gives it a symbolic meaning, allowing it to radiate its spiritual message outward from its prominent placement in relation to the other buildings. But it is placed with great subtlety on the rising land, nudged into a discrete arrangement with a series of larger structures.

Pfeiffer Chapel is a major achievement and one of the great triumphs of the campus. Certainly, it is one of the most important religious buildings of the mid-twentieth century and one of Wright's most successful late works. Its only rival in the modernist canon is Le Corbusier's sculpturally conceived Pilgrimage Chapel at Ronchamp (1950–55), which is also linked to a series of surrounding structures designed by the European architect.[37] Certainly, Wright's compares favorably, with its joyful play of air and light, combining in ever-fresh patterns in each twenty-four hour cycle.

The chapel is based on a plan of intersecting rectangle and hexagon, with smaller hexagons, lozenges and triangles present or implied throughout. Rectangle and hexagon articulate the seating arrangement and pulpit. A tower of stacked triangular forms, creating a sequence of open-spaced lozenge areas, rises above, capped off with triangular racks for various indigenous hanging plants and vines (fig. 17).

Unity is also created on a smaller scale. The carefully crafted pattern on the sand-blasted concrete blocks is an interconnected grouping of large and small rectangular boxes, with the small boxes leading the eye away from the larger shape toward an opposite and complementary pattern of boxes. Like all of Wright's designs, the pattern is a careful balance of symmetrical forms in asymmetrical arrangements that stimulate the eye. This pattern is integrated as an ornamental insignia over the entire campus.

More sensuous and ebullient than Wright's earlier Unity Temple, Pfeiffer Chapel is filled with the play of color and light as stimulated by the sun. Primary colors are featured in tiny colored glass plates set into apertures cut out of the perforated textiled concrete blocks. The colored glass continually reflects light inward to the chapel and outward to the campus stroller. Reds, yellows, and blues fill the interior with varying patterns.

The chapel expands Wright's continual evolution of crystalline themes in his work.[38] Here the diamond shapes of chapel and library emerge as further elaborations on the honeycomb hexagons of the Hanna house. Clearly Wright was still rotating the square and a rectangle in new ways, creating a sense of vigorous movement and flux, destroying the stagnation of the box, as he had done all his life, but now in still new ways. Thomas Doremus perceptively argues that Wright's juxtaposition of hexagonal and rectangular forms in the chapel successfully "resolves the centuries old conflict between centralized and longitudinal plans in a Modern way."[39] In terms of the formal relationships, the longitudinal shape of the rectangular portion offers direction and impulse to the design, while the hexagon creates centralization and stability. The superimposition of the two shapes creates drama and unity.

A stable rectangle, rotated, becomes a hexagon. Rotated still faster and further, it finally becomes a circle. Thus the vibrant interpenetration of diverse forms—superimposed combinations of hexagons, rectangles and circles—in Wright's work at Florida Southern can be viewed as a transitional achievement leading to the circles, arches and ovals of his last years.

The concrete screens of Pfeiffer Chapel are noteworthy. They shape open space as much as they decorate it. Angular patterns are cut out to let in air and light. They echo the stacked spaces rising in the tower outside and above the chapel. Whereas Unity Temple was designed to protect its worshippers from the intrusive noises of the city, the Pfeiffer Chapel's outside surroundings are invited inside. Nothing is sealed off. The patterns created by the glass, triangular ribbed bars, diamond-shaped seating arrangements, colored light, and arabic concrete screen in the interior are all based on open interaction between exterior and interior.

Wright's 1940 designs for three small seminar buildings were completed in 1941 at a cost of about $77,000. Originally punctuated by small garden courts, the seminars are now linked by glassed-in areas. These shapes are as low and close to the ground as any of Wright's earlier prairie houses, offering an important contrast to the larger masses of library and chapel.[40] However, the same textile pattern used at the Pfeiffer chapel is continued on the concrete blocks used here, and the use of colored glass in small interstices cut in the blocks is present here as well. Sand-blasted blocks left over from the Pfeiffer chapel were used in the construction of the seminars, thus combining Wright's concern for unified motivic design with a pragmatic use of existing materials. Three different kinds of concrete block were used here.[41]

The former T. R. Roux Library (1941), now The Buckner Building, presently houses the offices of the Dean and other administrative services. Groudbreaking ceremonies were in 1942, and the dedication was celebrated in 1945. Here Wright works with a combination of a giant circle and interlocking hexagonal and triangular shapes. Essentially, the union of hexagon and circle in the library replaces the union of hexagon and rectangle in the Pfeiffer chapel. The change in forms resembles musical modulation, in which some pitches are discarded while others remain as a new tonal center is formed. This is a metaphor of great importance in Wright's work, more conscious and crafted than latent and subconscious.

The original library had balconies opening over the circular reading room, dramatically highlighting the wedding of hexagon and circle. Inside the hexagonal stack, where the library holdings were originally housed, Wright creates a rotational organicism that resembles the passageways that could be found in an intricate honeycomb. Evident here is the same intrigue with three dimensional geometric forms that Wright displayed in the Hanna house and the Price tower in Bartlesville, Oklahoma. As Jeanne

Rubin has noted, this love of the crystalline possibilities of geometric form dates all the way back to Wright's youthful fascination with the Froebel blocks.[42] The structure ushers the human form through passageways that form a rotational grid of sorts. Eventually, the rotating angles emerge into the giant circle of the reading room.

The library is connected by cantilevered esplanades to other significant structures, but most important is its bonding via the esplanade to the stylistically related but contradistinct Pfeiffer chapel. The triangles, lozenges and hexagons of the modest library tower echo Pfeiffer Chapel and the circular library reading room parallels the much grander circle of the Waterdome. The library's concrete blocks have the same etched patterns as Pfeiffer Chapel and the seminar buildings. Thus, the library and the chapel are central works connecting the varied activities of the campus, both spiritual and educational, by means of the different geometric shapes that are thematically developed in the varied structures.

The Waterdome is adjacent to Wright's library and today it also borders on the new library, which was designed by Wright protegé Nils Schweizer. When the Waterdome was completed in 1948, the whole was a giant water circle, expanding the circular shape housing the intellectual fertilization taking place in the reading room into the fecund realm of tropical water and light. Today, college representatives say that the fountain in the center originally splashed water all over the place and had to be replaced. This is too bad, for photographs in old college publications show the original splendor of the giant water circle as it reflected the curves of the Roux Library reading room. Smaller fountains now take its place today, but the reflecting pools are still connected underneath the concrete surfaces, and the large circle of the original plan is still evident.

The Watson Administration Building is linked by a cantilevered esplanade to the old Roux Library. Today it houses the president's office and public relations services. Wright personally supervised the building of the Watson Building, which was finished in 1948. The cantilevered esplanade, supported with stoas on only one side, joins into a crowning walkway for the Watson Building, leading on an upward slope toward the office of the college president. One of Wright's most innovative details in the campus design is the large hexagons cut out to allow the penetration of sunlight for hexagonally arranged planting areas below. Sculpted space and architectural form complement each other remarkably here to shape the environment.

The Danforth Chapel (begun in 1954, completed 1955), a small chapel near the larger Pfeiffer Chapel, resembles a kind of blown-up "jewel box." The use of colored glass is intriguing and effective here too, as in the larger chapel. Triangular shapes evoke hands joined in prayer, a motif that Wright will recreate for the congregation at Beth Sholom synagogue in a more grandiose manner just a few years later.

Ordway Hall was completed in 1952. It now houses a testing center and registration facility. Originally, it featured a theater-in-the-round, art studios, and a large recreation lounge. The building features a number of Japanese-style courtyards exposed to sun and air, integrating indoors and outdoors in a carefully controlled environment of dynamic movement. One court is marked off from the rest of the campus with an esplanade. The other is surrounded by classrooms.

Ordway Hall recalls the charm and elegance of Japanese palaces, such as the Katsura Detached Palace, replete with the seclusion and tranquility of the Japanese tea house. Because of the enclosed gardens, long wings for classrooms, and large pavilions for major educational functions, Ordway Hall is in part a miniature reworking of Wright's strategy for the Imperial Hotel. Secluded areas are created for contemplation and conversation, integrated into the life of this particular structure and sealed off from the rest of the campus. But the building is inspired by the tropical light of Florida, which is reminiscent of the brilliance of the Mediterranean sun. A number of the classrooms are exposed to light and air, with doors opening onto courtyards on two sides. What is seen is shaped by the low roofs. The Japanese do that kind of spatial framing of nature in architectural form extremely well, and it is a technique that Wright absorbed for himself and uses masterfully. Wright uses his great skills of synthesis to make the classroom building a remarkable union of Mediterranean villa and Japanese country palace. Much of the literature on the campus refers to Wright's particular personal pleasure with this structure, which is purported to have been one of his favorites amongst the constellation of campus buildings.

The Polk Science Classroom, completed in 1958, is the last realization of Wright's extensive designs for the campus. Today, it is both a science classroom building and planetarium. It is a long horizontal structure on three levels, similar in its rhythmically organic articulation to the kind of desert lizard shape of Taliesin West, hugging the ground in a similar manner. As at Taliesin West, cantilevered, reinforced concrete covers passageways to create shade and intriguing tunnel effects. Glass is used in ingenious ways, enabling rooms and offices to open onto covered outdoor corridors that in turn lead to the open air. The Polk building stays close to the hillside, gradually emerging in long lines and sloping downward toward the lake.

The greatest poetry of the complex is in the interlocking esplanades (fig. 18). Perhaps the most intriguing of all the structures on campus, the esplanades link building to building, protecting strollers from rain and sun. Earlier in his career, Wright had emulated Jefferson's worm-walled brick walls with his own horizontal boxboard walls, marking out angular patterns in the desert at Ocotillo. Now the zigzags of wood evolve into undulating lines of concrete. Even the angular requirements of steps are smoothed out, moving gracefully with the curving lines of the esplanades. The overhanging eaves that first appeared decades before in the prairie house here evolve into a new plasticism that moves with the curvatures of the earth, or flow, when required, along horizontal planes of architectural form. They organically echo the slopes of the hill, leading in diamond patterns all over the campus and crisscrossing at a number of central points. They are a greatly expanded version of the same principle that Wright used to connect the guest house to the main house at Fallingwater in Mill Run. Both the Florida Southern esplanades and the Fallingwater canopy gently move with the shape of the land, moving up the slope of the hill which they echo in fluid architectural form. In the thirties and forties, the dense orange groves added to the shade and grew around the esplanades at Florida Southern. The orange groves are gone now, replaced by green lawns, and today the esplanades shield the pedestrian by themselves.

The whole plan rises from the topography, just as Wright insisted it should in many of his favorite aphorisms on architecture. At Florida Southern College, he shows us exactly what he meant. The campus is a symphony in space of triangles and diamonds and hexagons and circles that continually seem to be moving through the time of human experience as the body walks in continual motion from building to building via the esplanades, and elsewhere across the grounds, rediscovering each perspective as a source of wondrous insight into the subtleties of geometric forms. There is a stylistic interrelationship connecting the esplanade and the motive unit of design inscribed in the walls of the seminar buildings, Pfeiffer Chapel, and Roux Library. The horizontal line of tiny boxes leading to a larger square metaphorically capture the movements between esplanades and buildings.

In summation, there are five basic elements to the overall design for the campus that combine harmoniously for the pleasure of the naked eye: 1. esplanades serving as organic links to the buildings and reflecting the patterns of straight orange groves on the hill (on a larger scale than the esplanade at Fallingwater done at around the same time); 2. sand-blasted blocks colored with dye and coquina shell; 3. poured concrete in a white-cream color; 4. (oxidized) copper; 5. glass, used generously to reflect the tropical Florida light.

Today the campus is shorn of the original lush orange groves, and Wright's full conception of eighteen buildings was never realized. But Florida Southern is a striking testament to what Wright might have done if his large scale plans had received ample backing. The campus buildings, especially the chapels, are a particular delight at night, as they project their colored glass into the humid evening air of Florida. They are a joy from the interior during the day, as the sunlight plays upon them as if they were instruments of visual music. The play of light radiates outward at night, inward during the day. Light and structure join to make a complex organic rhythm that is changing during every second of passing time. The play of shadows in the esplanades is also a great drama worthy of a Florida poem by Wallace Stevens. Wright made the warm tropical air of Florida a stage for the play of interacting oxidized copper, patterned stone and colored glass as they transform in the flux of light, in day and night, in constant variation, giving constant delight.

VI

ARCHITECT AND AMERICAN PROPHET: THE FINAL YEARS

■

Melodic structure is absent in modern music for the same reason that gen-
uine ornament is absent in "functionalism." True ornament is the inherent
melody of structure and functionalism to date is a bad builder.

Frank Lloyd Wright, *Architectural Record*

In the 1940s and 1950s, Wright increasingly caught the attention of the national press. Negative publicity had been the plague of his middle age, but as he advanced in years, he managed to make almost all publicity work in his favor, and he learned to masterfully manipulate the media to broaden the reach of his message. In spite of his advanced age—he was seventy-eight at the end of World War II—Wright achieved the renown usually accorded to a pop singer or movie actor. His name became familiar to the readers of *Time, Life,* and the *New York Times.* Wright's familiar image, with his grey mane of hair and flowing cape, had become an American icon.

But the physiology of human life was catching up with Frank Lloyd Wright. After he contracted pneumonia in 1937, his physician recommended that he spend more time in a warm, dry climate. Wright was also aware that the outdoor lifestyle he encouraged for his Fellowship did not go well with the severe Wisconsin winter. In addition, the high cost of heating the complex of buildings at Spring Green also made him think of other alternatives for the winter months. All of these factors convinced Wright to move his practice and apprentices from Spring Green to Phoenix, Arizona every winter.[1]

For a number of years, Wright stayed with A. J. Chandler, the entrepreneur who had intended to finance the aborted San-Marcos-in-the-Desert project of 1929. Using Chandler's hacienda as a base, Wright toured the area around Phoenix, camping with his entourage at a variety of attractive locations. Finally, he settled on a site on the Maricopa Mesa, near craggy McDowell Peak and twenty-six miles from Phoenix. Wright became enchanted with the "mystic desert vegetation" that surrounded him, suddenly feeling as if he could "look over the rim of the world."[2] This site became Taliesin West, his winter residence. From 1938 on, Taliesin West served as the hub of his activities during the winter months. Wright continually upgraded and developed his estate on the mesa near Phoenix during the 1940s and 1950s, until his death in 1959.

Taliesin West, like the Ocotillo Desert Camp of the late 1920s, began as a temporary shelter made of wood and canvas. Unlike the camp, which was abandoned, Taliesin West eventually evolved into a great country estate in the desert. Originally, Wright stretched linen canvas tightly around redwood frames to provide shelter for large interior spaces at Taliesin West. After Wright's death, fiberglass and steel were used to replace much of the original materials, but the estate still retains the improvisatory feel of a desert encampment.

Following the pattern of Wright's literary descriptions of the desert environment, the shapes of Taliesin West are rich in metaphorical relationships with desert reptiles, the cactus, local stone shapes, a nearby mountain range, large nomadic tents, and sandships. The segmentation of the wood frames form a pattern that resembles the giant skeleton of a desert dinosaur (fig. 19). Unlike the large wooden trusses in the Hillside drafting room, which creates a kind of interior wooden forest (Wright called it an "abstract forest"), the trusses at Taliesin West are exposed to form a giant exoskeleton. These long beams penetrate outward from the interior of the structure into a magnificent pergola made of redwood beams supported by desert rock. Canvas (now fiberglass) was stretched around other portions of the redwood skeleton in the manner of a translucent skin tautly wrapped around giant bone. Indigenous pink and red stone is used with cement to shape the low walls of the structures at Taliesin West. These stones bring out the colorful variety of the native rocks and interrelate the surrounding landscape ideally with the manmade structure.

Characteristically, Wright has burrowed into the shape of the land, digging out shelter from natural irregularities of the topography, building shelter into the folds of the desert floor to create the feeling of cool, sheltering caves. The stonework in the lower portions of the structure evokes a sense of permanence and stability, the upper areas create a sensation of lightness and improvisatory flair.[3]

Like the earlier Taliesin, the heart of activities centers around a large drafting room, but at Taliesin West the drafting room is located in the heart of the main house. In Wisconsin, the drafting room was positioned several thousand yards away from the residence in the nearby Hillside School. That arrangement allows for greater seclusion at the main house. At Taliesin West, Wright clearly wanted to bring his apprentices and architectural activities close to his personal life. The compactness of the arrangements helps perpetuate the excitement of a spontaneous camp erected to study architecture in the desert.[4]

Since the 1930s, the Taliesin Fellowship had attracted eager young people to Wright's headquarters in Wisconsin and Arizona. Wright's architectural ideas were kept alive through his interest in the young, who came to him from all over the world to work as apprentices, as well as through his efforts in publication, public speaking, and in the media. Although Wright was far from the urban centers of the academic elite, and often at odds with powerful members of that community, Wright's magnetic personality attracted prospective apprentices from all over the world.

The commonplace assessment of Wright's efforts to spread his message by training fledgling architects in his Fellowship has been undeservedly negative. This may have been a result of the negative publicity generated by an F.B.I. investigation during the McCarthy era. Wright, always a vociferous critic of big government in Washington, had visited the Soviet Union, published an article in the leftist magazine *The New Masses* in the late 1930s, shown Russian films at Taliesin during the war years, and signed a World Peace Appeal in 1950.[5] Thus, in 1954 the F.B.I. informed the Veterans Administration that Wright's Fellowship was a nest of draft dodgers and conscientious objectors who did little academic and architectural work. Overlooking the significance of Wright's drafting room as an instructional tool, they insisted that Wright could not be an educator because Taliesin featured no classrooms. This was extremely damaging to Wright because his apprentices were dependent on Veterans Administration accreditation to receive federal support for participating at Taliesin. In addition, a Wisconsin State Supreme Court decided in 1954 that Taliesin did not deserve tax-exempt status as an educational institution. Wright was ordered to pay back taxes of over $18,000. Friends and admirers raised the $10,000 that was paid, and no apprentices were lost because of the incident.

In the 1930s, Wright had occasionally misjudged the fascists and advocated an anti-war position. This had led to an earlier F.B.I investigation of Taliesin, which was prompted when one of Wright's apprentices attempted to avoid the draft in World War II.[6] But in the 1950s, he accurately read the hateful political climate generated around Senator Joseph McCarthy, who was once a local judge from nearby Appleton, Wisconsin. Fearless as ever, Wright charged that the House Un-American Activities Committee was un-American itself. Calling McCarthy a "political pervert" in *The Capitol Times,* the Madison newspaper, Wright argued that McCarthy had caused Wisconsin to become a "a stench in the nostrils of decency."[7] America's xenophobic attitude towards Communism was, in Wright's opinion, largely a result of a false inferiority complex and he viewed rampant McCarthyism as the worst incarnation of this sense of inferiority. In *The Weekly Home News,* a small Spring Green publication, Wright took on McCarthy's committee directly: "If I were to list any un-American organization I would list this (house) committee . . . All of this fuss made over Communism is altogether too complimentary to our enemies and manifestly the best handle they could get hold of to destroy us."[8] Wright's stance, while heroic, caused him much grief in Wisconsin, complicating his legal entanglements over taxes at Taliesin and eventually causing the abandonment of an important commission, the elegant design of terraces for a civic center on the shores of Lake Menona in Madison.

Wright was particularly vulnerable because he had always taken great pains to deny any official designation as an educator in his role as founder and director of the Taliesin Fellowship. Nevertheless, the Taliesin Fellowship really did train and educate young architects. Surely, Wright was able to produce a significant number of practicing architects during the Fellowship years, among them talented former apprentices such as Edgar Tafel, William Wesley Peters, E. Fay Jones, Aaron Green, and Mendel Glickman. This new group of protegés compares favorably to Drummond or Mahony or McArthur, Oak Park apprentices of decades earlier.

The center of activities at Taliesins North and West revolved around the drafting rooms, for here Wright's theorizing, his teaching, his architectural practice, and his magical skills at the drafting table all came together at the point of a pencil. Wright would frequently arrive in the drafting room unannounced, generating great excitement. His style was mercurial, as he offered encouragement or criticism. Although he was a perfectionist, his work was continuously in flux, and he demanded continuous revisions. According to Edgar Tafel, apprentices would watch the master at the drafting table and emulate his work. But Wright was flexible, allowing students to interrupt this custom with questions and other interjections.[9]

Other features of Taliesin life are still etched in the minds of many former apprentices today: the formal dinners every Saturday evening; the films, lectures and concerts followed by refreshments and discussion; the frequent picnics with Wright and Olgivanna in the countryside. In the tradition of his Unitarian and Baptist ancestors, Wright would often preach to the young people who gathered around him after breakfast on Sundays for about two hours. But he did not talk of religion in any formalized sense. Instead, he spoke about architecture's calling and its relationship to human culture. He improvised, just as Emerson had a hundred years before, on the familiar themes that had concerned him all his life. Some of the material was a repetition of what he had already said or written, but he was able to find new insights as he worked over familiar material, like a great jazz musician improvising on a well-known tune.

A number of significant events marked the steady canonization of Frank Lloyd Wright in the early 1940s. In 1941, Frederick Gutheim published an important collection of Wright's essays and lectures spanning from 1894–1940.[10] Then, in 1942, Henry Russell Hitchcock published the first monumental assessment of Wright's work. Hitchcock was a respected member of the eastern art establishment that Wright essentially mistrusted. Wright, who was increasingly triumphant as America's foremost architect, still needed to win prestige amongst the northeastern elite, which had always preferred European repackaging of many of Wright's ideas. Hitchcock's study was written in conjunction with a retrospective of Wright's work at the Museum of Modern Art in New York. Both the book and the exhibit covered Wright's career from 1893 to 1940. Wright's uneasy relationship is best summed up in the architect's own words: "His opinions on architecture I have distrusted as being far too academic, but since it is safer to trust one's point of view to one's enemies than to one's friends, I asked him to record the show."[11]

Hitchcock's book, *In the Nature of Materials,* is still an essential source in Wright studies today. Working with the architect, Hitchcock covers the early work under Silsbee and Sullivan, the gradual maturation of the young artist, the prairie house period, the years of wandering in Japan and California, the later and grander designs of the 1920s, and the striking rejuvenation of the 1930s. Unlike Wright's own poetic autobiography, which reappeared in a revised and expanded version in 1943, Hitchcock's work is based in specific and meticulous observation of the works in sequence. The two works, Hitchcock's study and Wright's autobiography, form a comprehensive overview of Wright's life, work and ideas through 1940. Unlike the autobiography, which is essentially a belletristic literary work, Hitchcock's rigorous scholarly monograph places Wright firmly within the intellectual dialogue of art history and cultural criticism, showing Wright's clear position as a modern master.

Wright was active until his death in 1959. His intense productivity was in no way a mere repetition of his earlier accomplishments, however. He grew from his past achievements, using his instinctive knowledge of spatial form to constantly evolve in new directions. The chief development in his work was to move from rectilinear to curvilinear forms. But this change was established in stages. Wright had displayed a lifelong fascination with the architectural possibilities of crystalline rotation. Now this rotational sensibility caused fresh and diverse forms to come to life in space. First, the angular shapes of the crystal turned and twisted into dazzling new permutations. Gradually, Wright's sense of movement in architectural space caused him to smooth out his crystals into the continuous flow of the circle and sphere.

Wright realized that to posit one geometric form in space automatically projects the same form in other related spaces that are found along a rotating axis. One module of geometric structure automatically implies the generation of others. Wright's architecture resists the establishment of a fixed point of view. Rather, all points of view are important. Bruno Zevi describes this phenomenon in Wright's work as "anti-perspective tri-dimensionality," and points out that it enables Wright to eliminate façades and the "hierarchy of façades" from his buildings.[12] No single perspective dominates in a Wright work. Continuous movement is encouraged through a planned pattern of movement that enables the continuous discovering of formal interrelationships. These formal interrelationships, always organized in a three-dimensional scheme, in turn create stability and aesthetic harmony.

Lewis Mumford argues that Wright "achieved Cubism in architecture before the Cubists: and he [went] on to an integral architecture which creates its own forms with—not for—the machine."[13] Like Picasso, Wright destroys fixed-point viewing and forces the uncovering of simultaneous planes of space. But one can move through a Wright structure and live in it, while one can only look at a Picasso painting. Thus, the implications of Wright's architectural cubism, which are continually pervasive throughout his career, have a far more practical and far-reaching impact on world culture than the cubism of Picasso, Braque and their painterly disciples in Europe. On the level of pure ideas, the large-scale potential of Wright's cubist approach to architecture is clear in the Crystal Heights design of 1939, a pivotal work that was never actually constructed.

On a more pragmatic level, Wright's domestic designs have had a wide effect on the populace, especially though his many imitators, whereas the esoteric nature of painterly cubism has limited the scope of its influence. Nevertheless, the development of pictorial cubism and Wright's architectural cubism took place at around the same time, but with Wright anticipating Picasso by a number of years. Whereas the forceful impetus of painterly cubism died out by the 1930s, Wright never completely abandoned his multi-planar approach to architecture, working out its implications until his death in 1959.

It is as if Wright had been studying the architectural potential of crystal structures all his life, continually turning them, interlocking them, and combining them in new ways. Some of his late crystalline designs include the Price Company Tower (1952); the Boomer "Sunbonnet" house in Phoenix, Arizona (1953); Beth Sholom Synagogue (1954); Wyoming Valley School (1956); and the Mile High, Illinois skyscraper for Chicago, which is essentially a series of mutually reinforcing triangles in a rotational grid.

But Wright's conception of building design as an interlocking pattern of organic crystal also led him to design far more humble and practical buildings. Perhaps the prefabricated houses designed for Marshall Erdman in the mid 1950s are the best examples of these.

Another humble example is the tiny house, a compact, dynamic vortex of turning triangles, that Wright created for wealthy widow Jorgine Boomer and her servants (fig. 20). Asymmetrical slopes of the triangular roofs interpenetrate one another, creating a sense of movement and variety that is consistent with the internal movement planned within the structure. Its triangular theme is encapsulated in the zigzagging movements to the right and left required upon entering the house. These movements lead inevitably to the broad expanse of the sitting room. Then one mounts the stairs, turning in the torque of the planes, led through surprising exposures to the desert light. The ample eaves, breathtaking in the varied variety of extreme cantilevering, provide comfortable shade from the desert heat and inviting the "Sunbonnet" sobriquet. Here Wright displays a dashing new freedom with the jagged triangular shapes that had first stimulated his imagination when he visited Arizona in the late 1920s. His design is more dynamic than ever before, incorporating the natural flow of human movement into his plan with a striking new intensity. The rotating angles and edges of the house create a whirlwind in three dimensions, spinning sharp protrusions into a spiral of circular rotation. Movement and space are united in a new architectural metaphor.

The Price Tower in Bartlesville, Oklahoma was built in 1952, finally realizing a plan for a tall building that dated back to the St. Mark's-on-the-Bouwerie design of the 1929, a project that was abandoned during the Great Depression. In terms of interlocking, rotational forms, the Price Tower also evolves from the Romeo and Juliet windmill of 1896, which was a very early miniature tower conceived as a union of a mutually supporting diamond and octagon. In addition, the Price Tower design is related to the rotational pattern of the Honeycomb House, which generated great flexibility and freedom of movement for the Hanna family.

The lozenge and octagon of the earlier tower and the hexagons of the Hanna house evolve into a rotational grid of interlocking square shapes and triangular protrusions for the Bartlesville structure, allowing for an extraordinary range of variation for the artistic expression of space and creating a remarkable crystalline effect. No two views of the tower are exactly the same. Not one single point of view commands an obvious focal center of the building. The rotating pattern also features great stability, as the composite steel and concrete core of the building, made up of four interior columns, is mutually reinforced by the weight-bearing duties of the interlocking grid.[14]

The original plan for the St. Mark's plot on 10th Street in the East Village called for three residential towers to surround the existing church.

The honeycomb of rotated squares and hexagons for the St. Mark's project divided each floor into four apartments with four large rectangular living rooms. The turning of simple geometric shapes around a central axis affords great variety and flexibility in this earlier design.

For Bartlesville, Wright divided his tower into two complimentary halves that fit together like the antecedent and consequent clauses of a musical phrase. But the building is not simplistically symmetrical. Three offices are located on each floor. Each apartment is a duplex. An entrance to each apartment is thus placed on every other floor. Each residence has a lower level for living and dining, and an upper level for the bedrooms, balcony, and outdoor terrace. Separate entrances and elevator shafts provide entrances to each half of the building. By turning shapes in the grid, by rotating his forms on an axis, Wright creates great variety in his tower. One obvious example of this is the off-center rectangle of the bedroom floor on the domestic side of the tower. Turned against the axis of the shaft, it penetrates the outer wall of the tower, with a single line leading outward to a terrace, and inward to a balcony that overlooks the two-story living room (fig. 21).

Wright felt that the Bartlesville tower was so important that he took the trouble to publish a whole book on it in 1956: *The Story of the Tower: The Tree that Escaped the Crowded Forest*. Written in his seductive fashion, Wright's introductory essay for the book is rich in metaphorical language describing the structural conception of the building, a conception which is perfect for a broader application in imaginary Usonia:

> This type of tall building may enable you to imagine similar ones, though infinite in variety rising as gleaming shafts of light, tall as you please from every village in the country. Space in town, courting the sunbeams and the view—no masonry cavern standing on the streets—the areas thus thrown back into the village planted as green parks. Out of this varied mass of shade trees and flowering shrubs, see the spider—steel—spinning its web to enmesh glass—glass clear—glass translucent—glass in relief—glass in color. Iridescent surfaces of this light-fabric rising high against the blue out of the whole city, the city now seen as a park, the metal fabrication of the shafts themselves turquoise or gold, silver, bronze, the glass surfaces between the threads of the fabric shimmering with light reflected, light refracted—sparkling light broken into imaginative patterns.[15]

Wright's intuitive thought process enabled him to reach out into nature and draw structural analogies with his own forms as he needed to invent them. Here he tells his reader that steel is used as a giant spider web, spinning out from four shafts, which function in a manner analogous to the trunk of a giant tree. Concrete is poured around the steel, providing composite strength for the steel trunk and bark for the tree, and forming a union of great strength with the steel webbing.

Long an admirer of the power and economy of the modern airplane and ocean liner, Wright claims to use steel for the developing technology of the tall building in a manner that emulates modern marine engineering. In his view, the steel core provides a new lightness and strength in the tall building just like the implementation of the steel keel does for the great oceangoing ship. And it has been noted that the taut design of the interior provides the sense of sailing on board a tall ship.[16] Most important, the tower stands apart from the crowding of the city, on the open plain, available to the fresh air and light of the countryside. Wright compares this free-standing tower to the tall tree that is free of the unhealthy density of an overcrowded forest.

Herbert Muschamp argues that the Bartlesville tower is a displaced New York skyscraper, rescued from an abandoned project developed more than twenty years earlier. However, the later design is not exactly like the earlier one, but rather evolves naturally from it. Muschamp, however, is probably correct in detecting that Wright's anxiety about the failure of the New York project prompted him to publicize his success at this much later date, and to assert, once more, his dislike of the big American city. Thus, the old Saint Mark's Tower project is rewritten into a tower standing in Wright's imaginary Usonia. *The Story of the Tower* is the only one of Wright's seventeen books that deals exclusively with a single building.[17] The tower has special significance because it gives us a glimpse of an integral fragment of Wright's Utopian dream vision, demonstrating how a tall building can be an integral part of Wright's plans for decentralization.

Although he was continually working out ideas that had roots in the work of previous decades, Wright was also moving into a profound stylistic shift that characterized the last two decades of his life. Wright's intrigue with circular forms in his last years, already evident in the dendriform designs for Johnson Wax in 1936, led him to develop a variety of fresh spacial arrangements based on the circle. All circular forms became part of a highly integrated form of architectural grammar: arch, circle, dome, spiral, and sphere exist in coherent motivic relationship that gives structural unity to his late works.

The 1938 design for the Ralph Jester house is a taut series of circular forms integrating interior space and landscaping with the same rigor as the exterior and interior rectangles unifying the Coonley villa built so many years before. The circle is the theme of the Jester house just as the hexagon governs all aspects of the Honeycomb house. The Jester house, constructed near Taliesin West, signals Wright's evolution away from angular shapes. It anticipates by ten years the extraordinary fluidity of a number of later works based on circular forms.

Another significant transitional work was the "Solar Hemicycle" house, the second of the two homes Wright designed for Herbert Jacobs. The concept and plan for this home was developed in 1943, but the house was not built until 1948. The unbuilt designs of the "Wave House" for Stuart Haldorn (1946) and the Huntington Hartford house also mark Wright's growing fascination with curvilinear forms. Here crescent forms and half circles are used, shapes that are integrated on a larger scale with the spirals of the later Guggenheim Museum ramp.

By the late 1940s, a whole sequence of buildings had emerged from Wright's hand, all of them showing the organicism of the curve and the circle that had suddenly developed in his powerful imagination. The pivotal work in this sequence of late circular designs is the superb Morris Gift Shop (1948) on Maiden Lane in San Francisco (fig. 22). It was followed by the Sol Friedman home in Pleasantville, New York (1948); the David Wright House (1950); the spiral ramp in the Hoffman Auto Showroom (1954); the Guggenheim Museum in New York City (1956); the Greek Orthodox Church at Wauwatosa (1956); the Marin County Civic Center near San Francisco (1957); the Grady Gammage Memorial Auditorium in Tempe, Arizona (1959) (Wright's last public building); and Wright's last domestic design: the Norman Lykes residence (1959).

Like the tower at Bartlesville, other Wright works echo earlier achievements. Although Wright generates an entirely new series of buildings based on his work with circular forms, important features in his later works are clearly from the same artistic hand that designed buildings done many decades before. One such example is the band of carefully curved brickwork in receding arches around the entrance to the Morris Gift Shop. Wright's elegant use of brick for the shop exterior echoes the voussoir masonry at the Dana, Thomas, and Heurtley houses almost fifty years earlier. It also recalls Sullivan's highly elaborate "Golden Doorway" for the Chicago fair of 1893 (figs. 1 and 22).[18]

But Wright, developing continually from his lifelong experimentation with plastic geometric forms, also creates something completely new: a fluidity of form completely unknown in architectural history. The receding arches of the exterior conduct one into the arches of the tunnel entrance, which is half in brick masonry and half in molded glass. In a fluid progression, the circular forms of the exterior arches transform into the expanding circles of the interior ramps. The curves in the arch form of the entrance introduce the rising spiral of the interior. Bands of horizontal and vertical lighting contrast with the arches, providing a symmetrical relief to the pattern, as in the first Jacobs house in Madison. The horizontal band of lighting, too, leads the eye from the exterior to the interior of the structure.

Clearly, Wright's renewed fascination with the arch, circle and spiral is, in one sense, a return to his heritage in the works of H. H. Richardson and Louis Sullivan. This return is documented by Wright's short monograph on Sullivan, *Genius and the Mobocracy,* which was published in 1949—around the time that Wright's evolution toward curvilinear structures had already taken a clear direction. Sullivan's importance is the main topic of the book, especially in terms of his significance as Wright's mentor. Richardson frequently surfaces, however, as Wright describes Sullivan's passionate evaluations of Richardson's importance as *his* most important precursor. Wright also takes up a great deal of space in this curious book to expound his own views on architecture yet once more. Although *Genius and the Mobocracy* is strangely fragmented, it contains fascinating, enigmatic statements on originality, artistic rivalry, and Wright's notion of creative genius with respect to Sullivan. Rarely in the history of Western culture have any two such powerful creative personalities worked so closely together. In this particular case, one of the two has even left behind written testimony to describe the relationship.

Wright attempts to fully reconcile himself with the work of his artistic patriarchs in *Genius and the Mobocracy.* However, his strong praise for Sullivan still shows traces of rivalry and tension. He is careful to preserve his identity apart from his precursors. He describes Richardson as a "grand exteriorist," more interested in the picturesque aspects of the Romantic Romanesque than in structural innovations.[19] Wright argues that Sullivan, who he views as primarily gifted in his ability to invent original decorative patterns, never valued the inherent nature of individual materials. According to Wright, Sullivan used all materials—wood, stone, iron, or terra-cotta—as a kind of primal "clay" that served without distinction as raw matter to be manipulated by the will of his powerful imagination. Over the course of the years Wright spent as Sullivan's apprentice, Wright realized that he had something rather different in mind himself. Of all Wright's books, *Genius and the Mobocracy* makes this clearest:

> Not until toward the end of my service to Adler and Sullivan did I perceive that the nature of materials meant no more to lieber-meister [Sullivan] than their nature had meant to the ancient Greeks but with a nameless difference. Materials, all alike, were only grist for the marvelous sensuous rhythmic power of imagination he possessed. His spirit was deeply involved in the fluent organic expressions of form naturally appropriate to a plastic—and clay was (it is forever) the ideal "plastic." But whether executed in stone, wood, or iron, all materials were "clay" in the master's hands . . . Because of this effulgent sense of sympathy he possessed—for, all he cared or anything he seemed to want to know materials were pretty much all *one* to him. In the primal plastic—clay—his opulent imagery could triumph, and did so. As might have been the case with the Greeks had they the gift he had. But this inconsistency by its very constancy began to disturb me. Not much at first but an uneasy little. More and more, though, as years went by I would instinctively draw toward expressions more appropriate to other building materials by way of T-square and triangle: just as purely instinctively rhythmic—so it seemed to me—but more architectural ones.[20]

Still concerned about the possibility that he might be viewed as Sullivan's protegé, Wright constructs a distinction of great significance between the role of an apprentice and the role of a disciple. Wright freely admits that he chose to be the former in relation to Sullivan, but never the latter. To argue his point, Wright even quotes Sullivan's own statement to him to illuminate the distinction: "Frank, you have never been my disciple—but you are the only one who ever worked with me who understood. I couldn't do what you've done, nor could you have done what you've done but for me!"[21] And Wright insists, perhaps too strongly, that each artist always existed as a complete and separate entity:

> He taught me nothing nor did he ever pretend to do so except as he was himself the thing he did and as I could see it for myself. He ("the designing partner") was the educational document in evidence. I learned to read him with certainty just as you shall see him and see me if you are a good reader between the lines. I am sure he would prefer it—that way.[22]

The strangest aspect of all is the reversal of roles that Wright—perhaps subconsciously—works into his text. Teacher and student, master and apprentice, now change roles. Formerly, Wright had worked as Sullivan's draftsman, and he frequently described his purpose in Sullivan's office as that of Sullivan's "pencil-in-hand." Now Wright flips the implications of the metaphor the other way around, slyly praising Sullivan as greater in his draftsmanship and ornamentation than in his sense of overall architectural design:

> Beginning at the draughting board, it was my natural tendency to draw away from the mastery of his efflorescence toward the straight line and rectangular pattern, working my own rectilinear way with T-square and triangle toward the more severe rhythms of point, line, and plane. Never having been a painter I had never drawn more than a little "free-hand." So at this time not only was it my instinct to go away from free-hand exercise, but my technique (such as it was) condemned me to T-square and triangle, which I came to love and prefer, but they compelled me to stay behind the sensuous expressions the master so loved and mastered so surpassingly well.[23]

Clearly Wright intended to praise Sullivan (and Richardson indirectly) while leaving room for his own sense of superiority.

Wright's renewed interest in curvilinear forms reflects the final consolidation of his mature artistic personality, the final assertion of his distinctive stylistic differences with the work of Sullivan and Richardson. Now he could return to the shapes of his teachers, no longer needing to rebel by rejecting them outright. Reflecting these undercurrents in the text of *Genius and the Mobocracy,* the expanded use of poured concrete in Wright's later structures displays a flexibility of expression unknown to his precursors. Once again, understanding the nature of materials and the possibilities of technology enabled Wright to find new means of expression, even with the ancient forms of the arch and the dome. Spanning from the curves of the Richardsonian voussoir to the giant spirals of the Guggenheim, Wright's career encompasses at least a century of American architecture. It is a century that takes it shape chiefly from the force of his own imagination.

The successful Morris Gift Shop turned out to be a dry run for the controversial Guggenheim museum.[24] Through Baroness Hilla Rebay, Wright's Guggenheim commission eventually drew him into a working relationship with John D. Rockefeller, Robert Moses, and other prominent Easterners. Moses, who was related to Wright by marriage, offers a hilarious and insightful account of Wright in these years in a substantial profile of the architect he included in his lengthy memoir, *Public Works: A Dangerous Trade*.[25] The picture that emerges of the aging architect—already in his eighties—is that of a charming and difficult man, an unpredictable yet fiercely determined maestro who Moses felt occasionally obliged to placate and rescue from difficulty with the Guggenheim clients.

The search for a site for the new museum began during World War II. Preparations for the building went through a tumultuous seventeen years of sustained controversy that eventually required six sets of architectural plans and almost 750 drawings.[26] On the positive side, the controversy over the museum design sparked consistent coverage in the press. Unhappily, the struggle to build the museum as he wished it to be seems to have exhausted the architect during the last years of his life.

As work on the Guggenheim brought him repeatedly to New York, Wright took a spectacular second floor suite at the Plaza, which he redecorated in his own style, including his own wall hangings and his own custom-designed furniture. Wright spent so much time in the suite that it became known as "Taliesin the Third," and he became a familiar figure as he walked along Fifth Avenue from the Plaza to the museum site on 89th street.

But the Guggenheim commission was a challenge from the very start. With a limited budget of approximately two million dollars, Wright ironically found himself in a situation roughly analogous to the Unity Temple commission in Oak Park in 1904. Once again, Wright turned to the use of poured concrete, which he had first applied at Unity Temple. Early in the planning for the Guggenheim, Wright penciled in the word "ziggurat" on one of his drawings. Clearly, he had been pondering the great ramps that sloped up toward the sacrificial pinnacles of ancient Mesopotamian temples of the Middle East.[27] He may also may have been fascinated with the rectangular masses that the Mesopotamians built as manmade metaphors for mountains, and he probably noted the use of tiers to mark off different levels of a ziggurat.

The tiers of the ziggurat, which could number as many as seven, found a modern reincarnation in the seven revolutions (and floors) of the ramp at the Guggenheim.[28] Wright boldly opted for the fluidity of the circle rather than the stability of the square, and he designed a museum based on a pair of spiralling ramps, with a large ramp for exhibits and a smaller one (a "monitor") for administrative space.

The circular motion of the spirals is balanced against the interplay of crescent forms. At the base of the large ramp, a fountain that resembles a large eye when viewed from above nudges neatly against the opening of the ramp as it hooks around in a last turn toward the floor of the great space of the rotunda.[29] Echoing crescent shapes signify the tubular shaft that anchors the spiral all the way up to the seventh floor. In the small tower the crescent is also playfully present. Here, however, it penetrates the spiral, locking both forms together in an embrace reminiscent of the Romeo and Juliet tower of 1896.

The great rotunda defines the space of the Guggenheim just as the open cubic space of Unity Temple defined its form decades before (fig. 23). The rotunda realizes the museum as a cathedral in the service of art, opening toward a brilliant skylight that allows for natural illumination and the gradations of natural lighting transitions. The great volume of cylindrically-shaped open space emphasizes the social nature of museum going, allowing for viewers to look up or down or across the spiral at others. Thus, the contemplation of art is celebrated as a public process, involving both the creativity of the artworks on display and the social interpretation by a public. Open space underscores the interpenetration of creating and viewing in the sociology of this public process.

With the Guggenheim design Wright once again displays his commanding ability to combine the old and the new, the ancient and the modern, the foreign and the native. The Guggenheim "ziggurat" merges a vocabulary of traditionally non-Western forms with new Western technology to create an entirely fresh conception of museum architecture.

The larger of the two ramps enables the Guggenheim museum to show the continuous progression of a body of work by an artist or group of artists. The continuity of the spiral brings out the continuity of a sequence of works. Years before, in his 1912 book on the Japanese print, Wright had indicated that the spiral symbolized "organic process." Now the Guggenheim spiral was intended to illustrate the process of organic development in a body of painting. Viewers are intended to mount the spiral via an elevator and descend as the rings of the spiral decrease with each complete turn. Thus, the greatest circumference is at the top, the least at the bottom. This notion had intrigued Wright during his initial planning for the structure, when he developed the notion of an "optimistic ziggurat" that accumulated a greater mass as it accumulated height.[30] The engineering of the decreasing spiral is deceptively practical. Contrary to what at first seems like common sense, the decreasing size of each circular section causes greater, not lesser, stability.[31]

As a young architect, Wright faced the criticism of doubting members of the Unity Temple planning committee. Now, he faced growing opposition of a similar nature, in spite of his much greater stature. Wright, who consistently viewed architecture as the greatest of the plastic arts, came into conflict with James Johnson Sweeney, who replaced Hilla Rebay as museum director, and a group of painters allied with Willem de Kooning. Wright's critics attacked him for his alleged insensitivity to proper conditions for viewing a canvas. The museum's curved design, his critics argued, would conflict with the necessity for viewing a painting properly on a perfect horizontal plane. In a 1957 letter to Sweeney, a letter obviously prepared with Sweeney's approval, de Kooning, Robert Motherwell, Franz Kline, and eighteen other painters mounted an attack against Wright's design. The letter asserts that "the basic concept of curvilinear slope for presentation of painting and sculpture indicates a callous disregard for the fundamental rectilinear frame of reference necessary for the adequate visual contemplation of works of art."[32] It is ironic that Wright, who had championed the horizontal and right angle in his prairie house, came to face a vicious critical attack because he abandoned it in his design for the museum.

Wright, an Emersonian artist to the end, was never foolishly consistent and now he wanted a museum that would generate continuous human motion in one organic movement, a continuous motion that would reflect the fluidity of creativity recorded within a well-chosen sequence of paintings. He maintained, moreover, that the plan based on the two interacting larger and smaller spiralling ramps, would be of a sufficiently gentle slope to allow for pleasurable viewing and would in no way detract from the individual integrity of each work of art. Addressing his critics as "Dear Fellow Artists," Wright responded to Sweeney and his allies with characteristic vigor and determination:

> I submit over my own name that there is no 'rectilinear frame of reference' whatever for the exhibition of a painting except one raised by callous disregard of nature, all too common to your art. I am sufficiently familiar with the incubus of habit that besets if not befits your mind to understand perfectly that you all, curator included, know too little of the nature of the mother art: architecture.[33]

But the continuous contentiousness surrounding all aspects of the museum wore Wright down during his last years. Many battles ensued, including heated struggles over details of the interior color and design. Both sides repeatedly sought out the support of influential people like Robert Moses and Harry Guggenheim, nephew of the by then deceased Solomon Guggenheim. Sweeney particularly infuriated Wright with his intention to whitewash the interior walls with ivory white paint. Wright viewed white as the "loudest color of them all," a color that distracts viewing attention from the painting that it is intended to enhance and support. Wright preferred a darker color and the use of natural light from above to emphasize the paintings displayed along the ramp. For Wright, using white walls as a background for displaying paintings was like intoning high C to accompany a melodic line in a symphony. He detested the idea.[34]

The Guggenheim finally opened in 1959, six months after Wright's death. It has always generated continuous debate. Although Sweeney and his allies altered Wright's plans at the museum's opening, a recent renovation project has attempted to restore much of Wright's original vision and to provide badly needed exhibition space and expanded facilities. It remains to be seen, however, whether the original conception of the large ramp will be retained, whether it will still be used to display pictures or whether the ramp itself will be chiefly foregrounded as a work of art in itself and as a monument to Wright. A third solution—and not necessarily an unsatisfactory one—has been the middle course taken by the museum's directors to date. This has been to use the space for temporary exhibitions, such as the one Dan Flavin created for the reopening of the museum in June, 1992 or the flowing survey of Roy Lichtenstein's works on exhibit in late 1993. One hopes that renewed attempts will be made to capture some of Wright's original intention and that the ramp will be used to capture the organic unfolding of the creative process in a variety of well-chosen artworks, whether on temporary or permanent exhibit.

Throughout the 1950s, Wright's growing fame would easily have enabled him to turn away from domestic architecture. But his lifelong fascination with the connection between the American family and the possibilities of organic architecture continued unabated. The publication of yet another book in 1954, *The Natural House,* documents Wright's sustained intrigue with the American house during the last years of his life. *The Natural House* is a collection of both recycled and freshly written material. Some of the text had already appeared in *An Autobiography* and other passages were reprinted from an architectural journal, but Wright also added new improvisations on his dream of Usonia, turning his architectural vision on the domestic option available to the American of modest means. Since the book concentrates specifically on the possibilities of the single family home, it brings a special focus to his thought.

In *The Natural House,* Wright develops the notion of Emersonian individualism more sharply than before, emphasizing the need for abandoning the American city more forcefully than ever. Claiming that integrity of a home and an individual are one and the same, Wright declares that his style of architecture affords clients a unique sense of place:

> Naturally should you want to really live in a way and in a place which is true to this deeper thing in you, which you honor, the house you build to live in as a home should be . . . integral in every sense. Integral to site, to purpose and to you. The house would then be a home in the best sense of that word. This we seem to have forgotten if ever we learned it. Houses have become a

series of anonymous boxes that go into a row on row upon row of bigger boxes either merely negative or a mass nuisance. But now the house in this interior or deeper organic sense may come alive as organic architecture.[35]

Once again, the key principle needed is decentralization. Americans should leave the "anonymous boxes" typical in urban areas and head for the country. "How far out should we go?" asks a client. Wrights' answer is emphatic: "My suggestion would be to go just as far as you can go—and go soon and go fast."[36]

The book also features plenty of pragmatic examples illustrating how the new homes in a decentralized America should look. To begin with, Wright includes excellent photographs and descriptions of the Jacobs house, then already close to twenty years old. By this time, however, there was also an abundant variety of Usonian houses to draw on, offering new prototypes which had spun off into a variety of shapes and styles since the Jacobs house of 1936.[37]

Since Wright views himself as the one architect with the means to dominate the scene with the power of his vision, one tends to wonder what he means when he also argues for Emersonian individuality expressed in the nature of each home. Anticipating this query, Wright argues that he seeks emulation not imitation. Mere copying, a method of flattery he had derided in his *Architectural Record* article of 1914, was not suitable for him in 1954 either. Form, site, materials and needs of the client must be united in a unique way for each individual home. The strength of the architectural conception determines the measure of success.

Wishing to illustrate the customized possibilities in his own low-cost dwellings, Wright offers one of his nature metaphors to explain the flexibility of the Usonian design typical of the original Jacobs house. These homes are biomorphic forms, replete with trunks and tails:

A Usonian house if built for a young couple, can without deformity, be expanded, later for the needs of a growing family. As you see from the plans. Usonian houses are shaped like polliwogs—a house with a shorter or longer tail.[38]

Once again, Wright's rich metaphorical way of mind enables him to conceive of original forms by combining natural shapes and architectural shapes. The body of the polliwog is the complex of living room and kitchen, an economical unit which holds the vital organs of life. Plumbing, refrigeration, and electricity are analogous to intestine, stomach, and nerves. The tail is the bedroom wing, which can be varied in size, according to the needs and means of an individual family. Specific illustrations are provided to show how variety is achieved; among them are the Rosenbaum house (1939), the Pope house (1940), and the Adelman house (1953). All of these are highlighted by photographs of the Usonian House and Exhibition Pavilion, which was temporarily erected on the site of the Guggenheim museum in 1953. Other types of design are also featured, including the lakeside John C. Pew house (1940) in Shorewood Hills, Wisconsin, and the Jorgine Boomer house (1953) in Phoenix. Wright also includes materials on a variety of favorite topics, including passages on natural illumination, air conditioning, roofing, interior design, and the possibilities of berm architecture.

Wright's work in domestic architecture probably had the most far-reaching impact on American life, reaching into a variety of social strata. During his later years, Wright's diverse religious buildings also brought his architecture into the varied streams of pluralistic American culture. For each of them, he chose a geometric shape that was given a motivic presence which continuously informed the whole work. If he was unable to bring the great religions of America together within one giant steel cathedral as he had once hoped to do in the 1920s, he was able to attend to many of them separately.

The Unitarian church at Shorewood Hills, Wisconsin (1947) is formed in a series of jutting triangular prows that recall huge hands interlocked in prayer. Giant sunbonnets shelter the angular structure from the elements, protecting congregation members from rain, heat, and light. Shelter from blinding light is particularly important for the tall prow-windows rising behind the pulpit, but the low eaves also protect points of entry and exit to the church as well. Huge limestone rocks anchor the church in the earth, but the soaring roofline makes the church seem as if it is sailing over the hilltop on which it is perched. The subtle torque of human movement created by the interior design anticipates the use of space in the 1951 Boomer "Sunbonnet" house in Arizona. But Wright's bold return to religious architecture—his first sally into the genre since Pfeiffer chapel at Florida Southern College in the late 1930s—also prepared him for new innovations to come in larger structures required for houses of worship as well.

Drawing upon his tripod concept for the interfaith steel cathedral design of 1926, Wright sketched a plan for the Beth Sholom Synagogue at Elkins Park, Pennsylvania, near Philadelphia, in 1954.[39] As is often the case with the artist's buildings, Wright's linguistic metaphor for Beth Sholom—"a luminous mount Sinai"—is an aid in understanding the spatial metaphors of the structure.[40] The Pennsylvania synagogue is in many respects a sibling of the Unitarian church in Wisconsin. It also encompasses its congregation within its giant metaphor of folded triangles.

The synagogue, a huge work on the theme of interlocking triangular shapes, contains two chapels, a large hall seating 1,030, and a smaller sanctuary for 250. Here, too, the floor of the large chapel resembles huge hands folded to hold the congregation. The small chapel, in turn, is neatly tucked into a smaller triangular pattern under the large chapel, bringing larger and smaller gatherings of the congregation into a unique form of architectural dialogue. To make the synagogue, Wright hung blasted corrugated wire glass, reinforced fiberglass, and aluminum cover strips over giant steal beams. All of this was suspended on top of 2,221 cubic yards of concrete. The resulting shape—a complex of significant Jewish symbols—is a giant evocation of both Mount Sinai, with its jagged rocks, and the nomadic tent of the ancient Hebrews (fig. 24).[41]

In addition to the synagogue and church in triangles at Elkins Park and Shorewood Hills, Wright built a Greek Orthodox Church based on the two symbolic shapes of that faith: the dome and the cross.[42] The result is the church shaped in circles and domes in Wauwatosa, Wisconsin (1956). Here Wright's late curvilinear sensibility is displayed in a religious edifice.

Throughout his career, Wright did not shun reading meanings into the simple geometric shapes that initiate the derivation of his buildings. For him, the square symbolized integrity, the triangle, aspiration, and the circle, infinity.[43] It is not surprising that all of these forms turn up as basic motivic units in his religious buildings, with a steady progression from the squares and rectangles used at Unity Temple in 1904 to the complex interaction of geometric shapes in Pfeiffer Chapel, to the triangles and circular forms of the later buildings.[44]

We are fortunate that Wright agreed to complete the Marin County Civic Center commission of the late 1950s. When Wright appeared before the board of supervisors to sign his contract, he learned that he had come under attack from a local McCarthyite. A seven page dossier had been produced, defaming Wright as a follower of radical and subversive causes. Wright walked out of the meeting, later exclaiming "I am what I am . . . If you don't like it, you can lump it."[45] Similar criticisms had caused the scotching of Wright's civic design for Lake Menona in Madison, Wisconsin. In Marin County, however, Wright's supporters overwhelmed the opposition and the commission went through.

In the manner of the arch shapes subtly integrated into the circular ramps of the Morris Gift Shop and the Guggenheim Museum, Wright also returns to the Richardsonian arch in the Marin County Civic Center design. Here, however, the arch revolves into a dome and spiral, and each circular form is related to the dome of a nearby hill. Fortunately, we have the eye-witness account of architect Aaron Green, an ex-Taliesin Fellow, who had accompanied Wright on a visit to the chosen site of the civic center. Wright's sense of organicism enabled him to always adapt to the architectural possibilities at hand. Not surprisingly, Green recalls that Wright immediately conceived of the design for the civic center in terms of a metaphorical relationship with the rolling hills of Marin county. Wright, Green remembers, made waving motions with his hands and then stated that "we will bridge these hills with graceful arches."[46] The complex of nine buildings in circular, spherical and elliptical shapes was on the

Taliesin drafting tables during the last years of Wright's life. Its major structures were not finished until the 1960s and early 1970s. Like Florida Southern College, this civic center just north of San Francisco today gives us a glimpse of what Broadacre City might have been like had Wright been granted an opportunity to implement his utopian conceptions on a large scale.[47]

Interlocking circles also form a highly successful integrated structure for the Grady Gammage Memorial Auditorium, a large concert hall that seats 3,000. Here Wright works out a complete grammar of curvilinear forms, and in so doing pays homage to the early American arches of Richardson and Sullivan. The grammar of Wright's auditorium moves from the arches framed by the fifty concrete columns on the exterior to the intersecting circular shapes of the hall, stage, and other interior spaces. Even the parking areas extend the meaning of the circle in relation to the function of the building. Long, fluid ramps flow in arcs of poured concrete from the circles and arches of the hall to the rounded parking areas. Circles, semicircles and arches articulate the decorative patterns leading along the ramps (fig. 25).

Many years before, straight lines of the hollyhock trellis were incorporated into the textile design for the concrete blocks of the Barnsdall house. Now Wright's architectural detail incorporates the curves of palm fronds, abstracted from nature to grace the tops of the columns and highlight the relationship between the native palm trees and the character of the building.[48] Lighting fixtures, designed in circles, orbs and spheres, emphasize the geometric themes of the work in greater detail and highlight the unity of the building at night. This late structure, noted for its excellent acoustics, also completes the circle of Wright's life, for it is Wright's version of the large auditorium, the genre with which he had initiated his architectural apprenticeship with Sullivan. Now an aged master himself, Wright offered a final counterpoint to the work of Sullivan, his "Lieber Meister" of the 1890s. He had begun his apprenticeship with Sullivan by helping with the design for what was once the cutting edge of concert hall architecture. Now Wright ended his career with the same genre.

Wright's two last major publications were *A Testament* (1957) and *The Living City* (1958). *The Living City* is Wright's most extensive literary description of Broadacre City and Usonia. It is a rewriting and expansion of earlier material introduced in *Modern Architecture* (the 1930 Princeton lectures), *The Disappearing City* (1932), and *When Democracy Builds* (1945), as well as other books and essays. *A Testament,* published in a handsome volume by the Horizon Press, is also largely a working out of ideas that Wright had developed in earlier essays. For example, a nine point outline of his architectural principles adds essentially nothing new to what he had been saying and teaching for decades. But there are important indications of a summing up, of a final retrospective in this late publication.

His style in *A Testament* is even more epigrammatic and fragmented than usual. The text is divided up into short sections of prose poetry headed by a suggestive title that gives a sense of the material that follows. More evident than before is Wright's increased desire to place himself in the context of great creative figures who worked in other art forms, especially poets and philosophical writers. Chief among these figures in Wright's pantheon are the poets William Blake and Walt Whitman. In a section that borrows its title from Shelley, "Poet—'Unacknowledged legislator of the world'"—even Louis Sullivan is described as a poet, the only poet, in fact, among the architects. Wright was obviously aware of Sullivan's predilection for writing Whitmanian poetry, and he reflects on the impact of that sensibility on Sullivan's architectural designs. Sullivan alone had stood up to the sterility of modern life in America, a sterility that had made it difficult to equal in architecture the achievements of American writers:

> Except for Louis Sullivan among the many poets I knew and have named, there were then none among all the architects of this world. The poet had been too long absent from architecture. So long indeed, architecture was no longer considered as a great creative art. But where might the soul of any humane culture we might ever know be found unless in architecture?
>
> Thoreau, Emerson, were ours . . . And then, too, Walt Whitman came to view to give needed religious inspiration in the great change: our new Place for the new Man in our Time. Walt Whitman, seer of our Democracy!, He uttered primitive truths laying at the base of our new life, the inspirations we needed to go on spiritually with the brave "sovereignty of the individual." Might not the spirit of creative art, desperately needed by man, lie in the proper use of the radical new technologies of our times, and so arise? . . . Sixty years ago I knew that until the needed inspiration could be found forthcoming in architecture . . . we would probably look in vain for coherent interpretation of our time and our place in time.[49]

Much more than homage to the poets can be found in *A Testament*. Jeffersonian democracy, especially in terms of Jefferson's notion of a democratic "aristoi" (an aristocracy of merit), is treated in the context of Wright's own vision of creative originality. Jefferson's love of earlier "schools" is described as an inhibitive force blocking Jefferson's own best instincts. Laotze's notion of the importance of empty space defining the shape of architectural form is mentioned at least five times. There are frequent references to the writings of Emerson and Thoreau, as Wright attempts to pinpoint his own vision in relation to theirs.

Most important is Wright's statements on influence and resemblance, which are his most elaborate since *Genius and the Mobocracy*. He argues that resemblance should not be erroneously labeled as influence:

Resemblances are mistaken for influences. Comparisons have been made odious where comparison should, except as insult, hardly exist. Minds imbued by the necessity of truth, uttering truths independently of each other and capable of learning by analysis instead of comparison are still few. Scholarly appraisals?, Only rarely are they much above the level of gossip. So, up comes comparison, to compare organic architecture to the Crystal Palace of London, for instance.[50]

While artworks may resemble each other, real influence is another matter. Resemblance exists because art springs from what Wright sees as the common source of creativity: nature. In a burst of defiance, Wright once again denies his link to European architecture:

To cut ambiguity short: there never was exterior influence upon my work, either foreign or native, other than that of Lieber Meister [Sullivan], Dankmar Adler and John Roebling, Whitman and Emerson, and the great poets worldwide. My work is original not only in fact but in spiritual fiber. No practice by any European architect to this day has influenced mine in the least. As for the Incas, the Mayans, even the Japanese—all were to me but splendid confirmation. Some of our own critics could be appreciated—Lewis Mumford (Stick and Stones), early Russell Hitchcock, Montgomery Schuyler and a few others.[51]

Resemblance indicates kindred creative spirits, not copying of one by the other. The art and ideas of those he admired did not give him something to copy, he claims; instead, this esteemed work of others give him confidence in his ability to see something that was already there, something that they saw—from their own different perspectives—as well.

Once again, Wright shows his lifelong generosity toward the positive fertilizing power of other art forms that nourished his own. Classical music and Japanese prints, writers, philosophers and essayists from a variety of cultures and traditions—all these receive acknowledgment. There is very little in the way of praise for other architects of the world. They instead receive criticism rather than kudos, even at this very late date in Wright's life. To whom does Wright leave his "testament?" To the architect who can revive an art form that (Wright always claimed) had been sleeping for five hundred years and thereby reestablish a lost connection with the great creators of civilization—the artists, musicians and poets of the world.

The last years of Wright's career made up for the tragic stalemate of inactivity during the 1920s and early 1930s. While his work on large public buildings expanded, his activity in the field of domestic architecture was as intense as ever. He landed 270 commissions for new homes from 1946 until his death in 1959. In 1950 alone, Wright designed twenty-one architectural structures that eventually were seen through construction. The architect was then 83 years old.[52] From 1954–6, Wright created forty-one executed designs. In 1958, almost 170 varied commissions were on the drafting tables at Taliesin.[53]

The most poignant moments of Wright's late career are not recorded in the many new buildings actually erected by his thoroughly revived and thriving practice. They are to be found in his last visual dreams expressed in the realm of the architectural drawing, the medium in which he had begun so long ago as Sullivan's apprentice. In the late 1950s, Wright completed a final series of visionary drawings of Broadacre City. The sketches were prompted by preparations for the impending publication of *The Living City*. By now, the original material of *The Disappearing City* had more than doubled in size, and grown to well over two hundred pages.

Wright's revision and expansion of *The Disappearing City* is of greater importance than the revised versions of the autobiography. The increased size and scope and added visual information in each succeeding version reflect the elaboration of Wright's powerful optic imagination as it treated his utopian theme. The specific page lengths of the various first editions and the increasing scope of the various visual materials included in each of the editions is of great interest. *The Disappearing City* (1932) is only 99 pages with 6 interpretive photos. *When Democracy Builds* is 131 pages with 11 illustrations (photographs and drawings). *The Living City* is 222 pages with 51 illustrations and a fold-out color map of Broadacre City. Taken together, Wright's titles for the different versions reflect a movement from dystopian to utopian imagery. The city in its corrupt form must first disappear. Then democracy rebuilds it. Finally, it is living once again in its proper decentralized form.

New illustrations were needed to reflect Wright's continued meditations on his Usonian theme. The resulting sketches included in the first edition of *The Living City* are distinguished by a captivating mixture of the fantastic and the real, merged in a complex and subtle balance. This last book appeared in 1958, shortly before Wright's death.

One drawing from 1958, which was not included in the published version of *The Living City*, contains structures that he had actually completed, others that were fully realized projects, and still others that were intimations of what Wright might have developed if he had been granted time to do so.[54] The drawing is a perspective of Broadacre City, gently rendered in pencil on tracing paper with the assistance of delineator-apprentice John Rattenbury. In the foreground, land and water meet along the winding shore of a broad river. Rolling hills rise in the gently receding distance. In between are wide stretches of countryside. Buildings, greenery, and cultivated areas are combined in balanced but playfully asymmetrical patterns (fig. 26).

Here some of Wright's best known late works—including the Beth Sholom Synagogue, and the Marin County Civic Center—are placed in a landscape that also features other projects that were never completed. These unrealized designs include the Rogers Lacy Hotel, "Self-Service" garages, the Gordon Strong Automobile-Planeterium, the Pittsburgh Point Civic Center no. 1, and the Huntington Hartford Play Resort and Sports Club. An elegant design for a never-completed "butterfly bridge" cuts across the foreground of the sketch at an irregular angle, dramatically leading the eye into the heart of the perspective view. Other features, which remain to be developed in the twenty-first century, are also included. These include "taxi-copters," attractive flying machines resembling a hybrid of helicopter and flying saucer. They hover above the surface of Broadacre City. Envisioning new uses for nuclear power, Wright also conjures up a number of elliptically-shaped "atomic barges" to sail along the river. We can be certain that Wright had an "atomic barge" in mind because he specifically pencils in the suggestive label in the margin of the drawing, with an arrow pointing to one of them. It is a marvelous counterpart to the nuclear powered elevators planned for the Mile High, Illinois skyscraper design (but not included in *The Living City*).

In this work and other last sketches, Wright left us with a partial glimpse of an imaginary world of perfection that only he could see with clarity. It is tantalizing to wonder how it must have appeared through the powerful lens of his fertile eye. Even during the last decade of his life, the deft touch of Wright's masterful hand creates a sense of precision and mysterious possibility. This is even more evident in sketches made without the assistance of intermediaries and apprentices. Wright's *Road Machine* (1955), *Helicopter* (1958), and *Train and Right of-Way* (1958) all display the rugged power of his probing mind as he searches for the new machines of his utopia. These late drawings are streamlined shapes, combining his deep sense of poetic form and instinctive knowledge of engineering in the motions of his pencil.

Wright had been a great master of the sketch since his youth. His last utopian sketches should be compared to the last works of Beethoven. Both search beyond the limits of form and meaning available at the time in which they created. In their last works, both Beethoven and Wright were able to project beyond the possibilities of art apparent from their respective positions in the history of culture.

Wright's hand always displayed a characteristic elegance and flexibility. As an architect, he needed to position his images in an imaginary three dimensions on the flat surface of the sketch. He never had to rely on the academicism of linear perspective or the overstatement of bad salesmanship. His drawings are powerful, visionary and seductive. Art dealer O. P. Reed has spent much of his life studying the hand of the master as he sort-

ed Wright's work from the renderings of the many assistants and apprentices around him:

> As part of my experience while trying to evaluate Wright drawings and
> arrange them according to quality, as I do with old master drawings, I have
> had to separate Mr. Wright's actual draftsmanship from that of apprentices
> and associates. It is now fairly easy for me to find his work on any drawing.
> The drawing is light handed, searching in space and not too linear. It is deli-
> cate usually, seems to be made with joy. Sometimes it seems impatient,
> sometimes the style changes to a delicate touch. He always is aware of shad-
> ows and light, and placement of any emphasis or balance. He used his
> favorite Czech color pencils with a great deal of skill. Wright was never heavy
> handed. Lloyd [Wright] sometimes was. The Taliesin Associates were mostly
> heavy handed, although the results seem spectacular and bold when com-
> pared with Mr. Wright's delicate meanderings. It was apparent he [Wright]
> was thinking about every stroke while the others were copying a layout. That
> is one difference between fine drawing and a reproduced design. Wright
> thought on paper. Others rendered.[55]

At the age of ninety, Wright still commanded a youthful energy through
the pencil in his hand. His last drawings of Usonia demonstrate the same
rugged energy and searching imagination that characterized his work all
his life. His last visions of his garden of perfection, integrating nature and
human beings in a sublime balance of technology and sensitivity, record
hopeful possibilities for the next century.

Wright died on April 9, 1959 in Phoenix, shortly after taking ill at
Taliesin West. The family decided to move the body back to the ancestral
home of Spring Green and mourn their great loss there. Funeral services
were on April 12th. Afterward, two horses pulled his coffin in the funeral
procession. In 1886, seventy-three years earlier, he had helped his family
build Unity Chapel, thus beginning his long life in architecture. Now the
funeral procession brought him to a family burial site near the chapel,
where he was laid to rest, near the graves of Mamah Cheney and the Lloyd
Joneses, in the land he had loved all his life.

POSTSCRIPT

■

I have focused on what semiologist Jean-Jacques Nattiez would describe as the poietics of Wright's creative process. Leaving the most speculative forms of psychoanalytic inquiry to others, I have concentrated on the conscious intent of what Wright said and built in order to bring out the neglected structural rhythm of his thought and architecture. My own opinions have been hidden in the background, but I am well aware that there is latent interpretation even in the choice of presentation, the mode of analysis, and the ordering of materials. I have avoided passing judgment on Wright's controversial life and personality, as this has been done excessively in the many biographical popularizations of Frank Lloyd Wright. By now, Wright's brilliance and importance are obvious, in spite of the very human shortcomings that some have chosen to underscore and exaggerate.

Clearly, this modern master will be treated in a continuum of serious rethinking and reevaluation. Many more studies of Wright will follow this one. Convinced of Wright's enormous achievement, I add my own voice to the vast chorus of researchers who have been compelled to study the remarkable phenomenon of Frank Lloyd Wright.

APPENDIX

∎

AN INTERRELATED CHRONOLOGY OF WRIGHT'S WRITINGS AND BUILDINGS

Early Period:
Oak Park Through the Wasmuth Catalogue

1889, 1893   Frank Lloyd Wright home, Oak Park, IL

1891   James Charnley house, Chicago, IL

1892   George Blossom house, Kenwood, Chicago, IL

1893   William Winslow house, River Forest, IL

1894   "The Architect and the Machine," lecture for the University Guild, Evanston, IL

1895   Frank Lloyd Wright studio added to home, Oak Park, IL

1895   Chauncey Williams house, River Forest, IL

1896   Romeo and Juliet Windmill, Spring Green, WI

1896   "Architect, Architecture, and the Client"

1896–97   *The House Beautiful* (photos and page designs)

1896   Isidore Heller house, Hyde Park

1897   Rollin Furbeck house, Oak Park, IL

1899   Joseph Husser house

1900   B. Harley Bradley house

1900   "A Philosophy of Fine Art," lecture, Architectural League, Art Institute of Chicago

1900   "The Architect," *The Brickbuilder*

1901   "The Art and Craft of the Machine," Hull House Lecture

1901   "A Small House with 'Lots of Room in It,'" *Ladies Home Journal*

1901   Frank Thomas house, Oak Park, IL

1901   E. Arthur Davenport house, River Forest, IL

1901   Ward Willits house

1901   William Frick house

1901   Hillside Home School, Spring Green, WI

1902   Arthur Heurtley house, Oak Park, IL

1902, 1905 Susan Lawrence Dana house, Springfield, IL

1902–3 William E. Martin house, Oak Park, IL

1903 Edwin Cheney house

1903 Larkin Company Administration Building

1904, 1905–8 Unity Temple, Oak Park, IL

1904 Thomas Gale house, Oak Park, IL

1904 Darwin Martin house, Buffalo, NY

1905 W. A. Glasner house, Glencoe, IL

1905 Thomas Hardy house, Racine, WI

1906 Frederick C. Robie house, Chicago, IL

1906 Pettit Mortuary Chapel, Belvidere, IL

1906 River Forest Tennis Club, River Forest, IL

1907 Blossom Garage, Kenwood, Chicago, IL

1907 Burton Westcott house, Springfield, Ohio

1907 F. F. Tomek house, Riverside, IL

1907 Avery Coonley mansion, Riverside, IL

1908 Isabel Roberts house, River Forest, IL

1908 Meyer May house, Grand Rapids, MI

1909 Ingalls House

1909–10 "Sovereignty of the Individual in the Cause of Architecture," preface to the Wasmuth Introduction

Middle Period

1911, 1914, 1925 Taliesin North I, II, III, Spring Green, WI

1912 Francis Little house, Deephaven, MN

1912 *The Japanese Print: An Interpretation*

1912 Coonley playhouse, Riverside, IL

1913 Harry Adams house, Oak Park, IL

1913 Midway Gardens, Chicago, IL

1915 A. D. German warehouse, Richland Center, WI

1915 Emil Bach house, Chicago, IL

1915–16 Imperial Hotel, Tokyo, Japan

1916 Ernest Vosburgh house, Grand Beach, MI

1917 Aisaku Hayashi house, Tokyo, Japan

1917–21 Aline Barnsdall mansion, "Hollyhock House," Los Angeles, CA

1918 Tazaeman Tamamura house, Tokyo, Japan

1923 Mrs. George Millard house, Pasadena, CA

1923 John Storer house, Hollywood, CA

1923 Samuel Freeman house, Los Angeles, CA

1923 Charles Ennis house, Los Angeles, CA

Literary Exile

1927 Arizona Biltmore Hotel and Cottages (assists Warren McArthur), Phoenix, AZ

1928 Ocotillo Desert Camp, Chandler, AZ

1929 Richard Lloyd Jones house, "Westhope," Tulsa, OK

1922 "The New Imperial Hotel," *Kagaku Chishiki*

1923 "The New Imperial Hotel, Tokio," *The Western Architect*

1923 "In the Cause of Architecture: In the Wake of the Quake—Concerning the Imperial Hotel, Tokio," *The Western Architect*

1925 "Facts Regarding the Imperial Hotel," *Wendingen*

1927–28 "In the Cause of Architecture" series of sixteen articles in *The Architectural Record*

1928 "Towards a new Architecture," Wright's review of Le Corbusier in *World Unity*

1930–31 *Modern Architecture,* Kahn lectures at Princeton

1931 *Two Lectures on Architecture,* Art Institute, Chicago

1932 *An Autobiography* (first version)

1932 *The Disappearing City,* later reworked in *When Democracy Builds*

1932 Broadacre City Model

Wright's Renaissance

1933 Taliesin Fellowship Complex

1936 Edgar J. Kaufmann, Sr. summer house, "Fallingwater," Mill Run, PA

1936 Paul Hanna house, "Honeycomb House," Palo Alto, CA

1936 Johnson Wax Administration Building, Racine, WI

1936 Usonian House for Herbert Jacobs, Madison, WI

1937 *Architecture and Modern Life* (with Baker Brownell)

1937 Taliesin West, Scottsdale, AZ

1937 Herbert Johnson mansion, "Wingspread"

1938–54 Florida Southern College

1938, 1974 Ralph Jester house

1939 Rose Pauson house, Phoenix, AZ

1939 *An Organic Architecture; The Architecture of Democracy*

1941 *Frank Lloyd Wright on Architecture: Selected Writings 1894-1940* (edited by Frederick Gutheim)

1941–44   *Taliesin Square Papers*

1943   *An Autobiography* republished in an expanded edition, also, *An Autobiography, Book Six, Broadacre City,* published separately by Taliesin

1943   Second Herbert Jacobs house, "Solar Hemicycle"

1944   Johnson Wax Research Tower

Late Period

1945   *When Democracy Builds,* later reworked in *The Living City*

1947   Unitarian Church in Shorewood Hills, WI

1948   V. C. Morris Gift Shop, San Francisco, CA

1948   Sol Friedman house, Pleasantville, NY

1951   Roland Reisley house, Pleasantville, NY

1949   *Genius and the Mobocracy*

1950   David Wright house, Phoenix, AZ

1952   Price Company Tower, Bartlesville, OK

1953   *The Future of Architecture*

1953   Jorgine Boomer house, Phoenix, AZ

1954   *The Natural House*

1954   Beth Sholom Synagogue, Elkins Park, PA

1954   Hoffmann Auto Showroom, New York, NY

1956   *The Story of the Tower: The Tree that Escaped the Crowded Forest*

1955   Dallas Theatre Center

1956   Wyoming Valley School

1956   Guggenheim Museum, New York, NY

1956   Greek Orthodox Church, Milwaukee, WI

1957   *A Testament*

1957   Marshall Erdman Company, Prefab house #2

1957   Marin County Civic Center

1958   *The Living City*

1959   Norman Lykes house, Phoenix, AZ

1959   Grady Gammage Memorial Auditorium, Tempe, AZ

NOTES

■

Notes to I
Origins: The Wisconsin Hills, Chicago, and Louis Sullivan

1. Along with primary sources, the reader should consult recent treatments of Wright's colorful life and career. The most useful account is Robert C. Twombly, *Frank Lloyd Wright: An Interpretive Biography* (New York: Harper, 1974). Brendan Gill's *Many Masks: A Life of Frank Lloyd Wright* (New York: Putnam, 1987) is refreshingly insightful. Finis Farr's *Frank Lloyd Wright* (New York: Scribner's Sons, 1961) is the first full-scale popular biography of the architect. It also contains useful information. The most recent treatment of Wright's life is Meryle Secrest, *Frank Lloyd Wright* (New York: Knopf, 1992).

2. Twombly, *Interpretive Biography*, 5.

3. Grant Carpenter Manson, *Frank Lloyd Wright to 1910: The First Golden Age* (New York: Van Nostrand Rheinhold, 1958), 2.

4. Gill, *Many Masks*, 31–32. Secrest concurs with Gill's theories. See Secrest, *Frank Lloyd Wright*, 48.

5. Vincent Scully Jr., *Frank Lloyd Wright* (New York: Braziller, 1960), 14, and Manson, *First Golden Age*, 5–10.

6. Wright, *An Autobiography* (New York: Duell, Sloan and Pearce, 1943), 13. There are a number of important editions of this work, which first appeared in 1932. However, unless otherwise specified, all subsequent citations are from the 1943 edition.

7. Jeanne S. Rubin, "The Froebel-Wright Kindergarten Connection: A New Perspective," *Journal of the Society of Architectural History* 48 (1989): 24–27. See also Robert Downs, *Friedrich Froebel* (Boston: Twayne, 1978).

8. For a discussion of the similarities between Ives' and Wright's Emersonian aesthetics and ideologies, see my *Angels of Reality: Emersonian Unfoldings in Wright, Stevens, and Ives* (Carbondale: Southern Illinois University Press, 1993).

9. Twombly, *Interpretive Biography*, 310, n.14.

10. I have treated Wright's use of music metaphors in *Angels of Reality*, 242–60.

11. David A. Hanks, *Frank Lloyd Wright: Preserving an Architectural Heritage, Decorative Designs from the Domino's Pizza Collection* (New York: Dutton, 1989), 24.

12. Frank Lloyd Wright, *Genius and the Mobocracy* (New York: Horizon Press, 1971), 54.

13. Manson, *First Golden Age*, 12.

14. Robert L. Sweeney, *Frank Lloyd Wright: An Annotated Bibliography* (Los Angeles: Hennessey and Ingalls, 1978), xvi.

15. Twombly, *Interpretive Biography*, 19.

16. Henry-Russell Hitchcock, *In the Nature of Materials* (New York: Duell, Sloan and Pearce, 1942), 6.

17. Manson, *First Golden Age*, 42.

18. Recent revisionist treatments of Adler bring out his importance. See, perhaps the

most recent, James F. O'Gorman, *Three American Architects: Richardson, Sullivan and Wright, 1865–1915* (Chicago, University of Chicago Press, 1991), 79.

19. O'Gorman, showing Sullivan's Richardsonian roots, argues that since Sullivan's style was developed before the steel frame, he was never fully able to reconcile the new technology and new materials with his aesthetic sensibility. See O'Gorman, *Three American Architects,* 89.

20. O'Gorman, *Three American Architects*, 89.

21. Edgar Tafel, *Years with Frank Lloyd Wright: Apprentice to Genius* (New York: Dover, 1979), 20.

22. O'Gorman, *Three American Architects,* 115; Scully, *Frank Lloyd Wright,* 13.

23. Meg Klinkow, curator at the Wright Home and Studio in Oak Park, believes that the changing family needs stimulated Wright's developing style.

24. My account of the fair is based largely on Stanley Appelbaum, *The Chicago World's Fair of 1893* (New York: Dover, 1980).

25. Appelbaum, *The Chicago World's Fair*, 74.

26. Jack Quinan also points out that Wright may have been fascinated with the Ceylonese building; Anne Baxter mentions the Turkish pavilion. See Jack Quinan, "Frank Lloyd Wright in 1893: The Chicago Context," in *Frank Lloyd Wright: In the Realm of Ideas*, edited by Bruce Brooks Pfeiffer and Gerald Nordland (Carbondale: Southern Illinois Unversity Press, 1988), 131. And see the documentary film, *The Architecture of Frank Lloyd Wright*, (Arts Council of Great Britain, A. B. C. Videos, Chicago, Illinois, distributors), videorecording, narrated by Ann Baxter.

27. Appelbaum, *Chicago World's Fair*, 5, 14.

28. Ibid., 7.

29. Ibid., 58.

Notes to II
Early Triumph in Oak Park

1. Robert C. Twombly, *Frank Lloyd Wright: An Interpretive Biography* (New York: Harper, 1974), 21; Grant Carpenter Manson, *Frank Lloyd Wright to 1910: The First Golden Age* (New York: Reinhold Publishing Corporation, 1958), 34.

2. Manson, *First Golden Age,* 33.

3. Manson, *First Golden Age*, 60; Twombly, *Interpretive Biography*, 22.

4. Henry-Russell Hitchcock, *In the Nature of Materials* (New York: Duell, Sloan and Pearce, 1942), 18–19.

5. Hitchcock, *Nature of Materials*, 19–20. Hitchcock prefers the Colonial Revivalism of the Blossom house and notes that Wright was probably purposely trying to avoid Sullivan's style in these "bootlegged" homes.

6. Ibid., 20.

7. Manson, *First Golden Age*, 59.

8. Manson has observed Wright's curious emulation of the Renaissance master. See Manson, *First Golden Age*, 46. Note, however, that Richardson had a kind of atelier too. See also Jack Quinan, "Frank Lloyd Wright in 1893: The Chicago Context," in *Frank Lloyd Wright: In the Realm of Ideas*, ed. Bruce Brooks Pfeiffer and Gerald Nordland (Carbondale: Southern Illinois University Press, 1988), 131.

9. Wright recalls them in "Roots," *Frank Lloyd Wright: Writings and Buildings*, ed. Edgar Kaufmann and Ben Raeburn (New York: New American Library, 1974), 32.

10. Both Twombly and O'Gorman agree on this. See O'Gorman's account, in James F. O'Gorman, *Three American Architects: Richardson, Sullivan and Wright, 1865–1915* (Chicago: University of Chicago Press, 1991), 122.

11. Frank Lloyd Wright, *An Autobiography* (New York: Duel, Sloan, and Pearce, 1943), 134.

12. Wright discusses the tower in *An Autobiography*, 132–35.

13. Richard W. Bock, *Memoirs of an American Artist*, ed. Dorathi Bock Pierre (Los Angeles: C.C. Publishing, 1991), 67–68.

14. Hitchcock, *Nature of Materials*, 27.

15. For a variety of readings of the Williams house see Manson, *First Golden Age*, 71–72 and Hitchcock, *Nature of Materials*, 26.

16. Manson, *First Golden Age*, 77.

17. Hitchcock, *Nature of Materials*, 28.

18. Versions of these are published in the first volume of *Frank Lloyd Wright: Collected Writings* (New York: Rizzoli, 1992), 20–57.

19. See Hitchcock, *Nature of Materials*, 49–50.

20. Manson, *First Golden Age*, 130–34.

21. The edition of the lecture discussed here is taken from Frank Lloyd Wright, "The Art and Craft of the Machine," *Frank Lloyd Wright: Writings and Buildings*, ed. Edgar Kaufmann and Ben Raeburn (New York: New American Library, 1974), 55–73.

22. Frank Lloyd Wright, *Modern Architecture: Being the Kahn Lectures for 1930* (Carbondale: Southern Illinois University Press, 1987), 7.

23. Wright, "Art and Craft," 55.

24. Ibid., 56–57.

25. Ibid., 58–59.

26. W. J. T. Mitchell has discussed the implications of art envy in *Iconology: Image, Text, Ideology* (Chicago: University of Chicago Press, 1986). See also David Michael Hertz, *Angels of Reality: Emersonian Unfoldings in Wright, Spencer, and Ives* (Carbondale: Southern Illinois University Press, 1993), 222–60.

27. Wright, "Art and Craft," 60.

28. Ibid., 64.

29. Ibid., 64.

30. Ibid., 65–66.

31. Ibid., 69.

32. Ibid., 71.

33. Ibid., 72–73.

34. Wright, "In the Cause of Architecture: the Third Dimension," John Lloyd Wright Collection (Box I), Avery Library, Columbia University.

35. At least two commentators have noted the cavelike aspect of the entrance and the house in general. See Grant Hildebrand, *The Wright Space: Pattern and Meaning in Frank Lloyd Wright's Houses* (Seattle: University of Washington Press, 1991), 34, 38, and Vincent Scully Jr., *Frank Lloyd Wright* (New York: Braziller, 1960), 19.

36. Kathryn Smith, "Frank Lloyd Wright and the Imperial Hotel: A Postscript," *Art Bulletin*, 67 (June, 1985): 298. The article contains an excellent account of Wright's trips to Japan both before and during his work on the Imperial Hotel.

37. Manson has a complete list of the artists Wright put up for sale in New York in 1927. See Manson, *First Golden Age*, 215.

38. "Wright's Japanese Treasures," *Frank Lloyd Wright Quarterly* 1, no. 3 (Autumn, 1990): 8–10.

39. Bruce Brooks Pfeiffer, *Frank Lloyd Wright Drawings: Masterworks from the Frank Lloyd Wright Archives* (New York: Abrams, 1990), 18.

40. For Wright's thoughts on Japanese *noton*, see Bruce Brooks Pfeiffer, ed., *Frank Lloyd Wright: His Living Voice* (Fresno: California State University Press, 1987), 33.

41. See E. T. Casey, "Structure in Organic Architecture," in *Frank Lloyd Wright: In the Realm of Ideas*, ed. Bruce Brooks Pfeiffer and Gerald Nordland, 143–48.

42. Wright, *An Autobiography*, 154. Wright's description of the genesis of Unity Temple is found on pp. 153–60.

43. Wright frequently mentions Laotze in his writings. For an excellent example of this, written near the end of his life and recalling his lifelong fascination with Laotze, see Frank Lloyd Wright, *A Testament* (New York: Horizon, 1957), 106. Wright also quotes Laotze in *Two Lectures on Architecture* (Chicago: Art Institute of Chicago, 1931), 11. For apprentice Edgar Tafel's account of Wright's interest in Laotze, see Edgar Tafel, *Years with Frank Lloyd Wright: Apprentice to Genius* (New York: Dover, 1979), 46.

44. Wright, *A Testament*, 106.

45. Wright, *An Autobiography*, 150.

46. Sadly and pathetically, Edward Doheny, who prompted Wright to design a wondrous ranch resort, was later indicted in the great Teapot Dome scandal of the 1920s. As a result, that project, too, was never realized.

47. Manson, *First Golden Age*, 202.

48. Stanley Applebaum, *The Chicago's World Fair of 1893* (New York: Dover, 1980), 5.

49. Monroe's review is quoted in H. Allen Brooks ed., *Writings on Wright* (Cambridge: M.I.T. Press, 1985), 112.

50. Harriet Monroe Collection, University of Chicago. Twombly mentions this important correspondence also. See Twombly, *Interpretive Biography*, 84, 94–6, 132–3. Twombly dates the letter at around April 18th.

51. Harriet Monroe Collection, Joseph Regenstein Library, University of Chicago.

52. See John Lloyd Wright's list of articles about his father, John Lloyd Wright Collection, Avery Library, Columbia University.

53. Hitchcock points out that its taut "crystalline" structure made the Ingalls house more attractive to European imitators. See Hitchcock, *Nature of Materials*, 44–45.

54. Wright's most extensive account of Francke's visit is in one of his last books. See Wright, *A Testament*, 131–32.

55. According to Anthony Alofsin, German architect Bruno Moehring, not Francke, actually arranged for the publication of the catalogue. See Anthony Alofsin, *Frank Lloyd Wright—The Lost Years, 1910–1923: A Study of Influence* (Chicago: University of Chicago Press, 1993), 3.

56. Wright's collected essays for the *Architectural Record* are available in Frederick Gutheim, ed., *In the Cause of Architecture: Frank Lloyd Wright* (New York: McGraw-Hill, 1975).

57. My description of Lloyd Wright's account of work on the Wasmuth catalogue is taken from Lloyd Wright's letter to Mrs. Linn Cowles, which describes his work with his father in some detail. This intriguing document is published in Edgar Kaufmann, Jr., *Nine Commentaries on Frank Lloyd Wright* (Cambridge: MIT Press, 1989), 96–97.

58. Wright, "Sovereignty of the Individual," in *Writings and Buildings*, 84–85.

59. Ibid., 85–86.

60. Ibid., 89.

61. Ibid., 89.

62. Ibid., 90–93.

63. Ibid., 93.

64. Ibid., 94.

65. Ibid., 96.

66. Ibid., 99.

67. Ibid., 104.

68. Ibid., 104.

69. Ibid., 104.

70. Ibid., 105.

71. Ibid., 106. It is of great interest to note that Wright does not spell out which of his buildings are which in his Wasmuth essay. But in an earlier essay (1908) for the *Architectural*

Record, he does do so. Some of the earlier essay was obviously reworked into the later "Sovereignty" essay prepared for the Wasmuth catalogue. See Wright, *In the Cause of Architecture*, edit. F. Gutheim, 57. Working through the Frank Lloyd Wright Foundation, the editors of the projected series of Wright's complete literary works have published yet a different version which does include these added details, along with other textual variations. For a comparison, see Wright, *Collected Writings of Frank Lloyd Wright*, vol. 1 (New York: Rizzoli, 1992), 113–15.

72. The reader may refer to the reasonably priced edition of the catalogue published by Dover in 1983.

Notes to III
The Middle Years: Taliesin, Japan, and Much Mischief

1. Finis Farr, *Frank Lloyd Wright* (New York: Scribner's Sons, 1961), 119–20.

2. The clearest account of this confusing series of events in Wright's life is offered in Farr, *Frank Lloyd Wright*, 117–25.

3. Note, also, that the divorce was not granted until 1921, according to Twombly, and 1922, according to John Lloyd Wright. Robert C. Twombly, *Frank Lloyd Wright: An Interpretive Biography* (New York: Harper, 1974); John Lloyd Wright, *My Father Who is on Earth* (New York: Putnam, 1946).

4. See Anthony Alofsin, "Taliesin I: A Catalogue of Drawings and Photographs," Narciso Menocal, ed., *Wright Studies*, vol. 1 (Carbondale: Southern Illinois University Press, 1991), 98.

5. The argument here summarizes the content of two important new articles in Wright scholarship: Neil Levine, "The Story of Taliesin: Wright's First Natural House," and Scott Gardner, "The Shining Brow: Frank Lloyd Wright and the Welsh Bardic Tradition." Both are in *Wright Studies*, vol. 1, 2–27; 28–43.

6. Levine, *Wright Studies*, 17.

7. Ibid., 2–27.

8. Wright's statement to the press as quoted to Farr, *Frank Lloyd Wright*, 124.

9. Ibid., 124.

10. Ellen Key, *The Woman Movement*, trans. Mamah Borthwick Cheney (G. P. Putnam's Sons, 1912; reprint, Westport, CT: Hyperion Press, 1976.)

11. Donald Leslie Johnson, *Frank Lloyd Wright Versus America: the 1930s* (Cambridge: MIT Press, 1990), 134–35.

12. Johnson, *Frank Lloyd Wright versus America*, 134. Grant Carpenter Manson, *Frank Lloyd Wright to 1910: The First Golden Age* (New York: Reinhold Publishing Corporation, 1958), 212.

13. Because of the pure abstraction in the Coonley playhouse, Henry Russell Hitchcock thinks it is a particularly important work. See Henry Russell Hitchcock, *In the Nature of Materials* (New York: Duell, Sloan and Pearce, 1942), 61–62.

14. Frank Lloyd Wright, *The Japanese Print: An Interpretation*, (New York: Horizon, 1967), 24. This is a reprint of the original 1912 edition, and it includes a number of additional Wright commentaries on the print.

15. Ibid., 15–16.

16. For a more extensive discussion of Wright's idea of conventionalization, chiefly during Wright's work from 1910–1922, see Anthony Alofsin, *Frank Lloyd Wright—The Lost Years, 1910–1923: A Study of Influence* (Chicago: University of Chicago Press, 1993)

17. Here Wright anticipates Nelson Goodman and E. H. Gombrich, two of the best modern writers on the theory of symbols in the arts.

18. Wright, *Japanese Print*, 66.

19. Ibid., 65–67.

20. Frank Lloyd Wright, *An Autobiography* (New York: Duell, Sloan and Pearce, 1943), 180, 181.

21. See Farr, *Frank Lloyd Wright*, 151–57. Farr recreates the lively rivalry that later surfaced between Ianelli and Wright over who came up with the notion of abstracting anthropomorphic form into geometric shape.

22. John Lloyd Wright Collection (folder xviii), Avery Library, Columbia University.

23. Edgar Tafel, *Years With Frank Lloyd Wright: Apprentice to Genius* (New York: Dover, 1979), 81.

24. Frank Lloyd Wright to Harriet Monroe, April 13, 1914, Harriet Monroe Collection, Joseph Regenstein Library, University of Chicago.

25. Frank Lloyd Wright, *In the Cause of Architecture*, ed. by Frederick Gutheim (New York: Horizon, 1975), 124.

26. Ibid., 126.

27. Ibid., 128.

28. Wright, *An Autobiography*, 184–85.

29. For a more extensive accounts of Maud Miriam Noel and her meeting with Wright, see Farr, *Frank Lloyd Wright*, 146–48; Twombly, *Interpretive Biography*, 139; and Brendan Gill, *Many Masks: A Life of Frank Lloyd Wright* (New York: G. P. Putnam, 1987), 234–37.

30. Gill, *Many Masks*, 237.

31. Twombly, *Interpretive Biography*, 141.

32. Farr, *Frank Lloyd Wright*, 149.

33. An example of this view is Vincent Scully's well-wrought essay, "American Houses: Thomas Jefferson to Frank Lloyd Wright," in *The Rise of an American Architecture*, ed. Edgar Kaufmann, Jr. (New York: Praeger, 1970) 199–200.

34. Tafel, *Apprentice to Genius*, 97. Tafel mentions "Professor" Takeda and Aisaku Hayashi. For more scholarly detail, see also Kathryn Smith, "Frank Lloyd Wright and the Imperial Hotel," *Art Bulletin* 67 (June 1985): 296–310.

35. Anthony Alfonsin, "A Catalogue of Drawings and Photos," *Wright Studies*, 108.

36. Twombly, *Interpretive Biography*, 139; Cary James, *Frank Lloyd Wright's Imperial Hotel* (New York: Dover, 1968), 7.

37. The handful of structures that Wright designed for Japan are listed in Storrer. In 1918, he designed a residence for Tazaemon Yamamur in Ashiya, Japan. Another home was destroyed in the 1923 earthquake. Before leaving in 1921, he designed a small schoolhouse in Tokyo. See William Allin Storrer, *The Architecture of Frank Lloyd Wright: A Complete Catalogue* (Cambridge: MIT Press, 1986), 206, 212, 213.

38. Tafel, *Apprentice to Genius*, 96.

39. Antonin Raymond, *An Autobiography* (Rutland, Vermont: Charles Tuttle, 1973), 66.

40. Frank Lloyd Wright, *Frank Lloyd Wright: Writings and Buildings*, ed. Edgar Kaufmann and Ben Raeburn (New York: New American Library, 1974), 202.

41. Wright, *An Autobiography*, 217.

42. Raymond, *An Autobiography*, 67.

43. Nicolas Slonimsky, *Lexicon of Musical Invective: Critical Assaults on Composers Since Beethoven's Time*, 2nd ed. (Seattle: University of Washington Press, 1965), 42–52.

44. Louis Christian Mullgardt, "A Building That is Wrong," *Architect and Engineer* 81 (November, 1922): 81–9.

45. Louis Sullivan, "Concerning the Imperial Hotel, Tokyo Japan," 10. Unpublished text in the John Lloyd Wright Collection, Avery Library, Columbia University.

46. Ibid., 3–4.

47. "In the Cause of Architecture: 'He Who Gets Slapped'," 2, 11. This is an unpublished draft in John Lloyd Wright Collection, Avery Library, Columbia University. The revised version is now available in volume 1 of *Collected Writings of Frank Lloyd Wright* (New York: Rizzoli, 1992), 183–186.

48. "In the Cause of Architecture," 2. This is another unpublished draft in the John

Lloyd Wright Collection, Avery Library, Columbia University. The revised version is now available in Wright, *Collected Writings*, vol. 1, 183-192.

49. "In the Cause of Architecture: The Third Dimension." Essay dated February 9, 1923. John Lloyd Wright Collection, Avery Library, Columbia University.

50. Wright, *Collected Writings*, 206.

51. Wright, *Writings and Buildings*, 201.

52. Ibid., 200. Tafel points out that the mud was at least seventy feet deep. See Tafel, *Apprentice to Genius*, 102.

53. Raymond, *An Autobiography*, 95.

54. Wright, *An Autobiography*, 222.

55. Anaïs Nin, *Diaries of Anaïs Nin*, vol. 7, (New York: Harcourt, Brace and Jovanovich, 1980), 2–6.

56. Norman Bel Geddes, *Miracle in the Evening: An Autobiography* (Garden City, New York: Doubleday, 1960), 155–64.

57. Wright, *An Autobiography*, 234.

58. As O. P. Reed pointed out in an April 27, 1990 letter to the author, Wright has been unfairly described as "deriving" ideas from a variety of sources, including Mayan architecture. What commentators have missed is the bold and original manner in which Wright appropriates material in a totally fresh way. See David Michael Hertz, *Angels of Reality: Emersonian Unfoldings in Wright, Spencer, and Ives* (Carbondale: Southern Illinois University Press, 1993), 114–59.

59. Wright, *An Autobiography*, 234.

60. Muschamp puts 1924 as the date of Wright's announcement to return to Chicago. See Herbert Muschamp, *Man About Town: Frank Lloyd Wright in New York City* (Cambridge: MIT Press, 1983), 40.

61. Farr, *Frank Lloyd Wright*, 158.

62. Although scholars must begin with Wright's own account of these matters in his autobiography, I also have learned much from Twombly's psychoanalytic approach to Wright's relationship with Noel and with women in general. See Twombly, *Interpretive Biography*, 139–53. See also Farr, *Frank Lloyd Wright*, 177–200.

63. Donald Johnson and Tafel agree on this. Twombly and Farr note that Wright was already working out Book One of the autobiography when he was arrested at Lake Minnetonka in 1925.

64. Twombly's excellent account of Olga (Olgivanna) Wright sets out the facts of their courtship succinctly. See Twombly, *Interpretive Biography*, 145–46. See also, Farr, *Frank Lloyd Wright*, 190–94; and Gill, *Many Masks*, 290–92.

65. Twombly, *Interpretive Biography*, 145, 150, and Gill, *Many Masks*, 294. Also see Farr, *Frank Lloyd Wright*, 181–206.

66. Farr, *Frank Lloyd Wright*, 202–3.

67. With additional investors, the organization was later reformed under the name of "Frank Lloyd Wright, Inc." See Gill, *Many Masks*, 300.

68. Geoffrey Perrett, *America in the Twenties* (New York: Simon and Schuster, 1982), 417.

69. See the chart by John Lloyd Wright in the John Lloyd Wright Collection, Avery Library, Columbia University. John Wright's chart, as he himself describes it, includes only the "Executed Building Designs, using dates of conception." It includes a total of 371 executed buildings.

70. Wright, *An Autobiography*, 311.

71. See apprentice Henry Klumb's excellent account of life at Ocotillo Camp, included in the symposium published by Frederick Gutheim in his edition of Wright's collected writings for *The Architectural Record*, which span from 1908–1952. See Wright, *In the Cause of Architecture*, 12–15.

72. Wright, *Architectural Forum* 68 (January, 1938): 64.

73. Wright, *Writings and Buildings*, 222. See also John Sergeant, *Frank Lloyd Wright's Usonian Houses: The Case for Organic Architecture* (New York: Watson-Guptill, 1976), 185.

74. Wright, *An Autobiography*, 311, and Johnson, *Frank Lloyd Wright versus America*, 13–28.

75. Wright specifically mentions Jefferson's worm-walled bricks in relation to his concept of the wooden walls at Ocotillo in *An Autobiography*, 310.

76. Frank Lloyd Wright, "Desert Camp for Frank Lloyd Wright, Arizona. Frank Lloyd Wright, Architect." *Architectural Record* 68 (1930): 189.

77. Wright, *Architectural Forum* 68 (January, 1938), 64.

Notes to IV
A Literary Exile

1. Finis Farr, *Frank Lloyd Wright* (New York: Scribner's Sons, 1961), 215.

2. Wright, *An Autobiography* (New York: Duell, Sloan and Pearce, 1943), 388.

3. Alexander Woollcott reprinted his essay in his *While Rome Burns* (New York: Viking, 1934), 171–79.

4. Ibid., 178–79.

5. Wright, *Modern Architecture: Being the Kahn Lectures for 1930* (Carbondale: Southern Illinois University Press, 1987), 3.

6. Ibid., 12.

7. Ibid., 21.   For a comparison of Wright's earlier remarks with these, see *Collected Writings of Frank Lloyd Wright*, vol. 1 (New York: Rizzoli, 1992), 39–44.

8. Wright, *Modern Architecture*, 34.

9. Ibid., 37.

10. Ibid., 52.

11. In this passage, Wright is quite clear that he visited Athens. However, Professors Leonard Eaton, Neil Levine, and Anthony Alofsin do not believe that Wright visited Greece (I spoke with all of them in early 1994.) I, too, have been unable to ascertain when Wright could have visited Greece. However, he may have fooled all of us and taken a ferry from Brindisi to Greece during his year in Italy.

12. Wright, *Modern Architecture*, 57. I have not been able to ascertain when Wright visited Athens, as he clearly states in this text.

13. Ibid., 65.

14. Ibid., 70.

15. I treat the important trope of the hearth and tokonoma more extensively in *Angels of Reality: Emersonian Unfoldings in Wright, Stevens, and Ives* (Carbondale: Southern Illinois University Press, 1993), 141–42. See also Camillo Gubitosi and Alberto Izzo, *Frank Lloyd Wright: Three-Quarters of a Century of Drawings* (New York: Horizon: 1981).

16. Wright, *Modern Architecture*, 88.

17. Ibid., 88.

18. Ibid., 101.

19. Ibid., 108.

20. According to Professor Bob Clark of Princeton University, the Princeton talks took place in May 1930. My thanks to Alistair Gordon for tracking this down.

21. Farr, *Frank Lloyd Wright*, 222.

22. Herbert Muschamp, *Man About Town: Frank Lloyd Wright in New York City* (Cambridge: MIT Press, 1983), 65.

23. Brendan Gill, *Many Masks: A Life of Frank Lloyd Wright* (New York: G. P. Putnam, 1987), 335. See also Henry-Russell Hitchcock and Philip Johnson, *The International Style* (New York: Norton, 1966), 25–27.

24. A survey of early reviews of *An Autobiography* from the 1930s indicates that Wright received a basically positive reception.

25. Wright, *An Autobiography*, 309.

26. Ibid., 23.

27. Ibid., 369.

28. Wright, *Collective Writings*, vol. 2., 102–381.

29. *Vers une architecture* appeared in 1922.

30. See Chad Walsh, *From Utopia to Nightmare* (New York: Harper & Row, 1962).

31. *Oxford English Dictionary Supplement*, 2nd ed., s.v. "dystopian."

32. Frank Lloyd Wright, *The Disappearing City* (New York: William Farquhar Payson, 1932), 3.

33. The notion of an imaginary city that is "everywhere and nowhere" appears on numerous occasions in *An Autobiography*. See 320, 548, 560 for examples.

34. Wright, *Disappearing City*, 17.

35. Ibid., 43.

36. Ibid., 17. The passage swells to two paragraphs in the later *When Democracy Builds*. See Frank Lloyd Wright, *When Democracy Builds* (Chicago: University of Chicago Press, 1945), 23.

37. Norris Kelly Smith, "The Domestic Architecture of Frank Lloyd Wright," in *Writings on Wright*, ed. H. Allen Brooks (Cambridge: M. I. T. Press, 1985), 191.

38. Wright, *The Disappearing City*, 74.

39. Ibid., 78. Wright expands the list with colorful added detail in *When Democracy Builds*, 110.

40. Wright, *Disappearing City*, 76.

41. Ibid., 61.

42. Donald Leslie Johnson, *Frank Lloyd Wright versus America: The 1930s* (Cambridge: MIT Press, 1990), 111–12.

43. Pfeiffer, *Frank Lloyd Wright Drawings: Masterworks From the Frank Lloyd Wright Archives* (New York: Abrams, 1990), 265.

44. Johnson, *Wright versus America*, 115.

45. Wright, *An Autobiography*, 318.

46. Wright, *An Autobiography*, 323–24.

47. Ibid., 323–24.

48. H. G. Wells, *A Modern Utopia* (Lincoln: University of Nebraska Press, 1967), 215.

49. Ibid., 32.

50. Meyer Schapiro covers Wright's notions of Broadacre City and Usonia in his review of the one book Wright co-authored with Baker Brownell. See Meyer Schapiro, "Architect's Utopia," *Partisan Review* (March 1938), 42–47.

51. Muschamp, *Man About Town*, 184–91.

52. Wright, "The New Frontier: Broadacre City," John Lloyd Wright Collection, Avery Library, Columbia University.

53. Lionel March, "An Architect in Search of Democracy," in *Writings on Wright*, 205.

Notes to V
Wright's Renaissance

1. Meryle Secrest, *Frank Lloyd Wright* (New York: Knopf, 1992) 469–70; Edgar Tafel, *Years with Frank Lloyd Wright: Apprentice to Genius*, (New York: Dover, 1979), 10.

2. Frank Lloyd Wright, *Architectural Forum* 68 (January, 1938): 36.

3. Frank Lloyd Wright, *An Autobiography* (New York: Duell, Sloan aned Pearce, 1943), 494.

4. John Sergeant, *Frank Lloyd Wright's Usonian Houses: The Case for Organic Architecture* (New York: Watson-Guptill, 1976)

5. Wright, *An Autobiography*, 491.

6. Wright, *Architectural Forum* 68 (January, 1938): 78. See also *An Autobiography*, 472.

7. Wright, *Architectural Forum* 68 (January, 1938): 68.

8. Ibid., 88. He varied the construction somewhat in the 1943 version of the autobiography: "Organic architecture designed this great building to be as inspiring a place to work in as any cathedral ever was in which to worship. It was meant to be a socio-architectural interpretation of modern business at its top and best." See *An Autobiography*, 472.

9. Wright, *An Autobiography*, 472.

10. Ibid., 472.

11. Wright's own remarks on the lighting are found in Baker Brownell and Frank Lloyd Wright, *Architecture and Modern Life* (New York: Harper, 1938), 39.

12. Jonathan Lipman, *Frank Lloyd Wright and the Johnson Wax Buildings* (New York: Rizzoli, 1986), 59.

13. Lipman has the clearest and most extensive account of this episode. See Lipman, *Johnson Wax Buildings*, 51–84.

14. Robert Sweeney points this out in his annotations for the issue. See Robert L. Sweeney, *Frank Lloyd Wright: An Annotated Bibliography*, (Los Angeles: Hennessey and Ingalls, 1978), xiv, 64–66.

15. Thoreau as quoted by Wright in the *Architectural Forum*, 68 (January, 1938), cover foldout.

16. Philip Johnson, *Writings* (New York: Oxford University Press, 1979), 194. Philip Johnson's attitude toward Wright is an extremely complex mixture of oedipal anxiety and admiration. Readers should also consult pages 195–98 in the same volume. In the original catalogue for the International Style exhibition at the Museum of Modern Art in 1931, Johnson praises Wright as a great pioneer who has been outmoded by the new high modernism of the International Style. See the reprint of the exhibition catalogue published by Henry-Russell Hitchcock and Philip Johnson, *The International Style* (New York: Norton, 1966), 25–27.

17. Wright, *An Autobiography*, 513.

18. Robert Pond, former Taliesin apprentice, pointed this out to me during an informal conversation in Bloomington, Indiana, in January, 1993.

19. See Wright, *An Organic Architecture: The Architecture of Democracy* (London: Lund, Humphries, 1939). This is the first published version of the London Talks.

20. Wright, *An Autobiography*, 537.

21. Wright, *Organic Architecture*, 3.

22. Ibid., 4. We learn here (and elsewhere) that he first discovered Laotze in a book that Okakura Kakuzo, Japanese ambassador to America, gave to him.

23. Ibid., 10.

24. Ibid., 13, 14.

25. Ibid., 14.

26. Ibid., 38.

27. H. Allen Brooks, ed. *Writings on Wright*,. Anonymous article from *The Architect's Journal* 89 (May 11, 1939): 757 14.

28. Frank Lloyd Wright, *The Living City* (New York: Horizon, 1958), 81–118.

29. For one conspicuous example, see Wright, *An Autobiography*, 330.

30. Of Wright's biographers, Brendan Gill has the best account of this. One interesting similarity between Wright and Spivey is the manner in which they managed to make use of young people. Student labor at Florida Southern College was essential. The labor practices used to construct these buildings echoed Wright's own practices with his apprentices at

Taliesin. See Brendan Gill, *Many Masks: A Life of Frank Lloyd Wright* (New York: G. P. Putnam, 1987), 396–405.

31. Wright generally calls for an acre per family in his utopian writings. However, the late Ray Fischer of Florida Southern College—a man who possessed great scholarly knowledge of the history of the college—recalled that there were 800 students enrolled at Florida Southern College and that Wright viewed this as an ideal number for a county center in Broadacre City.

32. Note that O'Gorman compares Monticello and Taliesin. Wright mentions Jefferson in *An Autobiography*, 334.

33. See the excellent educational video, *The Eye of Thomas Jefferson*, National Gallery of Art Series, #110.

34. For a very different account of the campus, see Kimball Fiske, *Thomas Jefferson, Architect: Original Designs in the Collection of Thomas Jefferson Coolidge, Jr.* (Boston: Riverside, 1926), 80.

35. Frank Lloyd Wright, *Genius and the Mobocracy* (New York: Horizon Press, 1971), 100.

36. Robert C. Twombly, *Frank Lloyd Wright: An Interpretive Biography* (New York: Harper, 1974), 213.

37. Banister Fletcher, *A History of Architecture* (London: Butterworths, 1987), 1,354.

38. Wright first employs this pattern in the Romeo and Juliet tower, with its combined diamond and octagon.

39. Thomas Doremus, *Frank Lloyd Wright and Le Corbusier: The Great Dialogue* (New York: Van Nostrand Rheinhold, 1985), 150.

40. For some interesting observations along these lines, see Henry-Russell Hitchcock, *In the Nature of Materials*, (New York: Duell, Sloan and Pearce, 1942), 99–100.

41. Some of the observations fleshed out in this account of the Florida Southern College campus are indebted to remarks offered by my helpful guide, Kim Yang, during my personal tour of the site in March, 1991.

42. Jeanne S. Rubin, "The Froebel-Wright Kindergarten Connection: A New Perspective," *Journal of the Society of Architectural History* 48 (1989): 31–37.

Notes to VI
Architect and American Prophet: The Final Years

1. Donald Leslie Johnson, *Frank Lloyd Wright versus America: The 1930s* (Cambridge: MIT Press, 1990), 169.

2. Wright describes how he found the site in *An Autobiography*, (New York: Duell, Sloan and Pearce, 1943), 452.

3. See the salient remarks in Henry-Russell Hitchcock, *In the Nature of Materials* (New York: Duell, Sloan and Pearce, 1942) figures 352–59

4. For a more extensive commentary on the difference between the two Taliesins, see Robert C. Twombly, *Frank Lloyd Wright: An Interpretive Biography* (New York: Harper, 1974), 185–89.

5. Meryle Secrest's treatment of these incidents is incisive. See Meryle Secrest, *Frank Lloyd Wright* (New York: Knopf, 1992), 538–41.

6. Scholars may write the Federal Bureau of Investigation at the following address to review the Frank Lloyd Wright file: Attention: FOIPA Section / Federal Bureau of Investigation / 9th and Pennsylvania Avenue N. W. / Washington DC 20535

7. Twombly, *Interpretive Biography*, 271. See also Twombly's sources, *Madison (Wisconsin) Capital Times* (April 21, August 21, 1951; Sept. 22, 1952), *Madison (Wisconsin) Weekly Home News* (April 12, 1951), and *The Nation* 162 (June 2, 1951).

8. *Madison (Wisconsin) Weekly Home News*, April 12, 1951.

9. Edgar Tafel, *Years with Frank Lloyd Wright: Apprentice to Genius* (New York: Dover, 1979), 164–69, and my conversation with Edgar Tafel in New York City in July, 1991.

10. Frank Lloyd Wright, ed. with and introduction by Frederick Gutheim. *Frank Lloyd Wright on Architecture: Selected Writings 1894–1940* (Duell, Sloan, and Pearce, 1941).

11. As quoted in Donald Leslie Johnson, *Frank Lloyd Wright Versus America: The 1930s* (Cambridge: MIT Press, 1990), 36. Also see Johnson, 28–37, for an excellent account of Wright's relationship with Hitchcock and Frederick Gutheim, another prominent Eastern intellectual. Vincent Scully Jr., *Frank Lloyd Wright* (New York: Braziller, 1960), 30, also discusses Wright's problems with the Eastern establishment. Or see David Michael Hertz, *Angels of Reality: Emersonian Unfoldings in Wright, Stevens, and Ives* (Carbondale: Southern Illinois University Press, 1993), 293–94.

12. Frank Lloyd Wright, *In the Cause of Architecture: Essays by Frank Lloyd Wright for the Architectural Record, 1908–1952*, ed. Frederick Gutheim (New York: Architectural Record, 1975), 37–38. This useful collection also includes a symposium on architecture, including those who knew him personally.

13. Mumford, "Frank Lloyd Wright and the New Pioneers," in *Writings on Wright*, ed. H. Allen Brooks (Cambridge: M. I. T. Press, 1985), 149–54.

14. David A. Hanks' remarks are helpful in bringing out the interrelationship between interior and exterior. See David A. Hanks, *Frank Lloyd Wright: Preserving an Architectural Heritage: Decorative Designs from the Domino's Pizza Collection* (New York: Dutton, 1989), 118.

15. Frank Lloyd Wright, *The Story of the Tower: The Tree That Escaped the Crowded Forest* (New York: Horizon Press, 1956), 14.

16. Hanks, *Preserving an Architectural Heritage*, 118.

17. Herbert Muschamp, *Man About Town: Frank Lloyd Wright in New York City* (Cambridge: MIT Press, 1983), 70.

18. Wright tropes on Sullivan's arch, but his variation is better and simpler than the "Golden Doorway." It is more stylized because of the straight line of interstitial lighting that cuts across the facade and contrasts with the smooth brickwork.

19. Frank Lloyd Wright, *Genius and the Mobocracy* (New York: Horizon Press, 1971), 76.

20. Ibid, 74.

21. Ibid., 107

22. Ibid., 55.

23. Ibid., 71. Also see Hertz, *Angels of Reality*, 47–68.

24. Note that the Morris Gift Shop was done while the seventeen year development of the Guggenheim Museum project was well under way. For a sense of the vast expenditure of energy and time that Wright put into the Guggenheim museum, see Bruce Brooks Pfeiffer, ed. *Frank Lloyd Wright: the Guggenheim Correspondence* (Carbondale: Southern Illinois University Press, 1986).

25. Robert Moses, Public Works: A Dangerous Trade (New York: McGraw-Hill, 1970).

26. See Pfeiffer, Guggenheim Correspondence, x. See also, Bruce Brooks Pfeiffer, ed., *Frank Lloyd Wright Drawings: Masterworks from the Frank Lloyd Wright Archives*, (New York: Abrams, 1990), 148.

27. Pfeiffer, *Guggenheim Correspondence*, 27.

28. Banister Fletcher, *History of Architecture* (London: Butterworths, 1987), 66.

29. Connie Hormizda pointed this out to me at the celebration for the reopening of the Guggenheim on June 27, 1992.

30. Pfeiffer, *Guggenheim Correspondence*, 28.

31. My analysis benefits from Twombly's. See Twombly, *Interpretive Biography*, 232–35.

32. Pfeiffer, *Guggenheim Correspondence*, 242.

33. Ibid., 243.

34. Ibid., 248.

35. *Frank Lloyd Wright, The Natural House* (New York: Horizon, 1954), 130.

36. Ibid., 140.

37. See John Seargant, *Frank Lloyd Wright's Usonian Houses: The Case for Organic Architecture* (New York: Watson-Guptill, 1976) for a survey of the different plans (especially 31–94).

38. Wright, *Natural House*, 167.

39. Pfeiffer, *Masterworks*, 99.

40. Pfeiffer, *Masterworks*, 99.

41. See Rabbi Mortimer Cohen's excellent short book on the synagogue he commissioned from Wright. Mortimer J. Cohen, *Beth Sholom Synagogue* (Elkins Park, Pennsylvania: Beth Sholom Synagogue, 1959).

42. Pfeiffer, *Masterworks*, 101.

43. Frank Lloyd Wright, *Frank Lloyd Wright: Writings and Buildings* ed. Edgar Kaufmann and Ben Raeburn (New York: New American Library, 1974), 19.

44. Pfeiffer has included some interesting material for the Trinity Chapel project at Norman Oklahoma in *Masterworks*, 103–5.

45. Secrest, *Frank Lloyd Wright*, 543–44.

46. Aaron G. Green, "Organic Architecture: The Principles of Frank Lloyd Wright," in *Frank Lloyd Wright: In the Realm of Ideas*, ed. Bruce Brooks Pfeiffer and Gerald Wordland, (Carbondale: Southern Illinois University Press, 1988), 135.

47. David Gebhard, Romanza: *The California Architecture of Frank Lloyd Wright* (San Francisco: Chronicle Books, 1988), 112. Gebhard cleverly notes the utopian implications of a world entirely suited to the middle class inherent in the design for the Marin County Civic Center. Also pertinent as a partial vision of Broadacre City are the Usonian homes in Pleasantville, New York (1948–51).

48. Pfeiffer brings this out too. See *Masterworks*, 168.

49. Frank Lloyd Wright, *A Testament* (New York: Horizon Press, 1957), 59.

50. Ibid., 204.

51. Ibid., 205.

52. These figures are taken from John Lloyd Wright's chart, which gives an annual account of his father's activities. John Lloyd Wright Collection, Avery Library, Columbia University.

53. Frank Lloyd Wright, *Frank Lloyd Wright: The Crowning Decade, 1949–1959*, ed., Bruce Brooks Pfeiffer (Fresno: California State University Press, 1989), 19.

54. For more commentary on this drawing, see Pfeiffer, *Masterworks*, 265.

55. Unpublished letter to the author, October 20, 1992.

BIBLIOGRAPHY

■

Works by Frank Lloyd Wright

Wright, Frank Lloyd. *An American Architecture*. Edit. by Edgar Kaufmann. New York: Horizon Press, 1955.

———. *Ausgeführte Bauten und Entwürfe von Frank Lloyd Wright*. Berlin: Wasmuth, 1910. Reprinted as *Drawings and Plans of Frank Lloyd Wright: The Early Period (1893–1909)*. New York: Dover, 1983.

———. *An Autobiography*. New York: Longmans and Green, 1932. New York:Duell, Sloan and Pearce, 1943. New York: Horizon Press, 1977.

———. *Collected Writings of Frank Lloyd Wright*. 3 vols published, 6 vols. projected. New York: Rizzoli, 1992.

———. *Future of Architecture*. New York: Horizon, 1953.

———. *Frank Lloyd Wright on Architecture: Selected Writings 1894–1940*. Edited with an introduction by Frederick Gutheim. Duell, Sloan and Pearce, 1941.

———. *Frank Lloyd Wright: Writings and Buildings*. Edited by Edgar Kaufmann and Ben Raeburn. New York: New American Library, 1974.

———. *Genius and the Mobocracy*. New York: Horizon Press, 1971.

———. *The Industrial Revolution Runs Away*. New York: Horizon, 1969.

———. *In the Cause of Architecture: Essays by Frank Lloyd Wright for the Architectural Record, 1908–1952*. Edited by Frederick Gutheim. New York: Architectural Record, 1975.

———. *The Japanese Print*. Chicago: Ralph Fletcher, Seymour Co, 1912.

———. *The Living City*. New York: Horizon, 1958. Earlier editions are as follows: *When Democracy Builds* New York: Horizon, 1945; *The Disappearing City*: New York: William Farquhar Payson, 1932. *Democracy Runs Away* is a special edition comparing the 1932 text with the 1942 version.

———. *Modern Architecture: Being the Kahn Lectures for 1930*. Carbondale: Southern Illinois University Press, 1987.

———. *The Natural House*. New York: Horizon Press, 1954.

———. *A Testament*. New York: Horizon Press, 1957.

———.*Three Quarters of a Century of Drawings*. New York: Horizon Press, 1981.

———. *Two Lectures on Architecture*. Chicago: Art Institute of Chicago, 1931.

———. *When Democracy Builds*. Chicago: University of Chicago Press, 1945.

Wright, Frank Lloyd and Baker Brownell. *Architecture and Modern Life*. New York: Harper, 1937.

Archives

Chicago, Illinois. University of Chicago. Joseph Regenstein Library.

Oak Park, Illinois. Frank Lloyd Wright Home and Studio Archives.

New York, New York. Avery Library, Columbia University. Frank Lloyd Wright Collection.

Scottsdale, Arizona. Frank Lloyd Wright Archives, Taliesin West

Biographies

Farr, Finis. *Frank Lloyd Wright*. New York: Scribner's Sons, 1961.

Gill, Brendan. *Many Masks: A Life of Frank Lloyd Wright*. New York: G. Putnam, 1987.

Secrest, Meryle. *Frank Lloyd Wright*. New York: Knopf, 1992.

Twombly, Robert C. *Frank Lloyd Wright: an Interpretive Biography*. New York: Harper, 1974.

Willard, Charlotte. *Frank Lloyd Wright: An American Architecture*. New York: MacMillan, 1972.

Wright, John Lloyd. *My Father Who is on Earth*. New York: Putnam, 1946.

Bibliographies

Mehan, Patrick J. *Frank Lloyd Wright: A Research Guide to Archival Sources*. New York: Garland, 1983.

Sweeney, Robert L. *Frank Lloyd Wright: an Annotated Bibliography*. Los Angeles: Hennessey and Ingalls, 1978.

Monographs and Selected Articles

Alofsin, Anthony. *Frank Lloyd Wright—The Lost Years, 1910–1923: A Study of Influence*. Chicago: University of Chicago Press, 1993.

Blake, Peter. *Frank Lloyd Wright: Architecture and Space*. Baltimore: Penguin, 1964.

Bolen, Carol R., Robert Nelson, Linda Seidel edit., *The Nature of Frank Lloyd Wright*. Chicago, University of Chicago Press, 1988.

Doremus, Thomas. *Frank Lloyd Wright and Le Corbusier: the Great Dialogue*. New York: Van Nostrand Reinhold, 1985.

Eaton, Leonard K. *Two Chicago Architects and Their Clients: Frank Lloyd Wright and Howard Van Doren Shaw*. Cambridge: M.I.T. Press, 1969.

Fishman, Robert. *Urban Utopias in the Twentieth Century: Ebenezer Howard, Frank Lloyd Wright and Le Corbusier*. New York: Basic Books, 1977.

Gebhard, David. *Romanza: The California Architecture of Frank Lloyd Wright*. San Francisco: Chronicle Books, 1988.

Hanks, David A. *The Decorative Designs of Frank Lloyd Wright*. New York: Dutton, 1979.

Hanna, Paul R. and Jean S. *Frank Lloyd Wright's Hanna House: The Client's Report*. 2nd Ed. Carbondale: Southern Illinois University Press, 1987.

Hearn, M. F. "Japanese Inspiration for Frank Lloyd Wright's Rigid Core High-Rise Structures." *Journal of the Society of Architectural History* 20 (March 1991): 68–71.

Hertz, David Michael. *Angels of Reality: Emersonian Unfoldings in Wright, Stevens, and Ives*. Carbondale: Southern Illinois University Press, 1993.

Hildebrand, Grant. *The Wright Space: Pattern and Meaning in Frank Lloyd Wright's Houses*. Seattle: University of Washington Press, 1991.

Hitchcock, Henry-Russell. *In the Nature of Materials*. New York: Duell, Sloan and Pearce, 1942.

Hoffmann, Donald. *Frank Lloyd Wright: Architecture and Nature*. New York: Dover, 1986.

———. *Frank Lloyd Wright's Fallingwater*. New York: Dover, 1978.

———. *Frank Lloyd Wright's Robie House*. New York: Dover, 1984.

———. "Frank Lloyd Wright and Viollet-le-Duc." *Journal of the Society of Architectural Historians*. 28 (Oct. 1969): 173–83.

Jacobs, Herbert and Catherine. *Building With Frank Lloyd Wright*. San Francisco: Chronicle Books, 1978.

———. *Frank Lloyd Wright: America's Greatest Architect*. New York: Harcourt, Brace and World, 1965.

James, Cary. *Frank Lloyd Wright's Imperial Hotel*. New York: Dover, 1968.

Johnson, Donald Leslie. *Frank Lloyd Wright versus America:The 1930s*.Cambridge: MIT Press, 1990.

Kaufmann, Edgar Jr., ed. *An American Architecture: Frank Lloyd Wright*. New York: Horizon Press, 1955.

———. *Fallingwater: a Frank Lloyd Wright Country House*. New York: Abbeville. 1986.

———. *Nine Commentaries on Frank Lloyd Wright*. Cambridge: MIT Press, 1989.

Levine, Neil. "The Image of the Vessel in the Architecture of Frank Lloyd Wright." *C.G. Jung and the Humanities*. Ed by Karin Barnaby and Pellegrino D'Acierno. Princeton: Princeton University Press, 1990.

Lind, Carla. *The Wright Style*. New York: Simon and Schuster, 1992.

Lipman, Jonathan. *Frank Lloyd Wright and the Johnson Wax Buildings*. New York: Rizzoli, 1986.

Manson, Grant Carpenter. *Frank Lloyd Wright to 1910: The First Golden Age*. New York: Van Nostrand Reinhold Publishing Corporation, 1958.

Muschamp, Herbert. *Man About Town: Frank Lloyd Wright in New York City*. Cambridge: MIT Press, 1983.

Nute, Kevin. *Frank Lloyd Wright and Japan*. Van Nostrand Reinhold, 1993.

O'Gorman, James F. *Three American Architects: Richardson, Sullivan and Wright, 1865–1915*. Chicago: University of Chicago Press, 1991.

Pfeiffer, Bruce Brooks. *Frank Lloyd Wright Drawings: Masterworks from the Frank Lloyd Wright Archives*. New York: Abrams, 1990.

Pfeiffer, Bruce Brooks, ed. *The Guggenheim Correspondence*. Carbondale: Southern Illinois University Press, 1986.

———. *Frank Lloyd Wright: His Living Voice*. Fresno: California State University Press, 1987.

Pfeiffer, Bruce Brooks and Gerald Nordland, eds. *In the Realm of Ideas*. Carbondale: Southern Illinois University Press, 1988.

Quinan, Jack. *Frank Lloyd Wright's Larkin Building: Myth and Fact*. Cambridge: M.I.T. Press, 1987.

Riley, Terence, and Peter Reed. *Frank Lloyd Wright: Architect*. New York: Musuem of Modern Art, 1994.

Rubin, Jeanne S. "The Froebel-Wright Kindergarten Connection: A New Perspective" *Journal of the Society of Architectural History*. 48 (1989): 24–37.

Scott, Margaret. *Frank Lloyd Wright's Warehouse in Richland Center*. Richland, Wisconsin: Richland County Publishers, 1984.

Scully, Vincent, Jr. *Frank Lloyd Wright*. New York: Braziller, 1960.

Sergeant, John. *Frank Lloyd Wright's Usonian Houses: the Case for Organic Architecture*. New York: Watson-Guptill, 1976.

Smith, Kathryn. *Frank Lloyd Wright: Hollyhock House and Olive Hill*. New York: Rizzoli, 1992.

———. "Frank Lloyd Wright and the Imperial Hotel." *Art Bulletin*. 67 (June, 1985): 296–310.

Smith, Norris Kelly. *A Study of the Architectural Imagery of Frank Lloyd Wright*. Ph.D. diss., Columbia University, 1961. University Microfilms, Inc., Ann Arbor, Michigan, Mic. 61–2668.

Storrer, William Allin. *The Architecture of Frank Lloyd Wright*. Boston: MIT Press, 1986.

———. *The Frank Lloyd Wright Companion*. Chicago: University of Chicago Press, 1993.

Tafel, Edgar. *Years with Frank Lloyd Wright: Apprentice to Genius*. New York: Dover, 1979.

Tselos, Dimitri. "Exotic Influences in the Architecture of Frank Lloyd Wright." *Magazine of Art* 46 (1953): 160–69, 184.

Wright, Iovanna Lloyd. *Architecture: Man in Possession of His Earth*. Garden City, New York: Doubleday, 1962.

INDEX

■

ABOUT THE AUTHOR

■

David Michael Hertz was born in Bay Shore, New York in 1954. He studied comparative literature, music and the interdisciplinary arts at Indiana University, Bloomington (B.A., B.S., M.A.). He earned a doctorate in comparative literature at New York University in 1983, where he subsequently was a Mellon Postdoctoral Fellow in the Humanities and Assistant Professor. Currently he is Professor of Comparative Literature at Indiana University in Bloomington. Professor Hertz is the author of *Angels of Reality: Emersonian Unfoldings in Wright, Stevens, and Ives* (1993), which also deals extensively with the work of Frank Lloyd Wright, and *The Tuning of the Word: the Musico-literary Poetics of the Symbolist Movement* (1987). A pianist and composer, Hertz has most recently written a song cycle, *An American in China,* and a musical comedy, *The Rose Garden Conspiracy*.